CHILDREN WITH
VISUAL IMPAIRMENTS

More children with severe visual impairments or blindness are now being included in ordinary school settings than ever before. How best to provide an appropriate curriculum for them has raised some intriguing questions.

Do children with visual impairments have special characteristics or follow a unique developmental path? What impact does a visual loss have on a child's language development, concepts or problem-solving? How can we promote play, mobility, exploration and social skills?

This book sets out the basis for addressing the individual needs of children with a wide range of visual impairments within the Code of Practice. It includes information about the structure and functioning of the eye; the nature and treatment of visual conditions; the identification and assessment of aspects of vision and the role of different agencies; a comprehensive range of practical strategies; and advice on the use of low vision aids, appropriate decor and physical layouts, lighting and information technology.

Drawing on very recent research, this book presents new insights into the kind of learning experiences required to offset the impact of a visual loss, arguing that it is the quality of the child's social interactions which promotes play, language and development.

Alec Webster is Reader in Education and Director of the Centre for Language Studies, University of Bristol. **João Roe** is a teacher with the Bristol Sensory Impaired Children's Service – Vision Impairment Team.

CHILDREN WITH VISUAL IMPAIRMENTS
Social interaction, language and learning

Alec Webster and João Roe

London and New York

First published 1998
by Routledge
11 New Fetter Lane, London EC4P 4EE

Simultaneously published in the USA and Canada
by Routledge
29 West 35th Street, New York, NY 10001

Typeset in Garamond by Florencetype Limited, Stoodleigh, Devon

Printed and bound in Great Britain by Biddles Ltd, Guildford and King's Lynn

British Library Cataloguing in Publication Data
A catalogue record for this book is available from the British Library

Library of Congress Cataloging in Publication Data
Webster, Alec.
Children with visual impairments : social interaction, language and learning /
Alec Webster and João Roe.
p.   cm.
Includes bibliographical references and index.
1. Visually handicapped children – Education. I. Roe, João, 1960–. II. Title.
HV1626.W43   1998
362.4′1′083071–dc21   97–12609
CIP

ISBN   0–415–14815–4
0–415–14816–2 (pbk)

CONTENTS

LIST OF PLATES

LIST OF FIGURES

LIST OF TABLES

ACKNOWLEDGEMENTS

The authors would like to thank the children, parents and school staff who made the Bristol research possible. They would also like to thank the Bristol Sensory Impaired Children's Service – Vision Impairment Team for their support and interest in the project. We are also grateful to the Guide Dogs Association for the Blind who provided financial support for the research.

A special thanks is due to Sue Rogers for the photographs and to Sue Rogers and Mary Wight for their suggestions, comments and enthusiasm. We are also indebted to Tania Thompson and Tom Hutchison for comments on the chapter concerning vision and visual impairment, and to Liz Fisher for her helpful advice on aspects of optometry. Valerie Webster provided a very helpful editorial review that shaped the final organisation of the book. A special thanks goes to Patrick Roe for his support and to Simon Daniel, whose very first social encounters took place during the writing of this book.

1

INTRODUCTION: VISUAL IMPAIRMENT AND INDIVIDUAL NEEDS

This introductory chapter sets out how we have approached the individual learning needs of children with visual impairments, and emphasises, wherever feasible, a research basis for intervention. We explore contrasting images of children with visual impairments, highlighting unique differences in the way in which individuals adapt to their experience in contrasting contexts. To some extent these images are reflected in changes in policy and legislation over time, moving from the 'deficit' models that informed earlier provision to more recent concerns with the personal goals that underpin 'lifetime learning'. Throughout the text, practical advice is shaped by the framework of the Code of Practice for SEN as it is currently being implemented in mainstream primary and secondary schools.

We have been careful not to locate all of the factors that influence learning within children themselves, and we have tried to steer away from comparisons between 'sighted' and 'visually impaired' groups. In any case, the major variables that adults, particularly teachers, control are the conditions within which learning takes place, and the transactions that support the child's adaptive efforts to make sense of the world. A small sample of case studies illustrates the range of individual differences encountered in children with visual impairments, in terms of ability, learning style, persistence, motivation, adaptivity and resilience. However, we need to look at the strategies adopted by adults and the culture of teaching environments in order to find ways of optimising learning. Recent research evidence, introduced briefly here, probes key aspects of interpersonal contexts, such as the scaffolding of interactions between adults and children, and the processes that promote independent control of learning in children with significant hurdles to surmount.

This book is about the impact of visual impairment on the development and education of young children. In many ways this book is also about difference. We are all different in terms of age, gender, origin, ability and experience. We have many differences and from these we form our identities and our individualities.

A child or young person with a visual impairment is first and foremost an individual. Parents and teachers of children with a visual impairment gather abundant evidence from everyday encounters and events that supports this. A 4 year old attempts to uncover the rules of a game of hide-and-seek that his older siblings have involved him in. A 6 year old is helping a friend to program a computerised robot given as a Christmas present, which requires keying in codes to produce different manoeuvres, sounds and actions. A 10 year old interrogates her mother on the metaphor of 'rock bottom prices' as she waits at the checkout of a supermarket. Children from early infancy onwards act on the world and make sense of it in the complex social environments in which they live, play and learn. The fact that all of the children mentioned above are adapting to the presence of a visual impairment obviously impinges upon, but does not arrest, the momentum to construct meanings, to sustain social contacts, to discover rules and relationships, to make sense of the world and how it works.

A SPECIAL PSYCHOLOGY?

We do not believe that a special psychology is required (or would be helpful) to understand the development or individual learning needs of children with visual impairments. We do not find it fruitful to address issues such as whether blind children, or those with impaired vision, have special characteristics or follow a distinct developmental path. Neither do we believe that visual impairments simply result in a series of developmental, intellectual or linguistic delays in children's growth to maturity. Therefore children with impaired vision cannot simply be considered in terms of the normal developmental milestones achieved by all other children, but with well-defined gaps in some areas of experience and maturation. Instead we shall be highlighting the ways in which, for individual children, there are different routes and styles of development: no two children learn in the same way. In our view each child's developmental profile is uniquely determined by a complex interplay of factors that a visual impairment influences, including:

- individual differences in ability, learning style, persistence and motivation
- sensitivity to a range of cue and information sources in social and learning environments, including use of residual vision
- patterns of interaction established with parents or carers, siblings, adults and peers
- resources of adaptivity and resilience
- learning conditions, including the ability of adults to act contingently and flexibly
- school curriculum, in particular issues of differentiation, guided participation and independent learning

In discussing people with visual impairments we are concerned with an extremely diverse range of individuals with different types and degrees of visual loss, all of whom have responded and adapted to their experiences in unique ways. Visual impairment of any degree interacts in an unpredictable and often uncharted way with many other factors that serve to differentiate individuals from one another, such as confidence, resilience, determination, specific abilities or areas of immaturity, the particular social and cultural circumstances of the family, in addition to contacts with different parents, carers, teachers and schools.

So this is a text concerned with the richness and diversity of individual experience, the multi-form qualities of interpersonal, linguistic and intellectual encounters during the formative periods of childhood and schooling, as children face the wide range of adaptive tasks and situations associated with learning and growing up. In our view a visual impairment tests out the flexibility and adaptivity of children, their families and teachers, over the already somewhat hazardous course of parenting, growth to maturity and independence. These points are often unheeded and can lead to much misunderstanding and confusion when children are gathered together on the basis of medical or legal categories (such as 'blind' or 'partially sighted') for the purpose of making educational provision, interpreting research evidence, or handing over advice to families and teachers.

IMAGES OF CHILDREN WITH VISUAL IMPAIRMENTS

In this book we shall be arguing the case that the development and learning of children and young people with visual impairments is best understood in terms of the social environments in which individuals find themselves and the quality of interpersonal encounters that arise therein. We take as read that the social contexts of home and school are complex for all children, and that we must focus on children's everyday attempts to cope with these environments. Furthermore, one fundamental shift in our thinking in relation to special educational needs, referred to, for example, in the chapter by Webster (1992), concerns how adult perceptions of a sensory handicap influence attitudes and behaviour. A common view is that children with visual impairments can be understood only in terms of what they lack or 'cannot do' in comparison with fully sighted children. This comparative approach assumes a 'visual impairment as deficit' model, in which any discrepancies revealed between the two groups are attributed to the sensory impairment and are thus located within the child.

Deficit models in special education have informed much of government policy and legislation until very recently. Prior to the report of the Warnock Committee (DES, 1978) and the ensuing 1981 Education Act that implemented its recommendations, special education was defined in relation to categories of disability. For example, labels such as 'maladjusted', 'deaf', 'ESN(S)', 'blind' or 'partially sighted' were applied to children and used to determine the kinds of educational provision that were required. Special education, to many people, was synonymous with special schools or classes. An inherent danger of this approach is that the nomenclature used to label or classify children colours expectations and attitudes. For example, if it is generally believed that a severe visual impairment precludes children from achieving academic success, participating socially with peers and achieving personal independence, then adult expectations may be lowered, fewer opportunities created or challenges offered. This would apply to all individuals who suffer under such labels, since they carry with them self-limiting properties, no matter how determined or competent a child happens to be. The child becomes, and is perceived in terms of, the handicapping condition.

A positive perspective

We mention the Warnock Report and the 1981 Education Act at this point because, in many respects, the new Code of Practice has returned to pick up many of the issues that were raised by this earlier policy and legislation but never fully implemented. In Chapter 4 we shall be revisiting these important issues in some detail, such as early intervention; partnership with parents or carers; positive terminology and concepts of special education; pupil entitlements; the relative nature of special needs; the continuum of special needs' provision; how professional agencies collaborate; integration and inclusion; and a shift from notions of disability towards individual requirements for maximising learning.

An alternative model to the deficit view, and one that has gained increasing support from research, stems from evidence that differences between individuals facing similar obstacles to development, such as a visual or hearing loss, are just as great as those found between contrasting groups. Accounting for differential rates of progress often highlights salient factors in contrasting environments, rather than within children. Any learning difficulties encountered do not, *de facto*, reside wholly within the child, nor should they be considered as inevitable consequences of a visual disability. (For a detailed consideration of this view, see Warren, 1994.)

Once we start to think of a visual impairment, or any other facet of individual functioning, as part of a continuum of human differentiation, it then becomes apparent that some of the developmental difficulties observed in children are in fact caused by the strategies adopted by adults or by the limiting conditions found in certain environments. Drawing on some very recent research carried out by the authors, which has explored these images and assumptions of youngsters with visual impairments, the book aims to help families, teachers and other professional groups towards new insights into the needs of children with visual impairments as learners. We examine the research basis for believing that the long-term course of a child's development can be affected by improving aspects of the learning environment in the early years and through the period of schooling.

THE CODE OF PRACTICE AND CHILDREN WITH SPECIAL NEEDS

In this book we shall be mainly addressing class and subject teachers who may have no special qualifications or experience in working with children with special educational needs. The sections of the text that provide basic information about the functioning of the eye, identification and treatment of ophthalmic conditions, and how vision is implicated in children's learning and development, provide a general introduction for those new to the field.

The Code of Practice for children with special educational needs came into force on September 1st 1994. From that date onwards all schools have been obliged to pay due regard to the Code, which identifies new roles and responsibilities for all teachers in relation to meeting the individual needs of children in the mainstream school context. The framework of the Code of Practice and its related Circular 6/94 set out the agenda for schools in the foreseeable future, shaping policy and provision for identifying, assessing and drawing up plans for pupils with special educational needs, within a number of clearly defined stages. Responding to criticisms made of the way in which procedures under the 1981 Education Act were being followed by most LEAs, the new Code intends to focus on increasing accountability; improving the quality and consistency of support offered to families and children; shorter timescales for carrying out assessments and making decisions; widening parental choice; more careful planning and evaluation of pupil progress and the effectiveness of SEN provision; greater involvement of pupils themselves in negotiating learning routes; and the much more central involvement of all mainstream teachers and staff in designing flexible learning environments across the curriculum for pupils with special needs.

In Chapter 4, where we deal with the issues of educational policy and provision in some detail, we shall be casting a critical eye over the Code of Practice and its implications for pupils of varying ages with visual impairments in different phases of the education system. Although the majority of the children who are the subject of this book will have clearly identified needs, it is still the case that non-specialist teachers shoulder the major load of making day-to-day provision for children in mainstream settings. The last few years has also seen a gradual diminution in the level of LEA resourcing for support services to schools, such as visiting teachers of the sensory impaired, educational psychologists and generic SEN support teams. This move towards inclusion of children with visual impairments in ordinary school settings – as indeed for a whole range of special educational needs – is set to continue. The wider sharing of good practice, such as strategies for differentiating the curriculum, is upheld by the Code of Practice as the major component of SEN provision. It is still the case, however, that detailed knowledge of the needs of children with visual impairments rests with the expert few.

Promoting achievement

This book will be invaluable in enabling non-specialist teachers to implement their new responsibilities under the Code of Practice, to understand ways in which learning can be promoted, and to design more effective learning environments for children with visual impairments. We have included a wide range of tried and tested strategies appropriate to mainstream school contexts, including use of low vision aids, appropriate decor and physical layouts, lighting conditions and equipment, and relevant information technology. Promoting curriculum access through differentiating modes of presentation, ways of working and learning outcomes will enable all pupils to participate more effectively. In this sense, what is considered to be good practice for pupils with visual impairments will also promote more effective learning for other pupils. Parents and family advisers should all find the book rich in practical advice.

The Code of Practice has a great deal to say about how agencies can work in partnership in order to empower families and youngsters themselves. There can be few misgivings in anybody's mind about the importance of all individuals, whatever their needs, capitalising on their full potential, acquiring a wide range of competencies, being positively orientated to the changing world of work, and achieving independence and control over their own lives.

The book seeks ways in which all parents, carers and professionals can work together with youngsters to find optimal environments for learning, in other words where the pace of learning is determined more by what an individual can achieve with the help of responsive, facilitating adults, together with appropriate equipment and technology, rather than by the notional limits imposed by a sensory impairment or the narrow expectations of a stereotype.

LIFETIME LEARNING

A relatively unfamiliar concept to many educationists is the concept of 'lifetime' or 'lifelong' learning, which has recently been brought to prominence with the tactical merger of education and employment departments during the summer of 1995. Lifetime learning is a concept that underpins the DFEE's objectives in terms of the continuum of education and training that society provides, of which schools form a central but not exclusive part. Such a continuum of learning opportunities, from nursery to post-compulsory school age and thereby onto employment, is meant to provide a context in which all individuals can gain, refresh and update relevant skills to meet changing societal demands and economic circumstances.

At one end of the scale, lifetime learning aims to improve the nation's competitiveness by increasing access to a diversity of educational opportunities that extend beyond school, and which are recognised through a wider range of technical, academic and vocationally relevant qualifications. At the other end of the scale, lifetime learning is about setting personal, social, academic and vocational goals that are relevant, appropriate, challenging and

Plate 1.1 A blind child using a hoople to navigate along a school corridor. Lifelong learning means equipping children with skills for personal effectiveness, flexibility and autonomy. Although mobility for many children with visual impairments is synonymous with independence, it is also important for exploration and related conceptual growth

meaningful to the individuals concerned. One of the main reasons for supporting the intentions that underpin the Code of Practice and the new initiative of lifetime learning is because it brings an opportunity to address the central issue of what learning is for – the raising of individual achievement through good quality learning experiences – and the wider question of how schools can become more effective communities for learning. These new emphases would require nothing less than a seachange in some school contexts to be even partially implemented. However, they do reflect an educational climate in which school effectiveness and the raising of individual achievement have both political and popular currency.

Personal action plans

For individuals with learning needs that are special in some way, the notion of lifetime learning has profound implications. It is a concept that embraces such important areas as personal effectiveness, independence, self-direction, transferable skills, flexibility, vocational awareness and entrepreneurship. It is about investing in people's potential to help themselves. It stresses taking every individual forward, in areas of development that have personal significance, whatever the starting points. Crucially, it is a process of handing over responsibility for learning to individuals themselves. These issues are realised in transactions such as personal action planning with pupils. Under the Code of Practice, the drawing up of individual long-term education plans and shorter-term teaching programmes provides important opportunities for engaging pupils in thinking about their own learning styles and curriculum needs. Plans drawn up with pupils whose needs are 'Statemented' under the 1993 Education Act should also include, at each review following a young person's fourteenth birthday, arrangements for transition into adulthood, further training or education, and the world of work.

In Chapter 4 we shall be dealing with the details of how these issues should be managed, who should be involved, and what should be the main focus of consideration. However, at this stage it is worth noting that a context of policy and professional practice is emerging whereby individual learning needs are negotiated and planned for the lifespan. Schooling lays important foundations in helping individuals to achieve their full academic potential, but as the term itself implies, lifetime learning requires schools to equip children with a wide range of personal competencies, to be flexible and self-motivated, to be enterprising and independent, to communicate, to take decisions, to make choices, to be in control.

TERMINOLOGY IN THE FIELD OF VISUAL IMPAIRMENT

Whilst current policy and good practice is moving away from prescriptive labels and categories, there is still a plethora of specialised terms that are used to define aspects of visual impairment by different professional groups. For example, the certificate of registration for individuals with severe visual impairment, called Form BD8, signed by an ophthalmologist and giving access to certain services and benefits, still uses the terms 'blind' and 'partially sighted', although these categories are no longer used to define educational needs. We shall be covering the origins, diagnosis and assessment of visual impairment in more detail in Chapter 2, together with aspects such as registration for medical or legal purposes. Level of vision is often expressed as a figure (such as 6/6 or 6/12 on the Snellen chart), which indicates the performance of an eye in relation to an arbitrary 'normal' standard (see p. 23). This score is based on the task of identifying a stationary black-on-white image at a distance. In school, pupils require many other visual competencies, such as identifying near or far images under different lighting conditions, and viewing objects that are themselves in motion or whilst the individual is moving.

The vast majority of children with visual impairments have useful remaining or 'residual' vision. The legal definition of 'partial sight' is a visual acuity measure on the Snellen chart of between 3/60 and 6/60. This term is interpreted quite differently for educational purposes to mean those children with a significant visual impairment whose learning and achievement is impeded unless modifications are made to teaching methods, materials and the learning environment. Some children function better in higher or lower levels of lighting than average, others have sharp near vision but limited distance acuity, and some visual impairments result in good distance vision but almost no useful vision for reading. Since the effects of a visual impairment can be very specific, the acuity score on its own is a poor guide to how handicapped a child may be educationally.

For medical and legal purposes, 'blindness' is defined as an acuity of less than 3/60 in the better eye for corrected vision, wearing spectacles or lenses. Using the Snellen criteria, about 80 per cent of children classed as 'blind' have some useful vision that they can learn how to use, so that they become more skilled at interpreting the imperfect images they see. Just as with 'partial sight', there is an important distinction between medical and educational concepts of blindness. In educational contexts, the term 'blind' is typically used to describe those pupils who have no sight at all, or who have light perception only. Blind pupils will be highly dependent on tactile and auditory means of learning, and will require specialised equipment. Their curricular needs are likely to include aspects of socio-linguisitic interaction and conceptual development, mobility and personal independence, use of information technology and braille. Another important factor concerns whether the blindness is congenital (present at birth) or acquired (for example, through illness or accident). If children lose their sight after the age of 5, there will be a store of visual memories to draw on when constructing inner representations of different physical spaces for orientation purposes, in forming and refining concepts, and in understanding the relationships between objects or events.

Visual memories may not be retained if the onset of blindness is before the age of about 18 months.

'Handicap', 'disability' and 'impairment'

Throughout the book we have preferred to distinguish between the terms 'handicap', 'disability' and 'impairment' in line with the guidance offered by the World Health Organisation (1980). 'Impairment' is defined as any loss of normal functioning, however small. 'Disability' refers to those factors that restrict or hinder an individual in carrying out certain everyday activities in a given family or social context. 'Handicap' concerns those impairing or disabling factors that also lead to disadvantage by limiting or preventing the fulfilment of roles for the individual. The WHO definitions point up some important questions to ask about the implications of varying degrees of visual impairment in contrasting settings, rather than seeing any social or educational difficulties as residing within the child. For example, a child who has lost an eye following an accident will be impaired but may not be disabled, and will be able to participate fully in most school and family activities. If a career as an airline pilot, police officer or professional tennis player had been anticipated, then this may be seen as a personal disadvantage or significant handicap.

INDIVIDUAL NEEDS OF CHILDREN WITH VISUAL IMPAIRMENTS

A number of brief case studies are given here, taken from our own contacts with children, their families and schools, to illustrate the range of individual differences encountered and the complex interplay of factors that influence a child's behaviour, learning and development in contrasting social settings.

Impairment: any loss or abnormality of psychological, physiological or anatomical structure or function.

Disability: any restriction or lack (resulting from an impairment) of ability to perform an activity in the manner or within the range considered normal for a human being.

Handicap: a disadvantage for a given individual, resulting from an impairment or disability, that limits or prevents the fulfilment of a role (depending on age, sex, social and cultural factors).

Figure 1.1 World Health Organisation definitions of impairment, disability and handicap

Source: WHO 1980

Paul

Paul is a 9-year-old child with a moderate visual impairment who attends his local primary school. He has a measured visual acuity of 6/24 wearing spectacles, which means that he is unable to read most of what is written on the blackboard. He also has a severe lateral nystagmus, which is an involuntary, rapid movement of the eyeball. Paul's medical condition and details of his classroom needs are documented in the school's SEN register. During lessons the classteacher reads out any information written on the blackboard, whilst Paul is allowed to stand up close to the blackboard or to look over the work of his peers. Worksheets are usually printed in a large bold type face with generous spacing, and where possible, instructions are taped. Resources, activity areas, equipment and displays are clearly labelled. Although he is a very sociable child and is often chosen by peers to partner activities, there are some school situations in which his confidence has begun to diminish. This is usually when more challenging tasks are given involving reading and writing. His speed of working is affected when he has to decipher information in textbooks, and relying on informed guesswork means that mistakes are often made. Increasing handwriting speed leads to illegibility; hence Paul has touch-typing lessons and is preparing to use a laptop computer for word processing when he transfers to secondary school.

Laura

This 3-year-old little girl was born ten weeks prematurely and subsequently diagnosed as blind with some light perception in her right eye, due to retinopathy of prematurity. Laura has only a limited repertoire of single words in her expressive vocabulary, such as 'hot', 'Mama' and 'choc-choc'. On the other hand, she is a very physical child who loves to bounce or climb on anything she finds in her way, with good fine and gross motor co-ordination. Laura recently started to attend a nursery class in her local infant school. A daily routine was set out to help her understand the sequence of daily events, such as starting out with a box of objects of varying shapes, textures and weights, which Laura explores. The programme also includes play with water, sand, plasticine, paint, and familiar objects for representational play. Laura can identify items such as a hairbrush and uses this appropriately on her own hair, on dolls and teddies.

Given a battery-charged toy, such as bubble tubes, Laura responds more to the sound or vibration emitted than to the changing light or colours. She moves rhythmically to loud music and participates in action songs, such as 'head, shoulders, knees and toes'. Recently, frequent colds and chest infections have resulted in a lot of absences from nursery. Her mother began to worry about her hearing following an incident where Laura seemed unperturbed at the loud clatter of a pan lid falling on the kitchen floor behind her.

She was given a hearing test and examined by an Ear, Nose and Throat Consultant who diagnosed a conductive hearing loss and prescribed antibiotics and a decongestant for 'glue ear'. There is a possibility, if drug treatment is ineffective, that Laura may have surgery to drain and aerate her middle ear.

Nelly

This 7-year-old child suffered brain damage at birth leading to spasticity (diplegia): loss of power and control of muscles in some parts of her body. She is also totally blind in her left eye, but has some useful residual vision in her right. Her vision is mainly peripheral and therefore colour sensitivity is affected. She has difficulties identifying objects, but through a programme of training using closed circuit television (CCTV) has learnt to spot similarities and differences between drawings, and can identify some letters. In order to explore objects, Nelly has found a way of bringing items to the right of her face where she can mouth them, and then look with central vision to identify colours. A brailler was introduced via a group of her classmates which drew her into using it for scribbling. She also enjoys braille books and can track along the raised symbols. However, she still has a long way to go to develop tactile discrimination and the required control in her fingers for braille. A physiotherapist visits her school and has provided a programme to strengthen her muscles and to improve her posture and movement. Activities designed to help fine motor co-ordination include plasticine modelling, texture-matching games, threading and sorting, cutting and punching paper, and matching colours with pegs. Nelly now tracks text from right to left, finds gaps in a line and can distinguish differences between lines of braille. In school, practical activities are organised so that she has contact with actual objects, plants and animals, in order to link her language and conceptual development with real experience. Social interactions are not always subtle: she insisted on a close demonstration of her wobbly tooth to everyone around her and ended up being pushed away. Mostly, the problems are to do with overprotection: other children pick her coat off the peg, pull her along the corridor and move things out of her way.

Daniel

Daniel is a 6-year-old blind child with no light perception who attends his local school. At the age of 1, retinoblastoma was diagnosed: a malignant tumour of the retina. His left eye was surgically removed and he had to undergo a course of chemotherapy and then radiotherapy. Daniel relies a great deal on non-visual information. His teacher tries to arrange for lots of practical activities like weighing, measuring, cutting or pouring. When the group were covering three-dimensional shapes it was very helpful for Daniel to hold models of these during discussions. He enjoys braille books which he started to read just before he was 5. Initially, books were written around his interests, such as 'Rusty', the toy furry dog he slept with at home. Later, braille captions were stuck into books from the reading scheme in use at school. He writes and prints his own stories using 'braille 'n' print'. There are occasional gaps in Daniel's understanding of everyday things that are usually accessible to children through visual means. Never having seen a lion in the zoo or wildlife documentaries, much explanation was required to accompany a story the class listened to about a lion who went shopping. Daniel has been taught to face other people when talking to them so that they are aware he is listening. He can also make his own choices about toys or equipment and will ask for things he cannot find for himself. He moves independently from one area of the classroom to another using set routes that he has learned. He uses a hoople (a modified hoop with a handle) to walk along corridors at quiet times. The tendency of other children to help him move faster by pulling him along has been discouraged.

Ian

Ian is a 15 year old who lives in a block of flats close to a city centre. He has some peripheral vision in his left eye but is considered 'educationally blind'. He was born with a condition called Leber's amaurosis. Ian attends a local secondary school which has a unit for students with visual impairments. Because his single parent works in the evenings, it is often difficult to arrange social contacts outside of school, or to fix transport. An important aspect of Ian's growing independence is for him to negotiate public transport routes and to manage unfamiliar environments. At school he has a network of close friends. He has an assistant working with him in some areas of the curriculum, such as science, where he is supervised with potentially dangerous materials or equipment, and helped with delicate tasks such as taking readings. Because his vision has always been monocular, practical work has posed problems in subjects such as technical drawing, which require an understanding of perspective. He types well and has access to computers in school and at home for recording work. Support teachers adapt graphs, worksheets, tables and maps for students, but this requires frequent joint planning between subject teachers, who do not always have detailed schemes of work. He recently spent time in a garden centre for work experience and is hoping to go on to study media and computing at a local college of further education.

Habil

Habil is a 19 year old whose visual problems became apparent when he was at infant school, and it was later confirmed that he had retinitis pigmentosa. His parents were told that the condition was progressive and that he might become blind by his teenage years. During the primary school years he attended a small local school with support from a peripatetic teacher for the visually impaired. Habil remembers not being able to see well, particularly at night, from the age of about 9. His visual field has gradually reduced to the point where he has tunnel vision, and the quality of his remaining central vision has also deteriorated. He has the most useful vision in his left eye of approximately 3/60. When Habil moved to secondary school, a unit for students with visual impairments had just been set up, but many environmental aspects were less than ideal. The school was large – more than 1,200 pupils – and housed in a four-storey Victorian building with a maze structure. However, right from the outset Habil had to get used to the idea of negotiating his way around complex spaces. In lessons where teachers made regular use of the blackboard for presentation, he used a CCTV with a camera, although it was difficult to move this equipment from floor to floor. The unit had an enlarger for reproducing worksheets and handouts, but this was unhelpful for certain materials, such as diagrams, maps and graphs, because his tunnel vision meant that he could not read information distributed over a wide area. Tactile diagrams have helped to get around some of these problems.

Currently, Habil is completing a course in a specialist residential college for students with visual impairments, in order to develop his mobility, communication and independence skills. Next year he is rejoining mainstream education at a college of higher education where he will study languages. Although highly sociable, with a huge network of friends, adjusting to living away from home has not been easy. The prospect of starting a new course is both exciting and daunting. There will be support from staff and appropriate technology for accessing information, but the challenge of a large and complex campus, together with new teachers and peers, is still formidable.

These notes, drawn from current case work, illustrate something of the complex and unpredictable nature of children's individual needs, as the clinical aspects of visual impairment interact with an intricate web of psychological, social and family variables. Visual impairments span a continuum from the mild and correctable to the complex and permanent. However, we have guarded against the implication that all children with visual impairments *ipso facto*, have developmental or learning difficulties. Neither have we wanted to give the impression that, when any learning, social or emotional difficulties arise, they are necessarily the result of the visual impairment itself. In all cases, whatever arrangements are made for schooling, either within or outside mainstream contexts, the focus of planning will be the tailoring of provision to the unique circumstances of the individuals and families concerned. This is what we mean by considering visual impairment as an aspect of human differentiation. It is by looking at the strategies adopted by adults and the contrasting conditions of teaching environments that we can tailor intervention to individual differences.

CONTEXTS FOR LEARNING AND RECENT RESEARCH

It is a commonly held view that a severe visual impairment, or blindness, has such a significant impact on children's perceptual experience that they are impelled to make representations of the world and to make sense of things through routes that may be characteristically distinct from those of 'seeing' children.

For a long time, researchers have been content to speculate on the nature and extent of these distinctions, in line with what we have earlier described as the 'visual impairment as deficit' model. Many writers see the condition of blindness as a kind of 'natural experiment' that provides researchers with intriguing possibilities for exploring the relationship between visual information, language and other domains of thinking, and the characteristics that are displayed by children without vision in trying to circumvent their difficulties. (See, for example, Dunlea, 1989.) We have also avoided the kind of explicit comparison of children with and without visual impairments, which maps the course of development of contrasting populations of children along normative 'milestones' or 'benchmarks'. Our own research has rejected the simplistic view of a visual impairment simply delaying 'normal progress', with intervention mainly focused on redressing these immaturities.

There are a number of ways in which recent research evidence encourages us to shift attention away from attempts to catalogue the 'typical' performance of groups of 'sighted' or 'visually impaired' groups on factors such as object perception, spatial awareness, vocabulary, creativity and reasoning, referential skills, locus of control, social and moral judgements. A more productive focus of interest is felt to be the processes (rather than the products) through which children and adults interact with one another in the learning environment, the strategies that adults adopt and the active involvement that children are prompted towards, as they live, play and learn together.

The social basis for learning

One significant factor that has begun to inform current thinking about children's potential for learning language and for cognitive growth is the importance of inter-personal contexts. All children are born with the potential to use symbols in order to represent the world and organise their experience, and it is this capacity for symbolic thinking that makes it possible for children to learn language and to use language as a means of enquiring further. However, the basic impetus for learning is a social one. Most children have a need to discover more about objects and events in the environment, to pass on material wants and to express feelings. But all of this occurs, in the early years at least, through interaction with familiar adults as part of the tacit and routine arrangements of children's activities in the everyday social contexts of care and play, which are not perceived as instructional.

15

Plate 1.2 Early social interactions with a partially sighted infant. The way in which early social encounters are patterned is highly significant. A visual impairment may disturb processes such as establishing eye contact, shared attention and responding to one another's smiles and expressions

In these early encounters, the child is neither simply exploring the world nor being explicitly taught, since an important aspect is the sustaining and negotiating of social contacts with those who share the environment. For a child with no, or very limited, residual vision, these social and linguistic encounters with parents and teachers are intensified and highly strategic in how the child constructs the world. In our view, the way in which social encounters between adults and children are patterned is highly important in determining thinking and learning, especially in the early years. All disabilities, particularly sensory impairments, disturb adult–child interactions. Parents frequently adopt more controlling or didactic strategies in an effort to try and work on aspects of language or behaviour. (See, for example, Webster and Wood, 1989, for an account of the impact of a hearing loss on adult–child encounters.) In order to facilitate learning and development, parents may have to recreate more effective patterns of interaction with their children. In the case of both hearing and visually impaired children, this will depend to a great extent on the ability of the parent to tune in to the perceptual world of the infant, to make responses contingent on what the child is attending to, in terms of visual or auditory events, and to find effective ways for the child to make sense of everyday experience.

A distinctive feature of the way in which children interact with other people in learning language is the child's interpretation of the social context. Children are influenced by the setting in which language is used, as they endeavour to find out what a person means. What words themselves signify is only one element of how meaning is constructed. Visual information is normally highly significant in helping children read situational clues: to interpret what people do as well as what they say. Visually based strategies may also underpin aspects such as the monitoring of each other's line of gaze, turn-taking, and the matching of language and concepts to objects and events in the immediate environment.

If vision is implicated in early play dialogues between infant and caregiver, and forms the basis for the introduction of the child into a social world where linguistic and cognitive development takes place, what are the implications for children with a visual impairment? One intriguing possibility is that vision is not a necessary condition for these early interactions to take place. We shall be exploring in due course the idea that language itself can take on some of the characteristics of vision as an integrating and co-ordinating sense, as a basis for learning. This is one example of what we have called the adaptivity and flexibility of developmental processes, which a visual impairment tests out.

Purpose and meaning

Another important trend in recent child development research is to highlight the importance of purpose and meaning in learning. Thus, whilst we assume a social context in which an adult is trying to share meaning with a child, we must also assume that there is something meaningful to communicate.

Adults and children do not talk about nothing. Similarly, in accounting for the child's motivation to acquire the language being used by others in the social context, it is difficult to believe that language is acquired for its potential or future use. Children are interested in language for what it can achieve in the 'here and now'. Both children and adults are impelled to use language, to develop linguistic and cognitive strategies in situations (however mundane) that really matter to the participants concerned.

These issues of purpose and meaning are also highly significant in considering the devising of effective learning environments for children with visual impairments. 'Verbalism' – the use of word meanings unsupported by direct experience – has been a contentious area of debate in the education of blind children in particular, with some 'experts' recommending that visually based language and ideas constructed around visual imagery should be avoided. 'Word/world' differences are, however, common to all children learning language. The real issue is how parents and teachers make bridges between the child's current representation of the world and any new linguistic uses or concepts that challenge that. It is through dialogue that carers draw attention to new information, make links between objects and events, abstract rules and similarities, and gradually enable the child's inner representation of the world to be brought into line with the adult's.

Learning how to learn

A particularly important aspect in overcoming some of the potentially limiting effects of a visual impairment is the child's own awareness of the function and intention of learning. When children are put into the position of passive assimilators in any learning process, they will be increasingly less likely to take responsibility for their own learning, to learn how to learn. Equipping youngsters for a lifetime of learning, we have already argued, requires flexibility, self-direction and the exercising of independence when choices or decisions have to be made. We shall be pursuing this line of enquiry in relation to the child's classroom experience. An important key to educational success for all children, particularly those affected by sensory impairments, is how far they can be helped to become aware of their own thinking and language, and of the most effective ways in which they come to know and understand. In other words, successful children achieve conscious control of some important aspects of their own learning and enquiry.

The final and perhaps most important of recent trends in cognitive science is the focus on what children can do, as opposed to what they are incapable of. Studying very young infants is a research area of increasing activity and importance. One reason for this intense interest in infancy is what it tells us about psychological processes generally. It is not so much that we now think that babies are far cleverer than we had ever imagined previously, but rather that children from early infancy onwards act on the world and make sense of it, and are not simply passive recipients of information. This also has profound implications for teaching and learning. For children with visual impairments, how we harness the child's sense of enquiry in order to develop a full understanding of the world informs much of the school curriculum.

LEARNING AS 'GUIDED PARTICIPATION'

In several sections of this book, particularly Chapter 6, evidence has been drawn from a three-year research project carried out within the School of Education at Bristol University. A number of parallel research projects, including work with children with severe visual impairments, studies of pupils and adults with severe hearing losses, and research across mainstream primary and secondary school contexts, share some common themes. First, they consider children, families or teachers in authentic home or school settings, accepting that the conditions and environments in which people live, play and work are normally unpredictable, typically messy, often fraught, always complex. The real challenge for the researcher in these social contexts is to find ways of capturing relevant data without oversimplifying, and keeping in mind the intricate dynamics and organisation of family or classroom life.

Second, the research studies examine aspects of interaction between adults and children, or children and peers. 'Adult–child proximation' is a term we have coined to refer to those instances where adults enter into close exchanges with children where explanations are given, deductions and inferences are shared, events are interpreted, conclusions are drawn. Adult–child proximation is examined in the nature and quality of everyday interactions, such as processes of negotiation, conversation, question and answer routines, or how children are recruited into tasks. Our approach stems partly from recent attempts to study teaching and learning as socially mediated activity or 'guided participation' (Wood, 1988; Moll, 1990; Rogoff, 1990; John-Steiner *et al.*, 1994). A key idea is that adults frequently help children to accomplish things that they could not do by themselves. Similarly, what adults assist children to achieve collaboratively prepares children for more independent enquiry in the future. The gap between what children can do on their own and what they can achieve with others more skilled than themselves is known as the 'zone of proximal development', from the Soviet writer Vygotsky (1978). Through social interaction with the more mature, children are exposed to practices and examples of how others tackle problems and manage their thinking.

'Scaffolding'

The third theme that links our research studies is that they intend to highlight those elements of the learning environment, or interactions around a learning focus, that most effectively promote development. Effective teaching and learning is seen as much more than the transmission of information from one individual to another. Rather, successful teaching is constituted in certain styles of collaboration and joint enquiry. All of our studies point to the most effective ways in which adults may 'scaffold' or support aspects of children's development: how children are introduced to tasks, how experience is represented and clarified, how meaning is constructed in a collective space such as a classroom, and how mediation takes place through language or other symbol systems, such as writing. It is a common belief that the long-term course of development can be affected significantly by improving aspects of social and learning environments. But to achieve this effectively requires a form of intervention and practice informed by research evidence, not simply polemic.

Socio-constructive approaches have profound implications for understanding processes of teaching and learning in children with visual impairments in the realtime of social contexts such as the classrooom. Essentially, they focus on the processes by which children's thinking and development are stretched and bolstered in the immediate social contexts in which they are involved in different forms of joint problem-solving or enquiry. Importantly, it is not assumed that the skills and procedures of thinking are generic to all situations, or exclusive to one group of children in contrast to another. It is the specific nature of what individuals do when faced with a problem, the means adopted to achieve given goals within the confines of a given situation, that holds interest. To our knowledge, there have been few attempts to research or apply these important ideas from socio-interactive encounters to the learning needs of children with visual impairments.

2

VISION AND VISUAL IMPAIRMENT

In this chapter we give descriptions of the 'normal' eye, its structure and function, as a basis for understanding the processes of seeing and how these may be affected by different eye conditions. The optical and psychological processes involved are highly complex and not fully understood. Given the complexity of the visual system, it is not surprising that there is a very wide range of conditions that may affect individuals. Although this is a fairly technical chapter, we have tried to keep specialist terms to the minimum. However, there is much specialist language used by different professional groups, and the medical or legal definitions of blindness or partial sight differ considerably from those used in education. Population figures for different groups depend on official categories and the data for registration; nevertheless, we have provided estimates for the numbers of individuals with handicapping visual conditions, together with recent figures for the numbers of children receiving different forms of educational help.

Parents and teachers often ask for advice on the kinds of signs to look out for in identifying a potential visual impairment. We have covered issues such as early screening and the assessment of vision, including details of common testing procedures used by doctors, specialists and other professional agencies. Functional vision – how children use their eyesight in real settings – is obviously of interest to teachers concerned with how well an individual may cope with the challenges of a mainstream school environment. We have also highlighted some of the main agencies that may be involved with families, children and schools. The Code of Practice is emphatic in its recommendations regarding close and effective co-operation between families and other services, particularly at points of diagnosis, when information is communicated and when plans are being made.

Defining what we mean by 'normal' vision is by no means straightforward. In everyday usage, people tend to consider their eyesight as adequate if they can cope with the majority of mundane tasks, such as driving, preparing food or reading a newspaper. The clinical measurement of visual acuity using the Snellen chart has an arbitrary standard of normal vision that permits us to carry out routine activities. However, there are many people who manage with less than average vision, whilst many tasks can be carried out perfectly adequately with lower than usual levels of visual acuity. In educational contexts, far more interest is shown in an individual's functional vision, which relates to the specific demands of real situations.

In this chapter we shall be considering some of the basic facts of vision and visual impairment, such as the structure of the eye and the neurological processes involved in seeing, as the light signals received by the eye are transmitted to the visual cortex and interpreted by the brain. The intention is to give a brief overview so that those unfamiliar with the field of visual impairment are aware of the parameters by which visual loss is defined and described. Significant in this respect are those definitions that carry legal as well as medical implications, giving access to certain benefits and services.

It is also important to understand the varying ways in which visual losses may arise, how these are identified and diagnosed, what treatments are available, and the likely significance of a visual condition in terms of the child's learning and development. We shall be returning to this theme in some detail in Chapter 3. However, we shall be outlining some general points about the impact of different kinds of visual impairment, estimating their prevalence, and suggesting the range of professional support services that may become involved with children and their families at different points in time following diagnosis.

INDIVIDUAL DIFFERENCES

As we have said, individuals with visual impairment do not fall simply into homogeneous groups. Whilst it is important to know the answer to questions such as 'How was the child's visual loss caused?', 'What is the nature and severity of the impairment?' or 'Did the loss occur at birth or during infancy when the child already had visual experience?', in fact the degree and nature of a child's visual impairment account for only a few of the differences between individuals. Some children with relatively mild visual losses may have marked educational problems, whilst other children with much more severe visual impairments in clinical terms manage remarkably well, given appropriate services, support and teaching. Research indicates that the success of a child's educational placement in integrated settings is most *unlikely* to be determined by visual acuity *per se*. This is one of the main reasons why, in Chapter 6, we turn our attention to the research evidence that explores the fine grain of teaching transactions and the conditions for learning most likely to be associated with success.

There is a very great variety of eye conditions in children with visual impairments. Even when two children share the same condition and a similar degree of visual loss, they may behave very differently. For example, given a Russian doll to play with, one child may keep the toy on a table, using hands to explore the smoothness, hardness and symmetry of its sections, whilst another child may try to use any residual vision to acquire information about its colour and construction, either by getting up close to the object or by bringing it near to the eyes. Yet another child may use a combination of tactile information and residual vision, touching the shapes and textures of its segments, but visually inspecting the patterns of light reflected from shiny surfaces, as well as some of the features with which the doll is inscribed.

These differences between children are highlighted by an unfamiliar situation, such as joining a new playgroup. In exploring the environment, one totally blind child may be very lively and adventurous, using some light perception to avoid obstacles, and rapidly assessing the components of the space and its boundaries. Another child may be much more careful, making sure that there are no obstacles in the way before moving around, anxiously requesting help from adults, or engaging cautiously in a peripheral activity, such as exploring a box of toys.

It is also important to take into account the psychological and emotional implications of a visual condition on not only children but also their families. A child diagnosed as totally blind in infancy, due to a non-life-threatening condition, may have a very different set of experiences and expectations compared with a child diagnosed as having a life-threatening disease, one of the outcomes of which happens to be blindness. Each family reacts and comes to terms with their child's visual impairment in different ways, and these responses are inevitably influenced by whether a child has a stable visual loss, a progressive eye condition or a potentially life-threatening disease.

DEFINING VISUAL IMPAIRMENT

Categories such as 'blind' and 'partially sighted' as used for medical and legal purposes can carry different connotations from the same terms used in educational contexts. Although representing only one aspect of vision, and in some instances not the most salient, visual *acuity* is the basis on which an individual's visual impairment is usually categorised.

Tests of visual acuity demonstrate the resolving power of the eye: the ability to distinguish very fine detail. Visual acuity can be measured in a variety of ways, but the most common method uses the Snellen chart. The chart has rows of different size letters arranged in decreasing size, which can be read by a 'normal eye' at different distances. The largest letter has a viewing distance of 60 metres, with smaller letters for distances of 36, 24, 12, 9, 6 and 5 metres. A normal eye reads the 6 metre letters from a distance of 6 metres. Visual acuity for each eye is tested separately by asking the person to read the letters from a distance of 6 metres with one eye covered. The visual acuity for each eye is expressed as 6 over the smallest line of letters that can be read.

In the UK, 'normal' visual acuity is expressed as 6/6, whilst in the USA this would be recorded as 20/20, or as 1,0 in some European countries.

A visual acuity of 6/12 indicates that the smallest size of letters that an individual can identify is 12 at a distance of 6 metres. Effectively, this means that the individual can see at 6 metres what a person with average eyesight can see at a distance of 12 metres. Sometimes visual acuity is measured at a distance of 3 metres, or even 1 metre, and therefore we can find visual acuity expressed as a figure such as 3/60, which would mean that the smallest size of letters that an individual can identify on the Snellen chart is 60 at a distance of 3 metres. One obvious problem in defining visual function in terms of visual acuity is the difficulty in quantifying visual impairment in young children, or in individuals with learning difficulties or complex handicaps. In such instances, it may be very difficult for an examiner to interpret an individual's responses to the test, or to know whether instructions have been understood.

Apart from clear vision at a distance, a visual impairment may also have an impact on other aspects of vision, such as loss of peripheral vision, loss of central vision, or disturbances in the visual field. The discrimination of sharp images immediately in front of the eyes is important for close work involving fine eye–hand co-ordination and the perception of small details, such as reading textbooks and handwriting, interpreting tables and diagrams, working

Table 2.1 World Health Organisation categories of vision

Category of vision	Degree of impairment	Visual acuity with correction	Alternative definition
Normal	None	more or equal to 6/7.5	
	Slight	less than 6/7.5	Near normal
Low vision	Moderate	less than 6/18	Moderate low vision
	Severe	less than 6/48	Severe low vision, counting fingers at 6 metres or less
Blindness	Profound	less than 3/60	Profound low vision or moderate blindness, counting fingers at less than 3 metres
	Near total	less than 1/60	Severe or near total blindness, counting fingers at 1 metre or less or hand movements at 5 metres or less
	Total	no light perception	Total blindness (including absence of the eye)

Source: WHO, 1980

with computers, using tools and equipment. Loss of clear vision will affect a child in day-to-day classroom activities where fine discrimination is required. However, the same child may well be able to cope confidently with physical activities in the playground or gymnasium.

Loss of peripheral vision, in contrast, may lead to clumsiness in general mobility, and difficulties negotiating steps and furniture, although central vision may be normal. Tunnel vision, a term used to describe the effect of some visual field impairments, can impede skills such as skimming text, plans or maps to find information, or catching a tennis ball. Complex visual conditions often give rise to a combination of effects, with the result that individuals learn through experience the kind of visual tasks they can cope best with, in different environmental conditions. In Chapter 5 we consider the management of learning contexts for children with visual impairments and how teachers need to be sensitive and respond flexibly to the interplay of factors that may affect a child's performance.

MEDICAL, LEGAL AND EDUCATIONAL TERMS

Blindness

In Britain, the official definition of a blind person is 'a person so blind as to be unable to perform any work for which eyesight is essential' (Tobin, 1994). This usually corresponds to a visual acuity of 3/60 or less in the better eye after correction. Assessment of an individual's visual field is also implicated in some attempts to define blindness; this refers to the extent of the surroundings that we can see without moving our head or eyes (Aitken and Buultjens, 1992). If there is a loss in the visual field, an individual with a visual acuity superior to 3/60 may be considered blind.

In educational terms, individuals are considered 'educationally blind' when they require non-visual means in order to access the curriculum. Educationally blind children will rely mostly on tactile and auditory information in order to learn, and are potential braille users. However, most of these children, approximately 80 per cent of those classed as blind, may have some residual vision or light perception that they can use to help orientate themselves, avoid obstacles and interpret the environment. Learning to use residual vision is a process of becoming more skilled at interpreting less than perfect images in relation to a cumulative store of experience.

Two of the case studies presented in Chapter 1 – Nelly and Daniel – give brief pen pictures of educationally blind children. However, Daniel is totally blind with no light perception and he relies on non-visual cues to follow every educational task, move around, explore surroundings, use resources and obtain information. Nelly, on the other hand, has some useful residual vision. Her visual acuity is extremely difficult to measure, but at the latest attempt she identified one drawing, size 60, at 30 centimetres. She can use her residual vision to move around in familiar environments, identify simple drawings of a big size and with good contrast using a CCTV, and determine colours and contours. However, Nelly cannot easily cope with the amount of visual information required to follow the curriculum and frequently relies on non-visual means. She is learning braille and making use of auditory and tactile information for much of the time.

Partial sight

In legal terms, 'partial sight' is defined as a visual acuity of between 3/60 and 6/60. As mentioned earlier, partial sight is interpreted quite differently in educational contexts, where the term refers to individuals who can use their eyesight to follow educational tasks, but whose learning and achievement will be hindered unless some modifications are made to teaching methods and materials, and adaptations are made to the learning environment. Although in school settings children will need to use their sight in a variety of situations that are very different to those used during a clinical assessment, a Snellen visual acuity of between 6/18 and 6/60 is typically assumed to mean partial sight.

Even when children with a visual acuity of 6/18 have been able to follow the first phase of their primary education successfully in a mainstream school, they are bound to require some special methods, equipment or adaptations as the academic curriculum intensifies. In keeping with the underlying philosophy of the Code of Practice, the educational needs of children with visual impairment are best approached as fluid and interactive, rather than fixed: their needs depend on the nature of tasks undertaken in contrasting social and academic milieux.

HOW MANY PEOPLE HAVE A VISUAL IMPAIRMENT?

One of the problems in determining the incidence or prevalence of visual impairment in childhood is the wide variation in terminology found in different studies, in the definitions adopted for normal vision, and in the criteria used for varying degrees of visual handicap. (Incidence refers to the number of individuals with a particular difficulty being added to a population, for example the rate of occurrence of new cases during the course of a year. Prevalence refers to the proportion of people in a given population exhibiting a particular condition.)

There is a very wide continuum of visual loss, with many youngsters experiencing mild difficulties, such as short sightedness, that can be corrected by glasses. Loss of colour vision is another form of visual impairment that is unlikely to be significant enough to interfere markedly with learning. Unusual in girls, but occurring in about 8 per cent of boys, loss of colour vision leads to problems distinguishing different parts of the spectrum (typically red and green), and may preclude some career options later in life. However, this is unlikely to merit special attention in school, or to warrant involving outside agencies such as specialist teachers of the visually impaired.

Registration

Official figures for the population of people with visual impairments are usually based on registration. Social Services departments have an obligation to keep registers of people who fall within prescribed categories of need, and to ensure that certain services are provided, such as advice, resources, equipment, travel concessions and, in some cases, financial help. However, many individuals with significant visual impairments do not volunteer themselves for registration. They may be unaware of any benefits they might receive from this, or feel it is not worth the bother, since failing to register does not preclude access to most services. Because LEAs take much of the responsibility for meeting children's educational needs, registration is often considered to be less important for children than adults.

From surveys carried out in the UK by the RNIB it has been estimated that blindness and partial sight are under-registered by 64 per cent and 77 per cent respectively in the adult population (Baird and Moore, 1993). Children represent only a relatively small number of the total visually impaired population. However, figures for the prevalence of visual impairments in children based on registration figures are felt to be just as unreliable, underestimating the numbers of partially sighted children by as much as 84 per cent (Best, 1992). This kind of misinformation assumes great impor-tance when the basis for planning services and resources is registration statistics.

In the pre-school years, children with very severe visual impairments or total blindness are likely to be identified without too much difficulty. Normally, the more severe the visual impairment, the easier it is to diagnose in early infancy; however, many children with a mild form of visual impairment are not detected until they attend school. Therefore, in the pre-school years, most of the children registered as visually impaired are those who present with more severe or complex conditions. At these early stages there are usually more children registered as blind than as partially sighted. In contrast, in the school-age years there are more children registered as partially sighted than as blind (Best, 1992). This is due to the fact that many visual difficulties are initially detected, or more precisely defined, when the child is required to perform more demanding visual tasks such as reading and writing.

Children with multiple disabilities

Another difficulty in giving a precise estimate for the prevalence of visual impairments is the likelihood of a severe visual loss arising in association with other disabling factors. For example, a child presenting with multiple disabilities, where the main factor is not a visual impairment, may be considered as having severe learning difficulties. Reports compiled by the RNIB suggest that there are as many individuals with a severe learning difficulty who could be registered as blind as those who are already so registered, and the same happens for partially sighted children (Bruce *et al.*, 1991; Walker *et al.*, 1992). There is a general trend, reported in most epidemiological surveys, for the majority of children with severe visual impairments or blindness to have additional disabilities, at least in the more prosperous communities of Europe and North America (Baird and Moore, 1993).

Despite the questions raised above regarding registration and its representative value, these are the data from which official figures for the visually impaired population in England are derived. In 1991, a total of 229,972 people were registered in England (DOH, 1991). From this total, 136,195 people were registered blind and 93,777 were registered partially sighted. About 65 per cent of the population registered were over 75 years of age, a figure that expands over time as people tend to live longer. From the whole population registered as having a visual impairment in 1991, only about 2 per cent were under the age of 16: a total of 4,698 children, of which 2,554 were registered as blind and 2,144 were registered as partially sighted.

LEA surveys

The most recent survey of children known to LEA visual impairment services in England and Wales (as opposed to registered with Social Services) was carried out by Louise Clunies-Ross (1995). LEAs were asked to provide information about all the children with visual impairments they were aware of, whether they were provided with educational support or not. Preliminary results of this survey, which included 53 per cent of LEAs, indicate a total of 8,243 children with a significant visual impairment under the age of 16, 35 per cent of whom have multiple disabilities. These figures, although incomplete, confirm estimates provided by, for example, the RNIB (Walker *et al.*, 1992) which suggest a prevalence of 1 in 1,000 children having some form of visual impairment carrying educational implications. As suggested earlier, differences between population estimates depend mostly on criteria for inclusion and the representativeness of the data collected. It is probably fair to conclude that most surveys under-record the true prevalence of visual impairments in young children, but we can expect 1 to 2 per cent of school children nationally to have a handicapping visual condition, which represents approximately 25,000 children (Walker *et al.*, 1992).

In terms of educational placement, the survey by Clunies-Ross (1995) shows that 67 per cent of primary-aged children with visual impairments attend mainstream schools; 32 per cent are placed in special schools, mainly for pupils with learning difficulties, whilst less than 3 per cent attend special schools for the visually impaired. For secondary-aged children the same trends were observed, with 58 per cent of pupils attending mainstream schools,

41 per cent placed in special schools for students with learning difficulties, whilst just over 3 per cent received their education in special schools for the visually impaired. By far the greatest majority of children known to LEA services for the visually impaired and visited by specialist teachers are included in mainstream school contexts. One important implication to be drawn from these data is that the day-to-day educational needs of most children with visual impairments, albeit the children with less complex handicaps, are met by non-specialist teaching staff with varying levels of additional support.

Causes of visual impairment globally

Finally, we give here some brief details about the major causes of visual impairments globally. In areas of the developing world such as Africa, Asia and South America, primary health care measures such as vaccination, use of antibiotics, and better nutrition would have a major impact on reducing the incidence of blinding diseases. In many countries the incidence of visual impairments in children is an indicator of general economic status (Baird and Moore, 1993).

In the more prosperous parts of Europe and America, most severe childhood visual impairment, approximately 40 to 50 per cent, can be accounted for by hereditary factors, such as congenital cataracts, albinism or retinal dystrophies. Unlike in the developing world, disease acquired in later childhood due to infection is an uncommon cause of blindness in Europe. The second most significant cause of visual impairment is perinatal disease, such as visual pathway damage associated with birth hypoxia and retinopathy of prematurity (ROP). This condition typically affects premature infants exposed to high blood concentrations of oxygen and was a major cause of blindness in the 1950s, since when the dangers of this treatment have been recognised. Premature infants are still at risk of ROP, even though their blood oxygen levels are not allowed to become too high. ROP is a disease likely to affect very small premature infants weighing less than 1,300 grammes at birth, many of whom will have additional neurological impairments. Diminishing numbers of ROP-affected infants may well be offset by the developing capability of paediatrics to save premature babies of very low birth weight who have a high risk of a wide range of impairments. For children registered as partially sighted, some of the main causes include optic atrophy, congenital cataracts and nystagmus (Baird and Moore, 1993).

THE STRUCTURE OF THE EYE

We need to know something about the basic structure of the eye and the functioning of the visual system in order to be aware of how things may go wrong, and to gain a better understanding of the importance of aspects such as residual vision.

The eye depends on several accessory structures that support, move, lubricate and protect it. These include the orbital bones of the eye socket; the eyebrow, eyelid, eyelashes, tear glands and ducts; as well as the muscles attached to the eyeball. Most of the eyeball is enclosed and protected within the bony orbit of the skull; only the very front portion is exposed. A pad of fat between the eyeball and orbit also cushions the eye. The eyebrow shields the eye from sweat, sunlight and foreign bodies, whilst the glands that line the eyelid secrete an oily fluid that helps to keep the eye lubricated. The blink reflex of the eyelid can be brought on by potential threats to the eye, such as bright lights or particles of dust. As a reflex to irritation, lacrimal glands secrete tears which flow over the surface of the cornea in order to help remove foreign bodies. Normal blinking closes the eyelid every few seconds to move secretions across the eye to prevent drying. The tears eventually drain through ducts into a sac that is connected to the nasal cavity.

The muscles attached to the eyeball and to the walls of the orbit are responsible for the control of eye movements. There are six muscles in each eye, organised in three pairs, each with a main motor function (rotation, up and down, side to side). Together they allow us to move our eyes with precise control to shift direction of gaze to near or distant objects. The eyeball itself is made up of three layers: the fibrous coat, the vascular pigmented coat and the nervous coat.

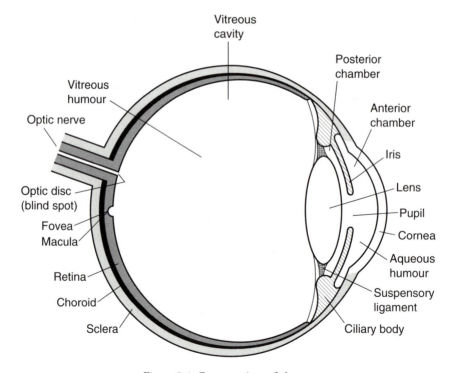

Figure 2.1 Cross-section of the eye

Fibrous coat

The outside fibrous layer of the eye consists of the posterior part, the sclera (the white part of the eye), which helps to maintain its shape, and the anterior part, the cornea (the transparent, curved surface at the very front of the eyeball), which initiates the focusing process necessary to see clearly, refracting light into the lens.

Vascular pigmented coat

The middle layer of the eye is made up of the choroid, the iris and the ciliary body. The choroid is a pigmented coat with many blood vessels which absorbs light and prevents leakage or scattering of light signals. At the front of the eye, the ciliary muscles adjust the shape of the lens to control accommodation: the eye's ability to focus on near or far objects. Extending from the ciliary body is a suspensory ligament that supports the lens. To view an object in the distance, the ciliary muscles relax and the suspensory ligaments pull the lens flat and thin. To view an object nearby, the ciliary muscles contract, reducing the pull on the suspensory ligaments, which allows the lens to bulge and become more rounded.

Blood vessels in the ciliary process produce a watery fluid, called the aqueous humour, which fills the anterior and posterior chambers of the eye. Behind the cornea is the iris, which forms the coloured part of the eye and controls the amount of light coming into the centre of the eye by changing the size of the pupil that it surrounds. The iris determines pupil size according to factors such as light intensity and emotional state. The pupil appears black because we are usually looking through the hole into an unlit eye cavity. Photographs taken with flash show the pupil as red because the blood vessels covering the back of the eye are then illuminated.

Nervous coat

The third, inner layer of the eyeball is the retina, or nervous coat, where light converges and images form. Covering the back of the eyeball, the retina is made up of a carpet of photosensitive elements, the photoreceptors. These photoreceptors are of two classes: rods (numbering approximately 125 million) and cones (approximately 7 million). Rods are found mainly in the periphery of the retina and contain one light-sensitive pigment (rhodopsin or visual purple). Rods operate under conditions of low light intensity; they detect weak visual stimuli, shape and movement, but not details. Cones respond to brightness and colour, and are more adept at detecting fine detail. Cones require more light than rods to be activated and contain pigments that respond to different light wavelengths (green, red or blue). Cones make possible high definition colour vision in bright light.

The photosensitivity of the retina varies over its surface. The blindspot is the point at which the optic nerve leaves the eyeball; this has no photoreceptors. The area of clearest vision is the macula. At the centre of the macula, the fovea is a point that contains only cone cells, providing images with detail and colour. The periphery of the retina, which contains mainly rod cells, is important for night vision and lower lighting levels.

The structure of the eye, as shown in Figure 2.1, also involves a number of distinct cavities or chambers. The front cavity of the eye is divided into the anterior chamber, which is in front of the iris, and the posterior chamber, which lies between the lens and the ciliary body. The front cavity is filled with aqueous humour. This provides nutrients to the cornea and the lens. Aqueous humour also helps to maintain pressure within the eyeball at a constant level. The vitreous cavity at the back of the eyeball is filled with vitreous humour, which makes up about two-thirds of the volume of the eye. In contrast to the anterior cavity, this is a closed system where the vitreous humour lasts for life. This clear gel helps to maintain eyeball shape, as well as the correct position of the lens and retina.

THE PROCESS OF SEEING

The functioning of the eye has frequently been compared to that of a camera: both allow controlled amounts of light through a lens to focus on a photosensitive surface. The crucial difference lies in how these images are processed, integrated and interpreted. Visual processes involve more than just receiving light signals in the eye, since information must then be transmitted to the brain, interpreted and made sense of, in order that the individual can decide how to respond.

Although there are some situations in which humans do not see as well as other species (for example, some animals have much better night vision), it remains the case that humans have a highly sophisticated visual system, capable of processing a very wide range of visual stimuli. We know that some aspects of our visual capacity are well adapted to the developmental and learning needs of humans. For example, evidence shows that newborn infants are active visual explorers and can track moving objects, preferring to look at patterns such as human faces. We shall be examining the role of vision in establishing adult–child interactions and extending the infant's early understanding of the world in some detail in Chapter 3. However, it should be said that both the physiological basis for much of our visual processing, and the psychological processes involved in perception and learning from visual experience, are highly complex and by no means fully understood.

Vision is sometimes described as a two-fold process, both optical and neural, combining sensory reception, perception and interpretation. The optical stage begins at the outer surface of the eyeball as light enters the cornea, and ends at the retina, a complex membrane of cells that specialises in transduction:

the conversion of one form of energy into another. Light interacts with the retina and is processed into electrical impulses; vision then becomes a neural process involving the central nervous system. These neural impulses are carried through the optic nerve of each eye to parts of the brain, especially the occipital lobe, where they are interpreted and given meaning.

Basic facts about light energy

In understanding the process of seeing it will be helpful to remember some basic facts about light energy. Light travels in straight lines as waves of energy at the rate of 300,000 kilometres per second. All visual sensations are produced by variations in three aspects of light energy: the length, amplitude and purity of lightwaves. The length of the wave determines the sensations we identify as colour. The amplitude of the wave determines our perceptions of the brightness or intensity of the light. Purity of the wave determines the saturation or depth of the colours we perceive.

Our eyes can respond to only a tiny fraction of the total range of wavelengths. Wavelengths are measured in nanometres (nm): units of measurement equal to one thousand-millionth of a metre. Visible light (between 380 and 760 nm) forms a small part of the electromagnetic spectrum. Wavelengths shorter than 380 nm (ultraviolet rays, X-rays, gamma rays) require special equipment for detection, as do wavelengths longer than 760 nm (infrared, microwaves, radiowaves). The longest wavelength visible to humans (760 nm) produces the colour we perceive as red. The shortest wavelength (380 nm) produces violet. We see objects as coloured when a particular colour wavelength is being reflected; so, for example, grass reflects the green wavelength. The purity of the colour we see depends on the homogeneity of the light waves. If only one kind of wavelength is seen, the colour sensation will be exceptionally deep. Black objects appear so because all the colour wavelengths are absorbed. White objects, in contrast, reflect all colour wavelengths.

Refraction

Another property of light energy we need to remind ourselves about is refraction, the change in direction of light when it passes from one transparent medium to another of different optical density, demonstrated, for example, by the apparent bending of a ruler placed in a tumbler of water. The eye refracts light so that it focuses to form a sharp image on the retina. The cornea is responsible for starting this process, while accommodation by the lens, changing its shape to increase light refraction, enables us to see fine detail sharply. Accommodation is an automatic response that changes the angle of incoming light rays to provide a sharper focus on the retina. The 'near point' is the closest point at which we can focus clearly on objects. The eye is working hardest for near vision, which is why protracted close work can lead to tired eyes.

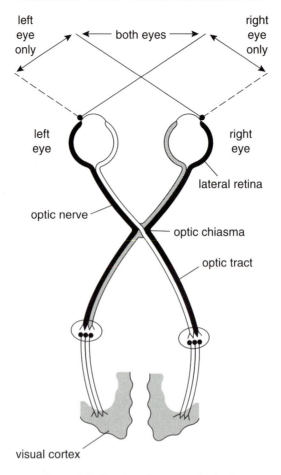

left eye only — both eyes → right eye only

left eye

right eye

lateral retina

optic nerve

optic chiasma

optic tract

visual cortex

Figure 2.2 Visual pathways to the brain

Transduction from light waves to neural impulses

Light passes through the cornea and lens to converge on the retina, forming a two-dimensional, upside-down image. The photoreceptors of the retina – the rods and cones referred to previously – differ in the nature of their sensitivity and give rise to different visual experiences. These cells undergo a chemical change when light falls on them. This change is converted, or transduced, into electrical energy which is transported through the optic nerve to the brain.

Each eye has its own optic nerve, but the two nerves converge at the base of the brain (see Figure 2.2) at the point known as the optic chiasma. The optic chiasma resorts the nerve branches so that information originating from each eye travels to both sides of the brain. This means that each side of the optic cortex receives nerve impulses from both eyes. The brain can then compare the slightly different information arriving from the same object viewed by each eye, and thus make decisions about positions in space. Children who lose an eye, for example through an accident, learn to interpret other cues to compensate for this loss of stereoscopic vision, such as textures, tones and the relative movement or occlusion of one object positioned in front of another. Adults may find it much more difficult to judge depth and relative positions of objects in space if they find they have to function with one eye.

It is the brain that organises our visual experience. In the visual cortex images are turned upright. From the succession of images that the eye takes in, the brain constructs and interprets a continuous visual 'reality'. Under instruction from the brain, the eyes select important details and ignore others. The role of the brain includes analysing and storing visual impressions, integrating information from different senses, and using information selectively within the complex processes of perceptual judgement, development and learning.

EYE CONDITIONS AND THEIR TREATMENT

Most of the common, less serious eye problems are related to refractive errors. In order for us to see, light rays pass through the cornea, aqueous humour, lens and vitreous humour to the retina, where neural encoding is initiated. The light rays change direction as they pass through these structures, due to their varying densities, and focus on the fovea of the retina. When parallel light rays are brought to a focus on the fovea without the use of accommodation or lenses, we say that we have an emmetropic, or 'normal', eye (Jose, 1983). Emmetropia refers to the absence of refractive errors.

Long-sightedness

Hypermetropia, or long-sightedness, occurs when the eyeball is too small and is not compensated for by increased curvature of the cornea or of the lens surface. As a result, when accommodation is fully relaxed, parallel light rays are focused behind the fovea, instead of on the surface of the retina. Individuals who are long-sighted will see things more clearly at a distance than near to. While it is true that adults with long-sight have difficulty seeing things near to, children with long-sight tend not to have a problem seeing things close up. Because their lenses are elastic, they have a high refractive power. With age this refractive power decreases. Children who are long-sighted have to accommodate much more to see near objects, but they generally have the 'reserve' power to do so. For some individuals the use of convex spectacle lenses or contact lenses makes it possible to correct the focusing point on the retina. However, some children who are long-sighted may find close work uncomfortable or tiring, even when wearing spectacles, and as a result may resist activities such as reading.

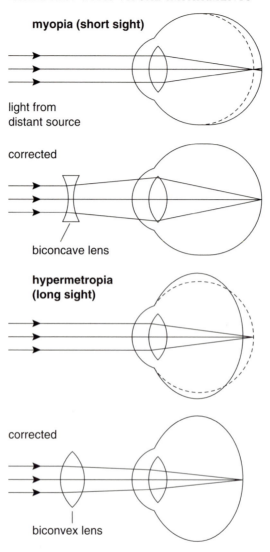

Figure 2.3 Refractive errors and their correction

Short-sightedness

Myopia, or short-sightedness, is an inability to focus the eyes on distant objects. This occurs when the eyeball is too big and is not compensated for by reduced curvature of the cornea or of the lens surface. As a result, when accommodation is fully relaxed, parallel light rays are focused in front of the fovea, rather than on the surface of the retina. The use of concave spectacle lenses or contact lenses compensates for this condition. Myopia tends to progress in young children and spectacles or lenses may have to be changed every six months or so. Children with severe myopia may need to hold printed material very close to the eyes to read it, whilst distance vision can also be poor. It has often been said that children with severe short-sightedness find it hard to follow much of what is going on around them in the classroom, opt out of group activities such as games, and seem out of step with their peers.

When children are prescribed spectacles or contact lenses it is important to remember that they provide optical correction, not a cure for visual impairments. This holds true so long as the glasses or lenses are worn at the appropriate times, are kept clean and continue to fit well. Because children's eyes change over time, vision must be monitored frequently. Contact lenses require more care and are difficult to manage, especially with younger children, although they can provide more effective correction in some eye conditions. We shall be returning to the issue of managing spectacles and contact lenses again in Chapter 5, when we discuss classroom contexts. Obviously, teachers need to be informed if any younger children are wearing contact lenses or have been prescribed spectacles, and should be given advice over their care and use.

Other conditions that affect the focusing of the eye include degenerative myopia, a condition associated with lengthening of the eyeball, and degenerative changes in the retina. Degenerative myopia leads to extreme short-sightedness, which may occur very early in life or, in some cases, be present from birth. As the disease progresses, there is a decrease in visual acuity, which is not always possible to correct. In some cases individuals complain of pain and flashing lights, which can mean that there is also detachment of the retina and subsequent loss of sensitivity in the visual field. The macula may also be involved, affecting central vision (Jose, 1983).

Astigmatism

Astigmatism is the term used to refer to a refractive error caused by irregularities on the surface of the cornea, preventing the eye from focusing a clear image on the retina and resulting in distorted or blurred vision. Astigmatism can be associated with either hypermetropia or myopia. Usually, astigmatism can be corrected with cylindrical lenses, though in some severe cases it may not be possible to achieve clear visual acuity. An affected individual may squint to try to get a clear image, and have persistent difficulties in judging depth or distance. There may be confusions observed in classroom tasks requiring shape discrimination, such as in the early stages of learning to read or using numbers (m/n, t/f, 3/8), in discerning details in maps, charts or illustrations.

Presbyopia

The term 'presbyopia' derives from the Latin for 'old person'. Because the elasticity of the lens decreases as we get older, so does the speed and power of accommodation. The lens cannot change its shape enough to allow the focus of light rays on the fovea. Instead, the light rays are focused behind the fovea. This reduction in the ability to accommodate is known as presbyopia. In effect, presbyopia moves the near point further away from the eye; hence older people read at arm's length. The condition affects almost all members of the population as they get older, and the use of biconvex lenses is necessary to correct it.

Certain types of myopia and astigmatism can be treated by surgery. In radial keratotomy, a scalpel or laser can be used to make incisions in the cornea to alter the way in which light rays are refracted. Lasers can also be used to shave microscopic amounts of tissue from the front of the cornea to change the eyeball's shape. The long-term effects of these surgical procedures to correct refraction errors are unknown.

Strabismus or squint

Strabismus, or squint, occurs when the two eyes are unable to work in unison, to direct their gaze simultaneously at the same object. Strabismus is caused by an imbalance in ocular muscle function, resulting in one eye being directed inwards or outwards, upwards or downwards, relative to the other. Squints are usually divided into concomitant (manifest) and incomitant (latent). If the squint is concomitant, it is observed in all directions of gaze. An incomitant squint means that it is observed only in some directions of gaze, but not others. In a concomitant squint, if one eye drifts inwards (converges), it is called an esotropia. Where an eye drifts outwards (diverges), the condition is termed exotropia.

Children with hypermetropia may have a convergent squint due to the link between accommodation and convergence. As we said earlier, children with long-sight have their eyes focused in the distance and have to accommodate much more to see near objects: both eyes will therefore turn inwards in order to focus on an object as it comes closer to the face. Correction of children's long-sight is usually done to help the squint and may have little to do with visual acuity.

In the presence of a concomitant convergent squint, the brain is receiving two contradictory images and double vision is produced. Children rarely complain of seeing double because the image from the squinting eye is suppressed by the brain. This can lead to abnormal development of vision in the squinting eye: a 'lazy' or amblyopic eye (Coakes and Sellors, 1995). The treatment of a convergent concomitant squint can be achieved in various ways, such as by the use of spectacles to correct for hypermetropia, the occlusion of the good eye with a patch to help develop vision in the amblyopic eye, or surgery. Surgery can be used to decrease or increase the pull of a muscle, or to change the direction of pull of a muscle.

Concomitant divergent squints are infrequent and usually intermittent, which allows the child to have binocular vision for most of the time. These squints can become more frequent with age and surgery may be necessary. Divergent squints are often taken to be indicators of a more serious underlying disease, and their sudden appearance should always be acted upon.

Nystagmus

Nystagmus is a repetitive, involuntary, oscillatory movement of the eyes. This condition can be congenital or acquired. In congenital nystagmus onset may be between 2 and 3 months, with no other pathology. However, it may be associated with serious pathology such as cataracts, albinism, aniridia or optic nerve hypoplasia. Congenital nystagmus can be 'pendular', which is observed when the vertical and horizontal movements are equal in opposing directions. 'Jerky' nystagmus is observed when the eye movements are fast and towards the direction of gaze. 'Latent' nystagmus refers to rapid eye oscillations that arise when one eye is covered. Nystagmus can be acquired through trauma, later onset of cataracts, exposure to toxic drugs or in association with disorders such as cone dystrophy or central nervous system dysfunction.

Individuals with nystagmus may have both distance and near vision affected. Children with nystagmus often have a 'null point', a position where the nystagmus is minimal. They may take up particular head postures, such as holding the head on one side or slightly askew, to utilise this. They may need to sit very close to the blackboard if the teacher writes up instructions or information. No attempt should be made to correct apparently abnormal head postures, although strained head or body postures can lead to fatigue and opting out of some activities.

Disorders of the cornea

Keratoconus is a progressive disorder in which the cornea acquires a cone shape. It is a disease that occurs mainly in females, with an age onset around puberty. Usually it occurs in both eyes. It seems that the condition may be hereditary, but it is not known how it is transmitted. Initially, the condition of keratoconus is noticed as a progressive decrease in visual acuity, associated with irregular astigmatism and a distortion of vision. Very rarely, blindness can occur if the disorder progresses to the point when the cornea ruptures. The use of spectacles or contact lenses can help to correct for the loss of visual acuity. Keratoconus is sometimes associated with syndromes such as Down's syndrome, Turner's syndrome and Marfan's syndrome. There are other corneal disorders called corneal dystrophies which are rare and progressive, and which also occur in both eyes. In some cases a corneal transplant may be necessary to improve visual acuity.

Ulceration and scarring of the cornea can be caused by infections or accidents, such as irritant substances entering the eye. These conditions may cause only temporary impairment to clear vision, and sensitivity to bright light or glare. Scarring of the cornea, often the result of an accident, can interfere with the passage of light rays into the eye and may also produce blurring of vision.

Disorders of the lens

The diagnosis of a cataract refers to the condition where, for one of a number of reasons, a section of the lens becomes opaque and prevents light passing through to the retina. Both eyes are often affected. Cataracts are one of the commonest causes of visual impairment across populations globally. Cataracts may be present at birth as a result of an infection, such as maternal rubella, that has crossed the placental barrier. They can also be hereditary, with other members of the family affected. Cataracts appear with increasing age, so most people over 70 years' old are at risk. Surgery may be necessary, and in some cases the whole lens is removed, to be replaced by an artificial lens. An eye without a lens is known as 'aphakic'. In this case a thick convex spectacle lens will need to be worn to help in focusing. Two pairs will be required: one for distant and one for near viewing, or alternatively, bifocals.

Cataracts vary in degree of density, size and location in the lens, and thus have different effects on visual acuity. The more dense and central the cataract, the greater the loss of vision for detail. Individuals with cataracts may also have blurred vision and experience difficulties with glare. When the cataract is situated in the centre or posterior part of the lens, the use of dim light may be helpful. When the cataract is situated in the periphery of the lens, working in bright light may be preferred. In severe cases of congenital cataracts, nystagmus may also appear. Surgery is often required as early as possible for dense cataracts in young children, so that the eye can still develop normally. Following cataract surgery, many children are able to see very well wearing glasses, whilst others have vision that cannot be improved above 6/60. There is an increasing trend towards intraocular lens implants in children, which obviously reduces the need for very strong glasses or contact lenses. Peripheral vision and associated mobility may well be affected. In classroom contexts, levels of lighting will need to be considered carefully for each child, and attention paid to print size and contrast.

Disorders of the iris

Aniridia is the term used to describe the condition characterised by the total absence of the iris. Aniridia is present at birth, affecting both eyes, and often occurs alongside other congenital abnormalities. Individuals with aniridia appear to have extremely large pupils. Because the iris controls the amount of light that enters the eye, those with aniridia are highly photophobic (light sensitive), and most have very poor visual acuity. They may also have nystagmus, and in some 50 per cent of cases, glaucoma.

Individuals with aniridia can have associated conditions such as cataracts, lack of development of the retina and displacement of the lens. The use of dim light, dark glasses and pin hole contact lenses can be helpful, the latter helping to increase visual acuity (Jose, 1983).

Coloboma is an absence of a sector of the iris, appearing as a fissure, crack or 'keyhole', caused by a malformation in early foetal development. This condition can also be associated with coloboma of the choroid, retina or optic nerve (Coakes and Sellors, 1995). The effects of coloboma can be very variable. In individuals where only the iris is affected, there may be no impact on visual acuity. Where there are clefts or gaps in the retina or choroid, there are likely to be permanent defects in central vision.

Disorders of the retina

A number of disorders affect the complex layers of cells that make up the retina. These typically prevent the light stimuli that are received in the affected area of the retina from being transmitted through the optic nerve to the brain. Usually, retinal disorders result in blurred vision. If the central area of the retina (or macula) is affected, then central visual acuity will be impaired. Activities such as reading, or focusing on objects at a distance, will prove difficult. If the peripheral area of the retina is affected, then the individual should be able to read or look at objects at a distance, but may lose peripheral vision. In such cases, playing team sports or crossing a busy road may prove difficult. However, even when an individual has lost some central vision, a small amount of useful residual vision may be retained. A small unaffected area of the retina leaves an individual with the potential to learn how to use residual vision, and to access and interpret less than perfect visual information.

Retinal detachment means that part of the retina has become separated from the middle layer of the eye and cannot receive nutrients from the choroid. The detached part of the retina atrophies and turns into a blind spot. The result of a retinal detachment depends on which area is affected. Usually, retinal detachments are caused by an increase in fluid between the retina and the choroid, which can in turn be caused by a trauma, such as a blow to the head. Often, surgery may be necessary, but it is difficult to predict the amount of vision that can be saved. Repair of the detachment is done by various surgical techniques. Retinal tears are often treated by laser, or cryotherapy (freezing), to try and re-link the retina to the middle layer of the eye.

Macular degeneration is a progressive deterioration of the macula that produces a central, dense scotoma, or blind spot. This means that the individual will retain some peripheral vision, but central vision will be poor. In young people the condition is usually inherited. Individuals will need to learn scanning techniques when examining things, moving the eye across details to focus unaffected parts of the retina on images. Close work will need to be facilitated using low vision aids or CCTV. Task lighting and good print contrast will be helpful.

Retinopathy of prematurity

Retinopathy of prematurity (ROP) is a condition that affects babies born pre-term, weighing less than 1,300 grammes at birth. Development of the vessels that supply blood to the retina continues from around 32 weeks of gestation to one month after delivery. Babies born prematurely are at risk of arrested growth of blood vessels, or of abnormal new growth, as a result of exposure to increased quantities of oxygen. Since the discovery of the deleterious effects of this procedure, premature babies are very carefully managed and their blood oxygen levels monitored. Infants at highest risk are those with the lowest birthweight, with an estimated 90 to 100 per cent of babies weighing less than 500 grammes affected by ROP if they survive (Good, 1993).

The consequences of ROP depend on the area of the retina that is affected. This can vary from total blindness to the presence of some residual vision. How useful the child's remaining vision turns out to be depends on which areas of the retina have been damaged. Children with some residual vision may also have myopia, squints and an increased risk of retinal detachments. In these cases the use of lenses will help to provide a clearer image to the part of the retina that is not affected. Children with ROP, especially those with a severe condition, may be affected by other handicapping conditions, such as cerebral palsy, hydrocephalus and delayed development.

Albinism

Albinism is a hereditary disorder caused by the absence of an enzyme (tyrosine), which has a role in the production of melanin. Individuals with this condition have a lack of pigment, or cannot produce pigment. All, or only one, of the pigmented structures of the body may be affected, such as hair, skin and eyes. There are different kinds of albinism. When only the eyes are affected, the condition is called ocular albinism: a recessive genetic disorder in which females are carriers and males show the condition. Another kind of albinism is oculocutaneous, which in turn can be divided into two groups. One form is tyrosine negative, which means that individuals cannot produce pigment: they usually have blond hair and very pale skin. The other form is tyrosine positive, which means that individuals can produce some pigment and present a varied complexion, though there is usually an impairment of visual acuity related to the functioning of the fovea. Albinism causes macula hypoplasia, or incomplete development of the macula. Usually, individuals with albinism show photophobia, squint, nystagmus and decreased visual acuity. Some individuals will be able to achieve distance acuity levels of only 6/36, but may be able to read by holding print close to the face. Appropriate lighting conditions at school or at work are also very important for those with albinism. Pupils with the condition may work more effectively away from windows, bright sunshine or glare.

Retinitis pigmentosa

Retinitis pigmentosa is a group of inherited disorders characterised by night blindness and a constricted visual field. Usually, the disease begins in the mid-periphery of the retina, affecting the macula and extreme periphery later. Peripheral vision is impaired to begin with. Both cones and rods are affected, but this condition has a particularly damaging effect on the rod system. There are different kinds of retinitis pigmentosa with different ages for onset, degrees of visual loss and rates of progression, depending on the form of genetic transmission involved. Night blindness, the first symptom to appear, may occur in young people during the teenage years or early twenties. Loss of peripheral vision, then poor central and colour vision occur. The visual fields are progressively reduced to produce tunnel vision, for which there is no available treatment. Other ocular features occur in some cases of retinitis pigmentosa, such as glaucoma, cataracts and keratoconus. Because of the age at which the effects of retinitis pigmentosa become most prominent, careful counselling of teenagers is required, particularly if new skills will have to be acquired, such as braille.

The retina of the eye is vulnerable to damage through many other kinds of infections or disease processes. Toxoplasmosis is a condition caused by contact with a parasite (toxoplasma gondii), present in cat faeces and raw meat, which affects some areas of the retina and which may also cause brain damage. Another parasite leading to visual impairment is roundworm in cats and dogs (toxocara); the infection is passed through the ingestion of soil or faeces by children. Achromatopsia (best known as cone dystrophy) is a genetically transmitted disorder that affects colour vision and visual acuity. In adults, long-standing diabetes can affect the growth of blood vessels in the eye, with complications such as retinal detachment, glaucoma and cataracts.

Disorders of the aqueous humour

Glaucoma impairs vision as a result of damage from increasing pressure within the eye. Pressure is created by a build up of aqueous humour, which normally drains away, leading to compression of the blood vessels supplying the optic nerve, so that nerve fibres degenerate. Where the condition is present at or soon after birth, surgery to improve drainage is usually required to prevent further damage, with further operations to keep the pressure at a safe level. Raised intra-ocular pressure alters the shape of the eyeball and the position of the lens, thus causing refractive errors. Children with glaucoma may have very seriously impaired vision and limited visual fields, including tunnel vision.

Adult glaucomas are not always easily recognised as they are often asymptomatic until well advanced. As peripheral vision is affected first of all, the individual may be unaware of the condition for some time and early symptoms, such as headaches, ignored. Pressure within the eye can be measured by a procedure called tonometry and the glaucoma can be controlled with eyedrops or surgery.

Disorders of the optic nerve

Optic nerve hypoplasia is a condition in which small optic nerves are visible on examining the eye. This causes low vision, with the possibility of nystagmus. Optic atrophy is a condition affecting the nerve fibres which transmit information from the eye to the brain. The condition can be caused by a variety of disorders, such as glaucoma, but probably the most frequent cause of optic atrophy is the presence of a tumour in the visual pathways. As in optic nerve hypoplasia, children will probably be required to undergo neurological evaluation (Good, 1993). The results of optic nerve atrophy are variable, depending on the degree of damage to the nerve.

Syndromes

Some medical syndromes, which are groupings of symptoms or characteristics that tend to occur together, are frequently associated with impaired vision. Down's syndrome, for example, is a congenital condition caused by an extra chromosome, which is characterised by learning difficulties, immature social and physical development, increased risk of heart defects, respiratory infections and conductive hearing loss, together with visual impairment. Associated with this syndrome are eye disorders such as myopia, nystagmus and cataracts.

Marfan's syndrome is a hereditary condition present, but not often obvious, at birth that affects the connective tissue of the body. Individuals with Marfan's syndrome have characteristics such as elongated limbs, fingers and toes. They may also have cardiac difficulties, muscular underdevelopment and ocular disorders. Typically, Marfan's syndrome produces blurred vision in both eyes as a result of upwards dislocation of the lens, which can also lead to glaucoma. Myopia is also frequent, and there is a risk of retinal detachment with visual field loss. Individuals with Marfan's syndrome may be near-sighted if they have useful vision through part of the lens, or far-sighted if they can see through the space around the lens. The ability to accommodate is retained.

Leber's amaurosis is an inherited condition that causes widespread dysfunction of the cone and rod photoreceptor cells of the retina. Affected children show poor vision under all light conditions. There may be associated anomalies such as cataracts, macular colobomata or kerataconus. Disorders affecting the kidneys, heart and central nervous system are also associated with the syndrome. Children with Leber's amaurosis tend to poke their eyes, whilst developmental delays and symptoms of autism may also be reported (Good, 1993).

Norrie's disease is another inherited syndrome characterised by blindness, hearing impairment and learning difficulties. Finally, people who inherit the condition known as Usher's syndrome are likely to be profoundly deaf and later in life experience a progressive deterioration of eyesight associated with retinitis pigmentosa, leading to tunnel vision and eventually blindness. These individuals, many of whom will have learned to communicate through sign, then have to learn strategies for the tactile reading of other people's signs.

Rubella

The discovery in the 1940s that women who had suffered from German measles (rubella) in early pregnancy later gave birth to damaged babies was the first evidence that it was possible for infections in a pregnant mother to cross the placenta and affect the growing foetus. The first three months of pregnancy is the period when the embryo's delicate organs are forming. In adults, a rubella infection may be so mild as to go unnoticed, the only symptom being a slight rash. However, an expectant mother who gets German measles in the first trimester of her pregnancy is at risk of having a baby with serious heart defects, visual disabilities and brain damage, together with a hearing impairment. Visual impairment may stem from cataracts, congenital glaucoma, retinopathy or microphthalmia, which means that the child has very small eyes. As a result, these children may have very reduced visual acuity and visual fields, nystagmus and squints. Because of the potentially serious effects of the rubella virus on the embryo, there is a national immunisation programme in the UK for children at 14 months and pre-school, to reduce the number of affected babies later on. All expectant mothers are tested for rubella antibodies to see if they are immune. If a woman contracts rubella during early pregnancy, then a therapeutic abortion may be recommended.

Other eye conditions

Hemianopia is a condition in which half of the visual field is lost. This condition is due to a lesion (or damage) at or above the optic chiasma, resulting in complete blindness on the affected side. As we discussed earlier in this section when we considered the process of seeing, objects on the right side of the visual field produce images on the left side of each retina, and vice versa. The visual cortex has inputs from both sides of each retina, via the optic chiasma, so that there is some overlap of information which enables stereoscopic vision (see Figure 2.2). Depending on the area affected, and whether this occurs before or after the optic chiasma, the individual loses vision in different ways. For example, if the lesion occurs on one side of the optic nerve before the optic chiasma, there will be total blindness in the affected eye although the other eye is not affected. If the lesion occurs after the chiasma on the right side, for example, the individual will lose vision in the right side of both retinas (left side of visual field). Field losses may cause problems in reading, where children will need to learn how to find the beginning of a line of print. In this condition, glasses and text enlargement will be of little help.

Cortical visual impairment is a term used to refer to individuals who have damage to the posterior visual pathways leading to the visual cortex. In this condition pupil reflexes, retina and optic nerve may appear normal. Typical causes include meningitis or encephalitis. Children with cortical visual impairment have severe visual difficulties, although there may be some peripheral field vision.

Retinoblastoma is a malignant tumour of the retina that can affect children under the age of 3 or 4 years. In a few cases the condition is hereditary, and genetic counselling is important. Both eyes are sometimes affected. The condition must be treated, as the tumour can spread to other areas, such as the brain. Treatment involves enucleation, or complete surgical removal of the affected eye, radiotherapy and chemotherapy (Kanski, 1994).

IDENTIFYING A VISUAL IMPAIRMENT

In this section we consider some of the ways in which a visual loss may be identified. Parents are often the first to suspect that their child may have a sensory difficulty, such as a hearing or visual loss (Webster and Wood, 1989). They may feel that there is something odd about their infant's eyes or looking behaviour. However, professionals may not take these concerns seriously enough and may appease parents with 'wait and see' advice. Generally, the more severe the visual impairment, the more likely it is to be identified early. Obviously, it is highly important to identify and diagnose sensory problems in young children as soon as possible, so that there is no delay in providing appropriate treatment or correction. The impact of even fairly moderate sensory impairments in infancy can have a very significant impact on the child's early interactions, learning and development.

The pattern of statistics for the prevalence of visual impairments in children, which we reported earlier in this chapter, shows that severe visual handicaps are typically discovered within the first few days or weeks of infancy, whilst less severe forms of visual handicap may not be detected until the child goes to school. At that point more demands are made requiring good visual acuity, such as reading and writing, which may serve to confirm early suspicions or bring new concerns to the fore. Mild impairments of a refractive kind may not become apparent until a vigilant teacher suspects a child's poor progress with some aspects of the curriculum are due to visual problems, and appropriate steps are taken to gain further information.

Some of the important underlying principles of the Code of Practice, which we shall be considering in some detail in Chapter 4, include partnership with parents, clear lines of communication between professionals, families and schools, and the earliest possible intervention. All of these principles need to be put into practice if early suspicions of a visual difficulty are to be acted upon effectively.

Children at risk

It is known that severe visual impairment is likely to occur in certain circumstances. In advance of a child's birth, genetic factors in the family history, or the presence of a visual impairment in siblings, may alert professionals to an 'at risk' baby. Similarly, there may have been factors in a mother's pregnancy, such as contact with rubella, that predispose a child to suffer a visual impairment. Prematurity, low birthweight, difficulties in the delivery of a baby, anoxia or other peri-natal factors should alert professionals to the possibility of a visual impairment, along with other potential problems, such as a hearing loss. Paediatricians in special care units, for example, will normally alert local vision and audiology teams when any factors have arisen that may be harmful for normal sensory functioning.

One way of proceeding is to keep a careful record of 'at risk' babies and to ensure that vision and other aspects of development are regularly monitored. Children with a known condition frequently associated with visual impairment, such as cerebral palsy or Down's syndrome, should also be carefully followed up. Good practice indicates that effective early detection of children at risk depends on a co-ordinated programme of surveillance of infants, rather than relying on one method, including 'at risk' registers, newborn screening, family questionnaires and follow-up interviews (Webster, 1994).

Screening

In the UK, early screening and testing procedures are usually organised by the community child health services, who see families with young children periodically to give advice on care and management and to make developmental observations. Run by the health authority or part of the provision made by an NHS Trust, community child health services usually include health visitors, clinical medical officers, general practitioners and district nurses. School health is normally part of the community child health services providing programmes of surveillance, immunisation, health promotion, advice and counselling for all children from birth to 19 years.

Health visitors endeavour to screen all babies at around 8 months and at other age points between 18 months and 3 years, for hearing, vision and general development, either at home or in a child health clinic. It is not easy to screen young infants objectively, so insights gained by health visitors from what parents themselves have to say about their children's development are very important. For this reason, health visitors in some areas ask parents to fill in a questionnaire that seeks details of the child and family history, gives an opportunity for parents to register any worries, and asks straight questions such as 'Have you ever been worried about your child's vision or hearing?'

Increasingly, GPs are taking responsibility for developmental screening, either in child health clinics or within their own practices. How extensive this screening review is varies from one area to another. Some health authorities simply review pre-school records with or without a parental questionnaire and then offer medical examinations to a selected group. Others organise medical and neuro-developmental assessments for all children, including gross and fine motor co-ordination, height and weight, hearing and vision, perceptuo-motor skills, language and learning. Measurement of visual acuity using the Snellen chart, and hearing 'sweep' checks, may be repeated at intervals throughout the child's school career, typically in Years 3, 7, 10 and 11 (British Paediatric Association, 1995).

Although health authorities have undergone major restructuring, the school health service continues to have a key role in detecting problems that may have implications for children's health or education (Dick, 1994). However, more emphasis is now being placed on providing information to help children make healthy choices as adults and to promote healthy environments. So the role of the school doctor or nurse is shifting towards a preventive one, providing information and advice, encouraging children to take responsibility for their own health behaviour and positive lifestyles, and supporting teachers in the delivery of health education programmes. Aims and objectives for health services for children, as expressed by the British Paediatric Association (1995), for example, extend the targets set out in the government's 'Health of the Nation' policy to the physical and mental health of its children. This is highlighted in relation to those children with known special needs, such as a physical, sensory or medical condition, who are integrated in mainstream school settings, and where questions regarding medication, diet, exercise, and a host of other issues may arise.

One controversial issue, examined in the study by Hall (1991), is the extent to which routine, comprehensive screening checks should be carried out on all children. Hall argued that most difficulties are known about before children come to school, and that parents are the best people to draw attention to any concerns arising subsequently. Recommendations from this study were that school health services should carry out only a limited number of screening checks for vision, hearing and physical development. A contrasting argument, put forward by Whitmore and Bax (1990), is that children and parents have a right to medical examinations, even if this simply confirms that the child is 'normal'. Furthermore, these authors point out that parental concern is not foolproof in identifying children's difficulties. Irrespective of the comprehensiveness of school medical examinations, issues taken up in the Code of Practice (see Chapter 4) unequivocally assert the need for professional agencies involved in screening to be open and accessible, to have good lines of communication with other agencies, and to work in close partnership with families and children.

Identification

Whether or not a child has passed a screening test, or has medical records that state normal vision, if an adult who knows the child well feels worried about aspects of vision, then concerns should be shared with parents and further professional advice sought. Teachers in school are in a good position to observe some of the signs that sometimes indicate a visual impairment, and it is important for school staff to know what to look out for:

- children whose eyes turn or squint, or who close or cover one eye to look
- children whose eyes appear crusted, red-rimmed, sore or swollen
- uncontrolled eye movements, misshapen pupils or drooping eyelids
- children who rub, poke, brush or screw up their eyes
- aversion to glare or bright light
- unusual head postures, peering, head-tilting
- holding printed material at odd distances or angles, or very close to the eyes
- frowning or facial grimacing during close work, with complaints of blurred vision, nausea, dizziness or headache
- resistance to group games and physical activities, particular difficulties in sports (such as using a small ball in flight), hovering on the periphery of playspaces
- problems in reading anything other than large print size
- difficulties dealing with textbook material, such as small print on diagrams, or with coloured overlays
- clumsiness in moving around or locating things, tripping over small objects, inability to locate small things dropped on the floor, lack of awareness of distant objects, walking carefully with hands ready or outstretched, poor balance
- difficulty in copying from blackboard and books, large or spidery hand-writing, pressing excessively hard on paper or going over letters to make them blacker
- visual confusions affecting early reading, frequently losing place in texts
- rapid fall-off in attention, confidence or standard of work in certain teaching conditions, such as bright sunlight or large open spaces
- quickness in tiring, distractibility, poor progress in areas dependent on vision, such as reading

Children with visual impairments may not know that others see things more clearly than themselves and therefore may not complain. Some common-sense is required in being alert to the signs given here, since features such as tiredness, moving around clumsily and reading difficulties may be due to a number of factors apart from vision. There is, however, no harm in elimi-nating a visual impairment as the cause of a child's educational difficulties. Concerns shared with parents in the first instance can then be referred to the family doctor, school nurse or medical officer, a visiting teacher of the visu-ally impaired or an orthoptist. It is at this point that a more systematic, objective form of testing may be attempted. There are several aspects of vision that can be examined, depending on the age of the child, including tests of visual acuity for near and distance vision. A helpful distinction can be drawn between the processes of identification and diagnosis: the former seeks to determine whether different aspects of a child's visual functioning are abnormal; the latter endeavours to explain why.

ASSESSMENT OF VISION

In this section we shall consider both clinical and functional assessments of vision. A clinical assessment examines a number of aspects: the ability to see clearly (both near and distance vision), the field of vision, and the physical appearance of the eye. Functional assessment determines the use of eyesight in everyday situations.

Preferential looking method

The preferential looking method is often used to assess children under a year old. Even very small infants, including newborns, show a preference for looking at an image with patterns or stripes, rather than a plain grey stimulus. In the preferential looking method, a child is presented with either two cards, one of which is blank and the other of which has black and white stripes, or a screen that is plain on one side and has a grating on the other. During the assessment, the child looks at different screens or pairs of cards, which vary in the width and contrast of the stripes. To estimate how much the child can see, eye movements are observed. If the child continues to show preferences between the images displayed, it is assumed that the patterns are being distinguished. When the child indicates, through observed eye movements, that no preferences are shown between the patterns displayed, it is assumed the differences cannot be distinguished. This test gives an estimated visual acuity based on the stripe width, colour or contrast of the patterns displayed.

There are some complicating factors to bear in mind with this procedure. Visual acuity develops rapidly in the first six months of life, together with infants' sensitivity to contrasts. Research reported by Rosenblith (1992) shows that there are maturational differences in the kind of patterns that infants prefer (vertical versus horizontal lines, sharp versus blurred edges), and in the distances at which a response is likely to be given, depending on how far away the stimulus is from the baby's eyes. Another procedure that uses the principle of preferential looking, but presents pictures instead of gratings, is the Cardiff Cards, developed by the Department of Optometry at Cardiff University.

When assessing very young children there are also some important mundane considerations to take into account, such as whether the child is hungry, tired, sleepy or frightened by the test setting, all of which could influence the child's observed looking behaviour.

Stycar tests

The Stycar vision tests (Sheridan, 1976) are a set of techniques used to assess visual acuity in young children, although they are considered to be obsolete by many practitioners. From the age of about 6 months the rolling ball test can be used. The child is sat on the floor and a small white ball is rolled on the floor, along the child's visual field and at a distance of about 3 metres. When the ball stops, the eye movements of the child are observed and it is determined whether or not the child fixates on the ball. If the child does not fixate on the ball, this can indicate a possible visual difficulty. Obviously, tests like this are open to a great deal of subjective interpretation and great care must be taken over their administration.

Another procedure in the Stycar tests involves displaying a series of small white balls mounted on sticks which the child is encouraged to spot at a distance of 3 metres. The observer hides behind a screen and watches the child's reactions through a small slit. The child is presented with balls of different sizes that crudely correspond to visual acuity scores. The test provides some approximate information about a child's vision and visual field.

The miniature toys procedure is also part of the Stycar vision tests and is used with children who are not able to read letter charts. In this test, a set of five miniature objects is presented at a distance of 3 metres. The set includes a spoon, fork, knife, chair and doll. The child is asked to name the objects or to point to the objects named by the examiner. The Stycar vision tests also include single letter cards, rather than a whole chart, which can be presented at a distance of 3 metres, to provide information about the child's visual acuity. For children who have very poor vision, the Panda test can be used, which is a variation of the single letter cards. This consists of cards with white shapes on black backgrounds which can be presented at any distance. The test is useful to gather some information about what the child can see, at what distance and in what conditions, particularly when it has not been possible to acquire information about the child's vision from standard testing.

Snellen tests

For children who can identify letters, the Snellen chart is generally preferred, which we discussed in some detail earlier in this chapter. This is the most commonly used test for screening of visual acuity, on which most of the official definitions of visual impairment, such as blindness and partial sight, depend. Children and adults are asked to read letters of different sizes, usually at a distance of 6 metres, permitting comparisons to be made between what an individual can see and an arbitrary standard. A variation of the Snellen chart can be used that consists of charts with shapes of common objects. The child is either asked to name the shapes, or to indicate the shapes on a separate card.

Another alternative, for children who do not know their letters, is a letter matching card which can be used with the Snellen test types. A further version is the E chart which can be used with non-readers. The child is presented with a chart depicting several E shapes pointing in different directions. The child is given a separate cut-out letter E shape and asked to turn it around so that it points in the same direction as the E selected on the chart.

Other tests of near and distant vision

The Kay picture tests allow the assessment of both near and distance vision. To assess near vision, a card with different size black drawings on a white background is shown to the child at a distance of 33 centimetres. The child is asked to name the drawings, which include items such as a house, hand, man, flower, aeroplane, boat. Distance vision can be assessed at a distance of 3 and 6 metres using a 'flip-over' book with one drawing on each page. The drawings are shown in sequence from the biggest to the smallest, and each corresponds to a given visual acuity score.

To assess near vision in children who are not able to read, the BUST cards can be used. This set of cards has black shapes of objects on white backgrounds. The shapes are of nine different sizes and the child is asked to either match or sort the cards. The cards depict shapes selected for their visual similarity, such as a clock and a wheel, a fork and a spoon, spectacles and scissors. Different pairs are used so that it can be observed if the child can discriminate between shapes of varying sizes and degrees of similarity. Thresholds are established for discriminating between similar looking pictures, the results of which correspond to visual acuity scores.

Another test of near vision is the Maclure Reading Test. A series of simple stories is presented, printed in different text sizes and at varying conceptual levels, depending on the child's age and maturity. The child is asked to read a story at an appropriate interest level printed in large text, which then shifts to smaller size text. The examiner records the smallest size text that the child can read.

Visual field tests

Another aspect of vision that it is important to examine is the visual field. Most people with good binocular eyesight have a field of vision of approximately 170 degrees, but this can be narrowed considerably in some eye conditions. In very young children it may be possible to make a very approximate assessment of the field of vision only using materials such as the Stycar balls. Attention is captured by presenting an object whilst the child is looking straight ahead. Another object is slowly introduced into the child's visual field, moving from the periphery to the centre. The position of this second object, when the child shifts attention to it, is carefully recorded. This can be done in all four quadrants of the field of vision. However, as might be expected with younger children, interpreting the results of this kind of test may be problematical.

More accurate assessment of the visual field involves the use of a perimeter in which the individual is placed and asked to face straight ahead. A small point of light is slowly introduced into the periphery, which must be identified in order to plot the visual field for each eye.

Tests of colour and other aspects of vision

Research shows that babies at 3 months of age discriminate colours and make preferences between red and yellow (long wavelength colours) over blue and green (short wavelength colours). Even newborns prefer coloured stimuli to grey ones (Rosenblith, 1992). Colour blindness, an inherited condition more common in males, is due to deficiency of the cone cells in the retina. In rare cases of total colour blindness, light is sensed in varying tones of grey. Typically, only a few of the colour wavelengths are affected, so that red may be perceived as black, or green as yellow. Testing colour vision involves matching or sorting colours, using cards or 'confusion' plates. The Isahara Test displays numbers or patterns on cards in small spots of contrasting colour. Different patterns are seen, depending on whether the individual has normal colour vision or not. If not, the nature of the colour confusions are highlighted, such as difficulty with red/green contrasts.

Other aspects of vision which may be examined include muscle imbalance, which involves checking the position of each eye and the use of binocular vision. The most common tests for squint involve 'cover–uncover' procedures, when each of the eyes is occluded in turn. The individual is asked to look at an object and the response of the uncovered eye is observed.

Contrast sensitivity can also be examined. This refers to the ability to discriminate a figure from its background. Contrast sensitivity is immature at birth but develops over the first few months of infancy (Rosenblith, 1992). In part, visual acuity also depends on contrast between the brightness of a stimulus and that of its background. In making sense of the environment, the brain uses information such as the edges of objects which serve to define foreground from background. Contrast sensitivity can be tested by a procedure involving the presentation of gratings, or parallel vertical lines, with different degrees of contrast. The threshold point at which the individual can no longer detect any difference between the gratings is recorded as the contrast limit for that individual.

Clinical examination

Clinical examinations are usually carried out by an ophthalmologist. In examining a child, some of the procedures listed above may be carried out again. However, the ophthalmologist will also examine the appearance of the eye and, where necessary, request electrical tests to check the function of the retina, optic nerve and visual cortex. The ophthalmologist will collate data from the range of assessments carried out, in order to reach a diagnosis about the likely cause of a visual impairment, and to share with parents the medical options for intervention.

The ophthalmologist will look at the appearance of the iris, cornea, lens and retina for indications of malformation or disease. The use of electrical tests provides information concerning the response of the retina and visual cortex to a stimulus, such as a flash of light, or black and white grating. An electroretinogram (ERG) is used to test the response of the retina, important in diagnosing retinal dystrophy, or other dysfunctions of the retina. The visually evoked cortical response test (VER) is used to test the response of the visual cortex and visual pathways. Following the stimulus, resultant electrical activity is measured through electrodes on the scalp. These tests provide important supportive evidence in diagnosing a visual impairment.

Visual perception

One aspect of vision, more frequently assessed by teachers of the visually impaired, concerns visual perception. We said earlier that vision is sometimes described as a two-fold process, both optical and neural, combining sensory information and psychological judgement. Perception refers to the ability to make sense of what we see. In these terms, perception does not depend exclusively on the correct functioning of the eye and its visual pathways. Perception is more properly considered as an active, constructive process that involves a great deal more than the registering of sensory information.

Cognitive psychologists who study visual perception are concerned with issues such as how we integrate pieces of information to make a composite whole, the relationship between linguistic concepts and our structuring of events, how context influences our interpretation of information, and the important role of memory and prior experience. This is one important reason why children who acquire a visual impairment later in childhood face a different set of obstacles to those children with congenital impairments. The former already have a bank of visual experiences, together with established conceptual and linguistic frameworks for coding, storing and making sense of the world. Any new data, such as from touch, can be mapped onto existing reference points. The latter group, however, must build their perceptual frameworks from the more limited sensory evidence available to them.

Some aspects of visual perception are appraised in Barraga's Visual Efficiency Scale (Barraga, 1970). This uses items presented in two dimensions. Generally, the child is asked to match items that vary in size, detail, light–dark intensity, or position in space. The scale also includes associated teaching activities and materials that were designed to help the development of visual perception skills.

The Look and Think checklists (Tobin *et al.*, 1979) test what children can do, in visual perception terms, with their residual vision. Extended from the Barraga scale, the material can be used with children from 5 to 11 years of age, and consists of separate skill 'units', each of which examines different areas of functioning. Initial areas that might be checked out include identifying and naming common objects without using touch, or the discrimination of similar objects (such as a watch from a bracelet). Tasks include searching and scanning across a set of objects to identify differences (such as one cube out of four with rounded edges). Other parts of the checklists assess understanding of perspective, facial expressions, patterns and symmetry. There are also tasks of eye–hand co-ordination, colour differentiation and naming. In using these procedures, not only the scoring is recorded, but notes are also taken about the child's visual behaviour. This information is very important for teachers who work with the child on a daily basis. The checklist allows the construction of a summary and profile sheet that provides information regarding the areas of a child's visual perception that are more mature than others.

Functional vision

Observation of the way in which a child uses vision in different activities, such as the tasks presented in the Look and Think checklists, contributes towards a picture of an individual's functional vision. We have defined functional vision as the use of eyesight in real settings. For the teacher concerned about how well a child may cope with some of the challenges of a mainstream school placement, there may be rather less interest in clinical data or standardised test scores, than in specific examples of a child's use of vision in the daily landscapes of home and school.

In real life settings, as opposed to clinical situations, we are often confronted with different levels of lighting, varying locations, familiar and unpredicted events, displays with high contrast or high ambiguity, objects that move, together with tasks that require accurate perception whilst we are in motion. How the child behaves perceptually, and how we can help the child to cope better in day-to-day environments, is extremely important for both parents and professionals.

For sustained close work, teachers can assess how much a child can fixate on and follow small objects of different sizes and contrasts at different distances, whether a child can shift focus from one object to another, or how much a child can discriminate between similar objects, shapes or drawings. Different objects can be used to build up an idea of the range of a child's vision according to object size, distance of presentation and background contrast. Children can also be observed while looking at a book or manipulating toys. When children play with toys it is important to note if they move their hands to find out where the toys are located, whether they pick them up straight away, and how they explore. Some children mouth or touch objects. Some objects may attract the child's attention more than others, because of bright colours, shiny surfaces or interesting textures. Does the child bring the object to one eye or both, while exploring it? Teachers will be interested to know the size of print the child can cope with in reading, and whether aspects such as letter identification vary according to the amount of information presented at any one time, the spacing of letters, the colour and contrast of print on the page, or the lighting conditions, angles and distances at which text is viewed.

Take the example of one of our case studies, Nelly, presented earlier. She uses an abnormal head posture to reduce her nystagmus when examining a drawing or printed text using CCTV. When trying to see the colour of an object or picture, she brings items close to her mouth on the right side of her face. These observations provide evidence about Nelly's visual field and her strategies for colour identification.

Observation in everyday settings

Relevant information can also be gathered by observing the child's mobility and negotiation of everyday environments, either in nursery or play-group, at home or in school. The focus of observation will vary from child to child. For example, it will be important to observe a child who appears to be totally blind in relation to light perception. Is the child aware of windows or other strong sources of light in the environment? If so, turning to the light from a window can then be used as a basis for orientation within a room. Observing how confidently the child moves around is also very useful. At what speed and how smoothly does the child move? Is the child aware of obstacles, even if they are low down (about knee height)? Can the child see patterns on the floor, such as lines in the playground, or designs on a carpet? Is the child able to judge depth, for example, in pavements and on stairs? Observing a child's head position whilst moving can also provide important information about the individual's visual field.

For older children, a functional assessment could include how well the individual identifies buildings and road signs, judges traffic and crosses roads, negotiates public spaces, shopping malls and bus journeys. A distinction will need to be made between those familiar environments that a pupil knows well, and surroundings that are new. What strategies does an individual adopt to identify unknown people or objects in strange settings? In school, different areas will throw up their own specific problems for pupils with visual impairments, but it is imperative to know how an individual can cope with the demands of a laboratory or workshop, computer room or resource area, narrow corridor with a crowd of people, or large open space such as a sports field.

Children's reactions to other people's facial expressions can also be noted, including the distance a child needs to be from another individual in order to be aware of such features. We can also observe whether children react to glare and the level of light they prefer to work in. If children have to read from a blackboard, it is important to observe at what distance this is comfortable for the child and how much information the child has access to. To summarise, a functional assessment involves observing the child engaged in a range of mundane activities in everyday settings. Valuable information is revealed about what children can do with their available vision, whilst also revealing circumstances that prove difficult and that require new strategies.

PROFESSIONAL ROLES

In the last section of this chapter we shall be summarising the professional roles of different agencies involved with children who have visual impairments, and with whom parents and teachers may have contact. The Code of Practice is emphatic in its recommendations that there should be close and effective co-operation between school, child health and other relevant services or agencies, particularly at points of diagnosis, when information is communicated and when plans are being made. The provision of specialist medical care and educational advice is important, but there needs to be effective liaison between regional services and local teams if the ongoing needs of children and their families are to be met.

Health visitor

Health visitors are involved in advising families on the care and management of young children, and make developmental observations. They work alongside clinical medical officers and district nurses in community health services run by the district health authority, or as part of the provision made by an NHS Trust. Health visitors are often the first professionals with whom parents share their concerns. Their continuity of contact with the family puts them in a good position to listen to parental anxieties, to recognise when babies are not responding to stimulation in the predicted way, and to link up with other medical agencies. Health visitors screen all babies at around 8 months (and at other age points between 18 months and 3 years) for hearing, vision and general development. Given the difficulties in screening infants objectively, insights gained by health visitors from what parents have to say for themselves about their child's development are also very important.

Clinical medical officer

Families may have contact with a number of medical services for children: doctors and other staff who work in the primary health care team at the GP's surgery, hospital services and those operated within the community. Doctors who are likely to be involved in identifying children with sensory impairments are the clinical medical officers who work in well-baby clinics, schools and other community health services. The precise role of doctors varies from one region to another. Increasingly, GPs are taking responsibility for developmental screening either in child health clinics or within their own practices. Where GPs do not provide this service, pre-school child health surveillance is part of the clinical medical officers' brief. Referral to community health services can be made by GPs, health visitors, school nurses or hospital staff, or the families can approach them themselves.

Clinical medical officers play a key role in identifying early difficulties in pre-school clinics. In some areas, community paediatric services will include a 'vision team', comprising a health visitor, nurse and orthoptist, who are trained and experienced in assessing vision in young children. Children who are identified as having a medical condition, developmental delay, or disability such as a sensory impairment, may be referred on for specialist investigation in a hospital unit. Where children are suspected of having a complex range of problems, highly specialised assessment may be sought at a regional centre, such as the Wolfson Centre in London, with access to staff such as developmental paediatricians, psychologists, ophthalmologists, neurologists and genetic counsellors.

If a teacher suspects that a child has visual problems, there are many routes to securing medical advice. Informally, parents may be asked to take their child to their family doctor. All schools will have a named contact (usually the school nurse or doctor) for seeking medical advice on children who may have special educational needs. Because of the number of different agencies involved and the varied arrangements that may operate in different areas, inter-professional communication must be effective if children's difficulties are to be identified as early as possible.

With the introduction of contractual arrangements for the purchase and provision of health services, a designated medical officer will be identified by each district health authority to work with LEAs on behalf of children with special educational needs, and to co-ordinate activity across DHAs, NHS Trusts and GP fund holders. The designated medical officer will ensure that LEAs are informed of children who are thought to have special needs, and that medical advice is provided towards a multi-professional assessment within prescribed time limits. They will also indicate the significance of any medical findings for later educational provision.

School nurse

School nurses are registered nurses, some of whom will also be registered sick children's nurses, and some of whom will have completed post-registration specialist school nurse training. They are key figures in ensuring effective communication between school-based services and primary health care teams, teachers, parents and other health professionals. They are also a source of information about local health services for the school community. An important part of their role includes the carrying out of a core programme of screening for vision, hearing, height and weight, and general health checks, as well as discussion with parents and teachers to identify concerns. At school entry, the school nurse may discuss issues such as behaviour, dental care, immunisation, other children in the family, any health problems or medication needs, and other health professionals seeing the child. One outcome of this health review may be referral to the school doctor for fuller assessment. The school nurse has an expanding brief in terms of health appraisal and the promotion of positive, healthy lifestyles through education programmes.

Ophthalmologist

Doctors who specialise in the diagnosis and treatment of eye defects are called ophthalmologists. They work in specialised hospital clinics where detailed clinical examinations of the eye are carried out. The ophthalmologist will work together with other hospital staff, such as the orthoptist and paediatrician, to establish the nature of a child's visual impairment and its severity, and to plan appropriate treatment and follow-up.

Optometrist

Optometrists work mainly in the community as part of the team involved in providing information towards the assessment, diagnosis and treatment of a visual impairment. They may carry out tests of acuity, and make recommendations about appropriate low vision aids, spectacles or lenses.

Orthoptist

Orthoptists make an important contribution towards childhood screening and the testing of children for visual acuity. They are involved in the diagnosis and treatment of anomalies such as squints. They may plan exercises for ocular co-ordination and the development or restoration of aspects of visual function. Within the multi-disciplinary team involved with children with visual problems, the role of the orthoptist is to provide an accurate assessment of visual acuity and of any ocular motility problem that may be significant.

Speech therapist

Speech therapists are involved in the assessment, diagnosis and treatment of communication difficulties, in the widest sense of the term. They may be called on for advice about the best ways of managing environments for enabling language development. The traditional view of speech therapists 'training' children's speech on weekly visits to an outpatients' clinic is an outmoded one. Handing on skills and strategies to those who have day-to-day contact with children with sensory or other impairments is a highly valued contribution of the speech therapist.

Physiotherapist

Physiotherapists who specialise in working with children also take part in the assessment and management of children with individual needs. Because one of the main concerns in the early development of children with visual impairments is mobility, exploration and the development of spatial awareness, physiotherapists may be called on for advice about planning appropriate activities and the design of materials or play environments for individuals.

Social worker

Under the Children Act 1989, Social Services departments have duties to provide a range of services for children regarded as being 'in need'. Whilst a child with special educational needs may not necessarily be 'in need' as defined by the Children Act, current government policy is very much in favour of an integrated approach to educational, health and welfare issues. For parents who have a child with a severe visual impairment, it may be advisable to make contact with a social worker who can act as advocate for the family. When a child has multiple and complex handicaps, including visual impairment, a number of decisions will have to be made about schooling and at points of transition into further or higher education, vocational training or employment.

The role of the social worker, as part of a multi-disciplinary team, has recently been outlined by Greenhalgh (1993). He suggests that the social worker can be an important family facilitator around the time of assessment and diagnosis, and when plans are made. The social worker can ensure that professionals are brought together at the right time, that information is coherent and assimilated, and that families are equipped to deal with the bureaucracy surrounding the network of services. Exactly which service becomes involved in family counselling, educational placement or careers advice will vary according to availability, but it is crucial that services assist, rather than direct or take over, the decision-making process.

Psychologists

There are a number of applied branches of psychology, although families with children who have visual impairments are most likely to encounter clinical or educational psychologists. Both have an academic background in psychology, followed by specialised training, although educational psychologists will also have qualified teacher status and teaching experience. We can assume that both will have a wide experience of ordinary children as well as those with developmental or learning difficulties.

Educational psychologists are usually employed by LEAs and visit groups of mainstream and special schools, as well as providing a service to the children and families who live in an area. They are often called on to give advice on ways of working with individuals or groups, and to provide in-service training on issues such as assessment, managing behaviour, effective learning environments, differentiation, and strategies for overcoming learning obstacles. They contribute to, and often help to organise, procedures for collating evidence at different stages of the Code of Practice, leading to the multiprofessional assessment of children under consideration for a 'statement' of needs. A few educational psychologists will have specialised in working with families and children with visual impairments.

The majority of clinical psychologists are employed in the health service and work with a range of adult and child psychological concerns. Most specialise in work with a specific client group, such as people with learning disabilities, drug users, adults or children with emotional disorders, people with chronic medical or disabling conditions, such as spinal injury, epilepsy or asthma. They may be involved in counselling families following the diagnosis of a sensory impairment, or may help to plan an intervention programme tailored to a child's developmental needs. Parents of children with severe visual impairments may be introduced to clinical psychologists as part of a paediatric assessment team working from a specialised assessment centre. Children can be referred to NHS psychology departments by social workers, GPs, health visitors, paediatricians and headteachers.

Advisory teacher

The first advisory services for children with visual impairments were set up in the 1970s, a move strongly supported by the Vernon Report (1972). The Vernon Committee made recommendations regarding the wider integration of children with severe visual impairments or blindness, and indicated that all LEAs should appoint staff with training and expertise who could support families and mainstream schools. All specialist teachers who work within schools for children with visual impairments are required to have a background in normal classroom experience followed up by further training or a qualification pursued whilst in post. Advisory services are not compelled to employ teachers with specialist qualifications, but advisory teachers cannot work for more than three years without undertaking specialist training. Evidence towards statementing procedures must be contributed by those who are suitably qualified, having attended a course in the education of children with visual impairment recognised by the DFEE. In the current climate of rationalisation and cost-cutting, services for children with visual impairments may become part of generic organisations concerned with supporting children with special needs generally.

Advisory teachers usually have close working relationships with community health services and will be involved with families as soon after the point of diagnosis as possible. At this time, even when a visual condition has been anticipated or suspected by parents, a great deal of information and support may be necessary to help families come to terms with their child's visual impairment. Parents are very vulnerable in these early stages and need very sensitive counselling. Effective specialist teachers must have resources of flexibility and empathy and an understanding of family systems and how they cope with stress, and be able to help parents meet their psychological needs in dealing with guilt, resentment, or feelings of inadequacy. Parents who have been given information about their child's medical condition in a hospital setting will need time to work over and digest the facts. The visiting specialist teacher is likely to be the person turned to for explanations about the effects of a visual impairment, and what the likely implications will be for learning and development.

The specialist advisory teacher will work together with other medical and support services, carrying out assessments on children and drawing up plans, helping to make decisions about school placements and evaluating progress over time. Advisory teachers fulfil a range of challenging functions: direct teaching of individual children, liaising with other professionals and LEA officers, giving and interpreting information, providing in-service training and promoting access to the curriculum in a wide range of educational settings. Increasingly, specialist teachers work indirectly in an advisory capacity, offering practical advice to those who have everyday contact with a child, such as parents and mainstream classteachers. Some families and schools may be visited once a week, other children are given a 'watching brief', which may mean visiting to sort out a problem, or a routine follow-up every term. Access to advisory services for families of pre-school children is usually by referral from health visitors, GPs or hospital ophthalmology departments. Parents and professionals can often contact services direct or through the LEA.

SUMMARY

This chapter has covered some of the physical facts of eye structure and the mechanisms of vision as a basis for understanding the ways in which visual impairments arise, how these may be identified and diagnosed, and the likely significance of different forms of visual loss for the individual concerned. We have stressed the view that the technical or clinical aspects of vision, such as measures of visual acuity, may bear little relationship to how well an individual functions in different settings. The ability to use eyesight in everyday contexts requires a number of skills other than clarity of vision, including tracking, fixating, changing focus, depth perception, figure–ground discrimination, and the ability to make sense of information in relation to prior experience. It is a combination of these factors, together with the individual's motivation, problem-solving and sense of enquiry, that determine functional vision. Many of the technological aids and specialised equipment for use in schools and other working environments enable individuals to develop or maximise their use of functional vision.

The medical aspects of a visual condition, like measures of visual acuity, have only limited power to account for the impact of a visual impairment on childhood development. There is little direct correspondence between the clinical facts of a visual loss and how well children achieve in aspects of language, learning, literacy and personal competence. It should also be borne in mind that when a visual impairment presents significant developmental obstacles to children and their families, these are rarely experienced in just one dimension. The effects of a severe visual impairment on a child may be obvious in terms of motor development, making sense of surroundings, language and conceptual maturity, but will also spill over in more subtle ways to affect the child's motivation, confidence, social and emotional well-being. In the subsequent chapters of this book we try to move away from using clinical categories and labels, to shift the focus of interest away from the child and onto the learning environment.

For every child with a visual impairment there is a professional responsibility to discover as much as we can of the individual strengths and possible immaturities of an individual. Much of the following chapter, where we discuss aspects of learning, examines the strategic role of vision in early interactions, and how the presence of a sensory impairment may disrupt early linguistic and cognitive processes. In much that follows in this book we shall be highlighting factors in the child's social and educational environments that have important effects and that are open to change. Wherever possible, although our knowledge is far from complete, we shall be seeking a research basis for improving environmental conditions and the social interactions that take place within them.

3

DEVELOPMENTAL PROCESSES AND THE IMPACT OF VISUAL IMPAIRMENT

This chapter is concerned with some of the important tasks of early infancy and later childhood, and the social contexts in which these tasks are addressed. All children arrive in the world sensitive to different kinds of perceptual experience and with an orientation to act on and make sense of their surroundings. There is wide variation in the characteristics that individual children, including those with visual impairments, bring to learning encounters. For this reason we have guarded against using the framework of developmental psychology to understand the relative progress of children with visual impairment, since this has tended to deal with 'normal' developmental milestones and has largely ignored environmental context.

The popular image, derived from Piaget, of the child as a 'little scientist' struggling to put together a personal understanding of the physical world, has given way to more recent accounts of children's learning and thinking as embedded in social relationships. It is this shift in perspective that informs our review here of important developmental processes likely to be affected by a visual loss. We have selected some key evidence sources from the literature on children with a range of visual impairments, including blind children, across a wide age span. The picture that emerges is one of a rich diversity of individual differences. Our own interest lies mainly with the learning processes that contribute to these differences.

The tasks we consider in some detail include children's adaptation to the physical world: learning the properties of objects, exploring space, tactile and motor skills. A second main area is language and cognition: the intellectual tools for ordering and categorising experience. The third main concern is with social development: how children acquire the behaviours that permit appropriate social relationships and entry into the surrounding culture. None of these areas of learning and adaptation can truly be considered in isolation. Their interdependence is clear when we consider that most of the infant's early understanding of the physical world, such as everyday objects, is facilitated by intense interactions with familiar adults.

Throughout this chapter we highlight the special place that vision holds in learning, for example in the processes that children typically adopt for extending their conceptual understanding. That children with visual impairments do learn to talk and think, and do gain a sophisticated understanding of the world, demonstrates the flexibility of human learning and the social systems that support it. Furthermore, knowledge gained from examining the problem-solving of children with visual impairments can inform more effective teaching of all children. A closer understanding of the relationship between language, learning experience, the intervention of adults and shifts in children's thinking is arguably the basis for raising all pupils' achievements.

It was the psychologist George Miller (1963) who made the famous remark that the most precocious child orator would be a blind girl, the only daughter of well-to-do parents. Miller was assuming that blindness would force dependence on adult caretakers who, with time on their hands and no other children, would stimulate language through a high degree of individual attention. The idea that a child with a visual impairment will be spurred on as a consequence to develop exceptional skills in listening, language and other areas of functioning has been called the 'myth of compensatory ability' (Erin, 1990).

In contrast, other researchers have used a variety of test materials, such as vocabulary tests, verbal reasoning and comprehension, to show that one of the outcomes of a severe visual impairment is a limiting of children's development in comparison with 'sighted' peers, most significantly in areas of linguistic and conceptual maturity. Furthermore, several researchers have suggested that there may be prolonged difficulties in some areas of language use, such as pronouns, questions, gesture, echolalia, and in the appropriate use of words that have a range of meaning (Dunlea, 1989; Mills, 1983).

The idea that a visual impairment might have a significant negative impact on areas of social interaction, together with language and conceptual development, has not always been fully appreciated. However, we are now more aware, from research evidence accumulated over the last twenty years or so, that vision plays an extremely important role in shaping early adult–child interactions, as well as providing information through which the world can be organised and categorised, and through which the child's linguistic repertoire can be extended.

In this chapter we consider some of the experiences that are formative in the development of children with visual impairments, and in particular the impact of a visual loss on teaching–learning interactions. In the introductory section of this book we made the point that neither a special psychology, nor notions of maturational delay drawn from developmental psychology, seem to account adequately for the early adaptive learning experiences of children with visual impairments. In studying some of the ways in which children do learn, despite their visual handicaps, we can discover a great deal about ways into language and the special relationship between visually based strategies, children's understanding of the world, and the course of normal language development in everyday social contexts for all children.

The range of individual variation amongst children as learners is unfathomable. It is also true that there are many more differences than similarities in a group of individuals identified as 'visually impaired'. Levels of achievement in aspects such as language, personal independence, social skills, together with academic attainments, show no clear or predictable association with levels of sight. In common with all other children, personality factors, family support, ability and adjustment, persistence and motivation, vary greatly and influence how well the child with a visual loss copes with school and other learning environments. However, we shall be making the case that we can most effectively influence the long-term course of a child's developmental progress by modifying social conditions and manipulating interactive encounters. If we can attribute lack of progress in an individual not simply to factors located within the child, but also to constraints that arise from teacher–learner interactions and the qualities of the learning environment, then we can design more effective contexts for learning.

DEVELOPMENTAL PSYCHOLOGY AND ITS CRITICS

The knowledge base of developmental psychology has recently been subjected to critical review and has its opponents (see, for example, Burman, 1994). Psychologists who have worked within this discipline in the past have typically selected the child as a unit of observation and abstracted development from its social and cultural context. Developmental psychology has often been driven by the demand to provide normative descriptions of behaviour. These have then been turned into benchmarks by which children's relative progress can be judged, whilst prescribing what children should be able to do, in different domains of development, by certain ages. Because of its focus on individuals as the object of enquiry, research has tended to ignore the situations in which children grow and change. Furthermore, the normative assumptions that have guided theory and research can lead to feelings of guilt, failure and victim-blaming, when parents or teachers perceive that development is proceeding along other lines.

Of course, as most parents will attest, the ideal 'normal' child is a fantasy, with no real child at its base. Developmental milestones present a picture of orderly progression through well-defined steps to ever greater competence. This picture is a homogenised one that leaves out most of the chaos, unpredictability and personal cost involved in the day-to-day bringing up of a family. We make these points here to remind ourselves that the presence of a visual impairment adds further complications to the already hazardous and sometimes stressful processes of parenting and growing up. The way in which childhood is depicted by those who write up research typically plays down its complexity.

In this chapter we shall be looking at aspects of development that are highly relevant to children with visual impairments: exploration of the physical world, language and thinking, mobility and social skills. However, our prime interest is in the conditions and processes that promote learning, and where vision forms a significant dimension, rather than in benchmarks or milestones. Much of what we consider here concerns learning in the family contexts of early childhood. To understand any cognitive process we need to know something of its origins. It is no longer held that learning processes from earlier stages of development are somehow discontinuous with those that follow. What infants and their caregivers achieve in terms of early patterns of communication, social interaction or exploration forms the foundation for, and is carried into, more mature behaviour.

THE SPECIAL SIGNIFICANCE OF VISION

Babies within hours of birth show considerable powers of discrimination and organisation. They arrive in the world already sensitive to very specific types of experience and with an inborn capacity to act on and organise those experiences. In this section we shall be considering the special qualities of visual experience, alongside other sensory modalities, in enabling infants to make sense of their environment, including their own position within it. Furthermore, as we shall discover, vision also holds special properties in enabling caregivers, from the outset, to introduce the child to the social contexts in which language and meaning are shared.

Newborn babies are not, as was once presumed, passive, unformed beings. A touch on the baby's cheek will elicit a 'rooting reflex', and any subsequent contact with appropriate objects will then evoke a pattern of highly organised sucking behaviour. Infants will also turn towards a sound source and respond selectively to sounds of different loudness or frequency. Gentle, low frequency, repetitive sounds tend to soothe, whilst loud, percussive noises often startle. Smells also evoke selective behaviour: offered a choice between the mother's breastpad and that of another breastfeeding woman, infants will typically turn to their own mother's and even prefer their mother's underarm odour! The power of visual experience, however, is very quickly established. By two weeks, babies are able to distinguish the mother's face from that of a stranger's. Although the visual acuity of newborn babies develops rapidly during the first 6 months, when it reaches approximately 6/60, they do show marked preferences for human faces, as well as voices, whilst the combination of human face and speech is irresistibly attractive (Rosenblith, 1992).

One of the problems facing researchers has been finding mechanisms whereby babies can demonstrate their intentions and exercise control. It is the weakness of the neonates' muscles that is one of the limiting factors. Given appropriate means, babies will strive to control the environment in order to sustain events that interest them. The use of videotape and the invention of clever experimental methods for studying infant behaviour have demonstrated that they react selectively to many different forms of sensory experience. For example, when provided with a teat containing a small switch that can be sucked to control lights or bring a filmed image into focus, infants soon discover how to turn lights on or how to maintain a picture in focus.

Continuity and immediacy of vision

Vision is implicated in all areas of children's development as a co-ordinating and integrating sense. Uniquely, vision has the quality of simultaneity: we can process information from near and distant objects at the same time, and know how objects are positioned in relation to one another, and to the observer. In contrast, although hearing gives clues with regard to distance and direction, our ears can only deal with auditory information arriving in sequence: a succession of events over a time span. Our sense of hearing is particularly well tuned to process verbal information, such as speech, which is produced and decoded serially, item by item. So, for example, our understanding of what a sentence means unfolds over the time we hear the words being spoken.

However, hearing can often provide only a minimal amount of information about unfamiliar objects in space. Auditory input cannot, without supportive data from other perceptual systems, reveal much specifically about an object's shape, size or colour, or about its surroundings. Many objects worth knowing about make no sound. It is because of the continuity and immediacy of vision in providing precise and detailed information about the environment that vision can be characterised as a powerful driving force in early learning.

Exploring through touch

Perception of the spatial forms of objects and their relative positions, in the absence of vision, must be achieved through touch. Although touch is a very important source of information about the environment for children with impaired vision, there are many limitations to tactile perception. Touch requires children to search out objects, to travel to their locations to discover their characteristics, and for objects to be within reach. Representations of objects through touch will require small fragments of information, acquired serially, to be put together to form an image of the whole.

For the infant with a visual impairment who is not yet mobile, objects have to be found nearby or be supplied in order to be explored. It may be difficult for the child to understand that the object still exists if it rolls away. For the child who sees clearly, checking whether an object still exists, though not immediately in view, is a matter of looking around to find its new location.

Without good vision, searching around to test the permanence of an object is much more uncertain. In terms of the conceptual development of infants with visual impairments, much has been made of the difficulties in establishing object permanence, which signals an important shift in understanding about the physical world 'outside oneself', and which is linked to vocabulary growth (Bigelow, 1986, 1990).

In order to understand the nature of the environment that surrounds them, children with visual impairments will have to explore single elements and construct a picture or map of the surroundings by adding together various sensory impressions. For example, asked to give directions on how to get from the playground to the school office, a child with a visual impairment may break the route up into a progression of locations: '. . . then there's a doorway . . . then a ramp . . . then the boys' cloakroom . . .'. This use of landmarks suggests that the route is experienced and represented by the child as separate segments encountered over time, and not as a whole entity.

There is some evidence to suggest that all children, including those with good vision, start out by representing spatial relations in terms of landmarks or a succession of points on a route. Integrated or survey-like spatial maps of whole situations are probably not typical of children's thinking until the age of 3 or 4 years (Spencer *et al.*, 1989). Even then, in more complex situations, children (and adults) may rely on landmarks and route sequences to find their way. However, by school age, most sighted children will be capable of constructing an inner map of the environment in order to locate things or find their way about. This kind of direct and effortless awareness of a whole spatial context would be very difficult to achieve through sensory information other than vision.

Vision enables us to construct a coherent sense of the physical environment and our place in it, without struggling to remember. On entering an unfamiliar classroom, a sighted child is able to take in something of the whole at a glance, and perhaps to work out the overall position of the room in relation to other, more familiar, places, such as the library, computer room, dining hall or the secretary's office. Paying closer attention to details, the same child will be able to focus selectively on a classroom charter pinned to the wall, signs that identify work areas, such as a listening centre or the writing corner, or children's work pinned to a display board. For the child with a visual impairment, constructing an inner map of this new classroom presents a problem of synthesising information from the interrogation of small, local details to achieve a functional sense of the whole, which must then be largely memorised.

Because children who see clearly do not have to touch objects to be aware of their existence, they can begin to learn much earlier (before they are mobile) about the characteristics of objects and their relative positions in space. Importantly, for many environmental features, direct contact is impossible (sky, stars, moon, smoke) or inadvisable (fire, boiling water). Some objects are too big to be understood by touch (buildings, mountains), some too small (insects, seeds), and some too fragile (soap bubbles, spider's web). Representations of objects or space achieved through sensory modalities other than vision may be less detailed, accurate, precise or continuous, and make greater demands on recall.

Conceptual 'bridging'

Children with severe visual impairments can build concepts that are just as elaborate as a sighted person's visualisations, but this will inevitably be a longer and less direct process. Since we have argued strongly that many of the child's discoveries about the physical and logical properties of the world do not take place in isolation, but in social encounters with familiar adults, this also makes more demands of caregivers and other interactive partners. In many respects, adults will be instrumental in making bridges between the child's inner world and the world outside, with language as the medium through which this is brought about.

By adding together impressions gained from touch, taste, smell and sound, sensory pictures can be constructed and recalled. The adult's explanations relate these images to prior experiences and other relevant reference points, extending the child's understanding in forms that are within the child's grasp. Reading a Beatrix Potter story, for example, a sighted child may have in mind a visual image of a rabbit, whereas a blind child may have an inner representation based on texture, shape, warmth, movement and smell. In both cases, a certain amount of adult 'bridging' may be required to explain differences between animals in stories, which eat at table, sleep in sheets, go to school, and are tended by a doctor when they get ill, and real animals. Sighted children, like their visually impaired peers, may have many conceptual confusions that need to be sorted out. The point is that for children with visual impairments, less can be gained from direct observation, requiring adults and other interactive partners to be more systematic and structured in their explanations and information-giving.

From early infancy onwards, the total loss of sight or a serious reduction in vision has an impact on the ways in which the child constructs the world, the relative salience of different information sources, and the time taken to build up a store of associations. But there are also profound implications for those involved in the child's immediate social world, in terms of adjusting tasks, materials and explanations to children's competences and needs.

There is an enduring belief that children who have reduced vision will compensate for this by a heightened acuity in other senses. Whilst children can learn to pay attention to information from touch and hearing especially, as indeed they can learn to make more efficient use of residual vision, there is no evidence that the acuity of other senses can be enhanced (Miller, 1992). The notion of sensory compensation is a myth.

THE VISUAL CAPACITIES OF YOUNG CHILDREN

In ordinary circumstances, newborn babies have the capacity to locate visual stimuli and keep them before their eyes and in focus. Infants do not have to learn or practise for their eyes to move towards a stimulus that appears in peripheral vision, even when they are already looking at something in their central vision. In the first month they can attend to and track moving objects, although smooth pursuit – anticipating the movement of a stimulus with continuous head and eye co-ordination to keep the object in central vision – does not develop until about 6 to 8 weeks of age.

Besides searching, tracking and keeping visual events in their centre of vision, by about 3 months of age sighted infants quickly accomplish pattern-scanning to make complex visual discriminations. Newborns generally look at a single feature or contour of an object. By 2 months infants are beginning to scan more broadly along the internal as well as external features of a display, for example shifting attention to the eyes as well as the hairline, chin or ear of a human face. At this stage the infant can discriminate between a scrambled and natural diagram of a face. Three-month-old infants can process internal features well enough to identify photographs of their mothers and to discriminate between some facial expressions.

Table 3.1 Sequence of visual behaviours in early infancy

Age of onset	Visual competence or behaviour
birth	focuses briefly on objects at different distances
	visual acuity 6/60
1 month	attends to and tracks moving objects
	prefers certain colours
	distinguishes lights of different brightness
2 months	smooth pursuit of objects co-ordinating head and eye movements
	fixates object and maintains gaze
	scans internal as well as external features of a display
3 months	scans complex patterns
	identifies photographs of caregiver
	discriminates some facial expressions
4–6 months	visually guided reaching and grasping at objects
	mature accommodation
7–8 months	prefers coherent messages (synchrony of recorded voice and facial expression)
12 months	shifts gaze from far to near
	uses eyes and hand together
	tracks across 180 degree arc
	visual acuity 6/18
24 months	inspects objects without touching
	visual acuity 6/6
	mature perception of visual forms
	awareness of space and relative positions of objects and self

Visual patterns give crucial information about the significance of objects that infants learn to attend to. Young babies are also good at distinguishing between lights of different brightness and show preference for certain colours by a few weeks of age. Even newborns prefer colours to grey stimuli. Visual acuity, often measured by preferential looking techniques (see Chapter 2), develops rapidly over the first year, from approximately 6/60 at birth to 6/18 at 12 months, as does the ability to accommodate the eye to look at stimuli at different distances.

The role of movement in object perception has also been studied in young babies. When objects move, their parts move together and are contrasted against changing background textures. Although this ability to use kinetic information matures with time, newborns are helped to recognise objects through movement rather than stationary patterns.

Visually guided reaching

When sighted infants begin to reach for objects that they can see at around 4 months, it is clear that they have notions of three-dimensional space, of the existence of things outside themselves, and of the graspable nature of objects. Children develop eye–hand co-ordination before ear–hand co-ordination. That is to say, infants generally try to grasp an object in view, prior to reaching for objects on the basis of sound. One explanation for this is that not all sounds, such as the television or a doorbell, signify a graspable object, so reaching towards sounds may be unrewarding. The net effect is that children with visual impairments may be delayed in their development of a co-ordinated reach and in object permanence (Bigelow, 1986; Dunlea, 1989).

Visually guided reaching depends on the integration of information from different sensory modalities, such as vision and touch, and shows how important it is for these separate sensory sources to be assimilated to make a whole. In fact, when competing information is presented in different perceptual domains, most infants show a marked preference for coherent messages. When shown a film of faces with contrasting expressions, such as angry or happy, alongside recordings of different tones of voice, sighted 7 month olds prefer looking at faces displaying the same emotions that are being expressed on the soundtrack. Younger infants are more interested in videos of faces that are moving in synchrony with the voices recorded on the soundtrack (Walker-Andrews, 1988).

All of these early developments in sensory perception, especially vision (for a summary, see Rosenblith, 1992) show that infants come equipped with an orientation to make sense of things. Newborns show interest in, and preferences for, certain colours, patterns, brightness, and things that move. All sensory systems are functional at birth, although it takes some months for some aspects, such as visual acuity, to mature. In the first few months infants begin to utilise clues, such as linear perspective and texture gradients, to perceive depth.

Most of the evidence reported above on the visual capacities of young sighted children is derived from experiments where aspects of the social context and the role of caregivers is largely ignored. It should be said that, in normal circumstances, the infant's growing understanding arises from the integration of sensory information from a wide range of cue sources, in social contexts where adults actively support the child's efforts to make sense of things.

EARLY SOCIAL INTERACTION

Children do not grow up in isolation. Depending on the culture and other social conventions, there are usually numerous opportunities to interact with parents, siblings, relatives and other children, in exchanges that actively involve the participants. The fact that most children come into the world already equipped with the ability to interact with other humans is not fortuitous. The importance of interaction in promoting cognitive and linguistic development is widely acknowledged. Many researchers have begun to view the child's thinking, learning and intelligence as socially mediated behaviour: what the child can achieve with the assistance of others (Garton, 1992; John-Steiner *et al.*, 1994; Light *et al.*, 1991; Rogoff, 1990; Woodhead, *et al.* 1991). This is a theme we shall be returning to in later sections of this chapter, and in some depth in Chapter 6, when we consider some recent research evidence derived from social encounters involving children with visual impairments and their interactive partners.

Early parent–child interactions are heavily dependent on visually related mechanisms. The evidence that vision is implicated in fostering interaction is highly important for our understanding of some of the effects of visual impairment on processes of learning and development. In fact, it is through vision that the very core of reciprocal human relationships begins. The sighted infant's first exposure to the world consists of the mother's facial expressions, eye gaze and vocalisations. The mother's handling, talking, tone of voice, rhythmic movements and attempts to gain eye contact establish an intense social relationship from the outset. The infant of a few weeks of age can recognise and distinguish the primary caregivers. The sensitive reading of clues and intentions, as demonstrated by the child's attention to the adult's face, imitation of mouth, tongue or arm movements, or the mutual responding to facial expressions and smiles, has been called 'intersubjectivity' (Trevarthen, 1979). A wide range of behaviours seems to be available to very young infants, both to initiate and respond to the signals and intentions of the caregiver. But they mostly depend on vision.

'Proto-conversations'

The emergence of a child's first words is the culmination of a process of communication, not its beginning. Early patterns of interaction establish a 'conversational framework' for initiating and maintaining social exchanges, out of which linguistic interchanges arise. These early processes of language development, particularly the conditions for contingent interaction established by caregivers, have profound implications for the management and teaching of young children with visual impairments. This is most obviously the case for children who are blind or who have only very limited functional residual vision.

One of the most interesting programmes of research on young sighted babies, carried out by Trevarthen (1979), has explored the way in which the social conventions of these early 'proto-conversations' are established. In one experiment, split-screen film of mothers sitting opposite their babies of 3 months of age show that the infant's social interactions are already highly structured. The infant's gestures and actions, such as frowning or tongue-protrusions, alternate with similar responses from the mother. During feeding there may be periods of intense sucking, alternated with pauses when the mother may talk to or 'jiggle' the child. There may be deliberate attempts to stimulate or gain attention through singing, handling or cuddling. Mothers typically use a combination of eye gaze, exaggerated facial expression and vocalisation to obtain mutual watching in face-to-face position with the infant. Once the infant is attending, a kind of play dialogue ensues until the infant disengages by looking away. The best predictor of when the mother will respond again is the moment when the infant chooses to glance at her face.

Caregivers use these intimate encounters to talk about the baby. The baby's changing facial expressions, smiles, sounds and movements are likely to be interpreted as meaningful by the adult and put into words: 'You've had enough of that now, haven't you?'; 'You're ready for a sleep, aren't you?'; 'Let's get rid of that horrid nappy'. The baby's crying, gurgling and laughing is often reciprocated by the mother taking a turn to respond. Many early interactions have this on/off, first you/then me pattern, as both infant and mother read signals in each other's behaviour.

Adult contingency

In all these contexts, the child's activity is suffused with adult commentary, which overlays and offers an interpretation of events, whilst also sustaining the child's engagement. By making their reactions contingent upon the infant's initially spontaneous activity, the child's responses are taken up, made sense of in relation to the surrounding context, and attributed with meaning. The infant may then respond reciprocally, by repeating a movement, gesture or sound that 'caused' an adult's earlier reaction. These rudimentary exchanges are structured along the same lines as the adult discourse system and can be considered as foundations for later conversation skills. The conventions of giving a message and eliciting a response are rehearsed and perfected until a communicative framework is developed whereby increasingly linguistic exchanges are made possible.

By being treated as though they had intentions, well before the emergence of the first word, the baby is thus playing a part in communicative exchanges in which infants come to expect that things will happen as a result of their own actions. This sharing of meaning between adults and babies is also supported by some other features of early infant environments. For example, the infant's world often presents repetitive cycles of bathing, dressing, feeding and changing, interspersed with play. Within these familiar formats, which are largely structured and regulated by caregivers, infants come to discover connections between tones of voice, vocalisations, persons and events. A child of one of the authors would begin thumb-sucking on hearing the words 'night-night', in anticipation of being laid in her cot. The mere production of the changing mat was enough to bring screams of protest at the anticipated hassle of a nappy change. The familiarity of these routines or formats, with their predictable accompanying actions and commentary, enable infants to discover regularities, patterns and acts of communication in their encounters with others.

During this period of infancy, children spend a lot of time doing a very limited number of things. Another child of one of the authors, at about 12 months of age, would sit opening and closing cupboards for hours on end, later extending this to doors, tins with lids, drawers and boxes. These repetitions of a narrow range of actions on similar objects have been called 'systematicity', whereby the infant tries out routines, deals with objects in a systematic way, makes a lot out of a little, seeking or imposing order and rules on everyday things in the environment (Bruner, 1983). In early play, as in later language activities, children are geared to generate and combine a small set of elements, in order to create a larger set of possibilities. We shall be returning to this idea of how the child imposes rules and generates categories when we consider concept development and also play. Here, too, the salient underlying features that propel the child's strategies for organising the world are mainly visual.

ADULT–CHILD INTERACTIONS AND VISUAL IMPAIRMENT

Most babies, then, are programmed at birth to respond to touch, taste, smell, sight and sound, and these senses mean that they have many ways of coming to know the world and of establishing contact with it. They are immediately orientated to test out the environment, to manipulate and to explore, to recognise patterns and regularities, to achieve goals and make sense of things, but above all else, to interact with their caretakers and maintain social contact. There is no reason to believe that babies who are born blind, or with severe visual impairments, are any less prepared than other infants to socialise, explore their surroundings, seek out regularities and respond selectively to adults' touches or sounds. But conditions must be right for this potential to be realised. One of the early hazards that families of a child with a visual impairment must overcome is the barrier to social interaction: the initiating and maintaining of early exchanges that introduce the child to the social contexts out of which language and problem-solving themselves emerge.

Much of the patterning of early interactions between parents and their infants, which we have described above, depends on visually based strategies. All of the following interactive processes depend to some extent on a visual component: obtaining an infant's attention; interest in faces and mutual gazing; looking away to signal disengagement; reciprocal imitation of gestures, actions and tongue movements; turning to locate a sound source; reading and interpreting a partner's intention; recognising familiar situations and events; and extending and linking exploratory play from one object to another. The structure of rudimentary interactions, mutual sensitivity to the signals and intentions of partners (or 'intersubjectivity') is obviously interrupted by a reduction of visual information. The important question is: how far is vision central to establishing an interactive framework between adult and infant?

Eye contact and responsiveness

In some families, the problem of establishing eye contact with a baby with a severe visual impairment leads to parents feeling that their child is unresponsive (Preisler, 1991). Some infants with visual impairments do not smile or gurgle when picked up, as most babies do in response to being cuddled or a face coming into view. Babies who quieten and still when being touched or hearing a voice may be more difficult to engage with in the early stages. However, parents can usually find other forms of contact to stimulate social interaction, and observe ways other than facial expression through which the child anticipates being picked up or enjoys the mother's attentions, such as arm or leg movements.

Tobin (1993) provides an illustration of how a child, aged 12 months and blind from birth, engages in social interaction whilst sitting on her mother's knee. Ruth begins to scratch the rough fabric of the armchair whilst her mother is being interviewed. The mother reciprocates and a dialogue of scratching proceeds, first Ruth, then her mother, at a gathering pace. As Tobin points out, there has been no eye contact in this situation, no reciprocal reinforcement on the basis of visual signals, and yet turn-taking, timing and communication are all being rehearsed.

The incident reported by Tobin shows that vision is not an essential requirement for all of these early foundations of communicative exchanges. However, vision does contribute towards the spontaneity, ease and frequency with which these exchanges take place. In Chapter 5, when we consider strategies for intervention, we shall also be examining ways in which parents of children with visual impairments can take positive steps to enhance early social encounters.

The reference triangle

By 6 months of age the sighted infant's predisposition towards other humans, and the willingness of adults to respond, have established the basis for communication. Turn-taking games such as 'Clap hands', 'Peek-a-boo' or 'This little piggy went to market' encourage the child to listen to the sounds and rhythms of speech and, at a critical point, the child is expected to respond in turn. Activities such as these, rehearsed and confirmed in familiar settings, distribute joint attention over a patterned sequence of events. They act as prototypes for later dialogues, in which a fundamental part is knowing when to talk and when to listen.

When, at about 6 months, the infant's attention turns to objects and events in the environment, the patterns of interaction change. An object or 'happening' attracts the child's interest. The infant's visual exploration is typically 'mirrored' by the adult, who looks where the baby looks and talks about what is being looked at. The infant may point to, reach for, or simply show an object to the adult, which invites commentary. In this way the outside world is brought into the mutual attention of the adult and the child. By following the infant's line of attention, drawing inferences about what is being looked at, or what the baby is feeling, the adult puts into words that which is of apparent interest to the child.

More remarkably, by the second half of the first year, the baby begins to follow the adult's line of gaze. Such shared attention to common objects and events increases the probability that adult and child will be looking at the same things, and when the adult names things or interprets an event, the shared visual experience of the world is tied to the patterns of language that refer to it. This shared attention helps bring the infant's experience into conjunction with language, emphasising the relationship between speech sounds and events. This process has been called the 'triangle of reference' and forms the basis of the development of shared meanings and, eventually, words (Webster and Wood, 1989).

Interpreting the significance of different experiences is also helped by the adult's tone of voice or mood, well before words are recognised. A strong 'No' from an adult to a child just about to eat soil in the garden, or in danger of pulling over a lamp stand, conveys meaning through intonation. Speech contours and rhythms help children to begin to recognise questions ('What's that?') and statements ('That's a . . .'), to register delight, surprise, caution or danger. The beginnings of verbal meanings do not simply reside in word sounds, but depend also on interpretations conveyed through speech tones. At around the age of 10 months, the infant will begin to point at objects whilst also looking at the mother, whereby the reference triangle, involving two minds trained on the same object, becomes increasingly more intentional.

This period of language acquisition, which begins well before first words, depends on a number of factors. Children come into the world orientated towards human faces and voices, and resourced for means–end exploration and language. They are active enquirers, programmed to seek rules and regularities. Adults provide the right conditions for these processes to materialise, such as predictable formats for social interaction, reading intentions in the

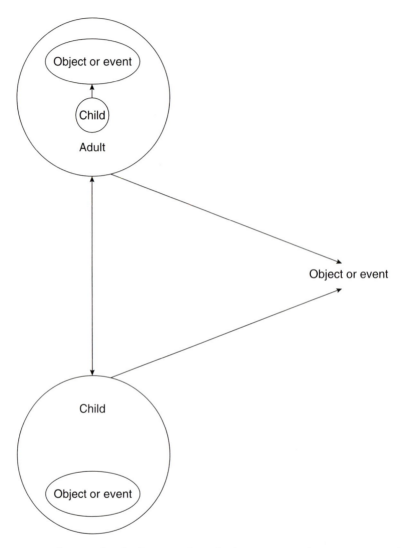

Figure 3.1 The triangle of reference. The infant's attention is drawn to a particular object or event. The adult follows the infant's line of attention and hypothesizes what is being looked at, imagined or felt (such as fear at seeing a dog; joy on catching sight of the mother). This influences the adult's verbal response and tone of voice. When a child has a visual loss, joint reference may be much harder to achieve: the adult may be unable to read the child's focus of interest and thus unable to put into words what the child is experiencing

child's behaviour, and bringing the child's perceptual experience into juxta-position with language, such as by naming things which the child looks at. Where conditions for learning include reduced access to visual information, how are these early reference patterns affected?

Joint reference and sensory impairment

We might predict that shared attention and joint reference are much harder to establish with infants who have a sensory impairment. We have depicted the reference triangle as a shared visual experience suffused with language. As described above, the adult's commentary, intonation and tone of voice are tied to familiar events, so that when attention is drawn to a particular object, the relationship between words and their referents is emphasised. In the situation where a deaf baby turns to look at a shared object or event, the accompanying voice-over is missing. In the case of a child with a visual loss, the triangle of reference is disrupted because the social experience lacks the dimension of vision, as opposed to language.

In situations where a child is unable to use visual information, adults cannot always interpret the focus of attention from the child's direction of gaze. If a blind child stills as a signal of interest in some new stimulus, it is much harder to infer what might be the source of arousal, or to interpret the child's train of thought. Pointing or reaching may be absent, although blind children do gesture. Adults may find it much more difficult to read the infant's cues, intentions and preoccupations, to draw inferences about what is being looked at, imagined or felt, and to put into words that which is of apparent interest to the child.

Adults interacting with children with severe visual impairments have to learn to pick up other signals of the child's interest or arousal, such as hand movements and vocalisations. One important question for parents and teachers of children with visual impairments is how far language itself can take on some of the functions of vision, for example in establishing the child's target of attention, directing the child's interest to new objects, and providing information about the immediate environment, what we referred to earlier as forms of 'bridging'.

EARLY EXPLORATION AND COGNITIVE DEVELOPMENT: THE CONTRIBUTION OF PIAGET

People's views about the nature of children's learning and conceptual development have changed markedly in recent years. There will be few teachers who are unfamiliar, at least in part, with the work of Piaget. His work continues to hold significance for our understanding of conceptual development in relation to vision. For children with visual impairments, the implications of Piaget's theories are profound. In his review of research on emerging understanding of the physical world, Warren (1994) points out that there has been virtually no research done involving children with visual impairments that has not taken a Piagetian perspective.

Although Piaget's influence has been great, his analysis of children's cognitive competence at different stages of maturity has not been accepted uncritically. We have already expressed some misgivings about the way in which developmental psychology has tended to observe individuals outside of the contexts in which they grow and change, and to present a picture of orderly progression through well-defined stages.

Piaget's method, for example, was to provide a child with novel materials or situations, and then observe and question what the child did with them as evidence of emerging understanding. Piaget's research on problem-solving has generated some important notions about children's active involvement in making hypotheses about the world, their capacity to reflect on experience and to formulate their own proposals about how things work. However, Piaget promoted an image of the child as a solitary thinker, struggling to put together a personal account of the mathematical and logical properties of the physical world, through self-directed exploration. The role of the adult or teacher in Piagetian theory is low key and indirect, restricted to providing resources or structuring activities. Many people have made the point that Piaget was more interested in the nature of knowledge than in processes of education: he did not see teaching as his business.

What has been added more recently to Piaget's theoretical accounts of changes in children's thinking – their role as 'scientists' or 'explorers' – is that they are not alone in their voyages or experimentation, and that adults have a significant facilitative part to play. This shift in perspective has drawn on the work of writers such as Vygotsky and other socio-constructivists, who see children's learning and thinking as embedded in social relationships (John-Steiner et al., 1994; Light et al., 1991; Rogoff, 1990; Wood, 1988; Woodhead et al., 1991). Importantly, for promoting the development of children with visual impairment, these accounts have begun to analyse the nature of adults' scaffolding of children's thinking and enquiry. We shall be referring to this work in some detail in Chapter 6.

Acting on the physical world

At the heart of Piagetian theory, which has had a seminal influence on most primary classrooms, is the idea that learning arises out of the child's own actions on the physical world. The child becomes aware of objects and events in the environment primarily through visual and tactile exploration: pointing, reaching and grasping; the urge to become mobile; exploring spaces; coming to know that objects exist outside oneself and are permanent, even though hidden from view. All these discoveries about the world are much harder to achieve for a child with a visual impairment.

Piaget argues that exploratory play is the beginning of the baby's mental life

through anticipation. Simple, repetitive games mark the foundations of thinking as infants begin to imagine and anticipate the effects of their
actions on events. Eventually, the consequences of actions can be imagined
internally by the child, without actually having to carry them out. This learned
co-ordination between actions and their outcomes has been highlighted as the
'bedrock' of children's thinking, and it is this process that lies behind Piaget's
famous phrase that 'thought is inter-nalised action'.

The strategies that all children use to explore are described by Piaget as
'schemata'. Grasping and mouthing of objects like plastic containers are good
examples of this. The child will have an existing schema for grasping and
mouthing objects such as beakers, bottles and cups in order to drink. Any
new container can be successfully assimilated into the existing schema.
However, some of the child's basic concepts or schemata will have to be
adjusted, or accommodated, in order to cope with new situations. For example,
if a beaker is hidden or placed out of reach, the child must now crawl to find
it before grasping, mouthing and sucking.

Vision and sensori-motor intelligence

It is because the first two years or so (what Piaget refers to as the sensori-motor
stage) are dominated by physical explorations such as reaching, pulling or
mouthing, that vision is so important in exploring and interacting with the
world. Vision provides an important incentive for the infant's exploration and meaning-making, the linking of words to objects, and the tying of
concepts and categories to the environment. In the sensori-motor period,
according to Piaget, children do not initially distinguish between their own
bodies and outside objects or events. In other words, the child's movements and
its effects are part of a continuous flow of experience. Gradually, through an
accumulation of experience in play, infants begin to discover the physical limits of their bodies and begin to distinguish 'self' from 'objects' (including other
people).

In Piagetian terms, the point at which infants can begin to imagine different
ways of achieving the same ends without actually performing them is the
onset of practical intelligence. In other words, internalised mental actions start
to represent physical actions. For example, a child of 2 begins to use bricks
to play cars, and makes drawings of people. The child is capable of representing the world in other symbols. Pretend objects are assimilated into existing
ideas about the world, with the important shift that one thing can represent
another in the child's imagination.

Intuitive thinking and visual perception

Piaget invented a range of ingenious techniques to explore and illustrate the
emerging nature of children's thinking. In the second, 'intuitive', stage, chil-

dren's thinking often seems idiosyncratic and rather capricious as they centre on irrelevant aspects of situations. For example, in one experiment Piaget asked young children to make judgements about the amount of liquid in two containers. If the containers are identical in shape and size and the liquid in each comes to the same level, 4 and 5 year olds usually have no hesitation in judging that both contain the same amount. However, if, in full view of the child, the content of one is poured into another container with a different shape (for example, taller and narrower), children at this stage will probably say there is more liquid in the new container than the one left untouched.

Children base their judgements on one feature of the situation (usually height) but may ignore others (such as width). In Piaget's view, children cannot co-ordinate more than one focus of attention in order to reach a logical judgement. Thus, a change in appearance may be interpreted as a change in volume.

Concrete operations and perceptual evidence

In the third stage, one of concrete operations, from around 7 to 11 years, schemata such as addition, subtraction and multiplication are gained. Children become aware that certain properties of objects, such as weight, volume or quantity, stay the same even when visible changes take place, as in the water jar experiment. To do this the child must step back from the perceptual evidence, and marry all the relevant aspects together, including the relationships between them.

The child's thinking is no longer intuitive, based on single points of comparison. Inductive logic also characterises this stage: the child can abstract features of objects to form generalisation of classes, such that balls, oranges and marbles are all round. It is generally assumed that this shift from intuitive thinking to concrete operational thought parallels important developments in children's understanding of social relationships and the perspectives of others. Initially, children cannot assume another person's point of view; later they realise that others may see things differently, and finally they understand that a third person may have a separate understanding of a situation that contrasts with that of the child or a second person.

Logical thinking and the real world

In the last period of cognitive development, from age 12 years on, which Piaget called formal operations, the structure of the child's thinking shifts towards increasing levels of abstraction, released from the here and now. Eventually, the adolescent is able to reason about hypothetical events with no material evidence. For Piaget, the natural culmination of intellectual growth is the achievement of formal, logical thinking that enables the internal setting up of hypotheses and propositions about the world. Formal thinking has often been felt to be associated with the kind of intellectual demands made by secondary schooling in the later stages, in subject areas where a high level of abstract or conceptual understanding is required.

Piaget's work has been re-examined critically by a number of researchers who have re-run experiments and established that changes in conditions or instructions make a difference to the child's performance. Other researchers, such as Bruner (1986) or Wood (1988), have suggested that individuals do not utilise a single method or logic in their thinking, characteristic of a particular stage, but that they adopt one of any number of strategies that differ in scope, power and efficiency.

Furthermore, there may be important distinctions to be drawn between the kind of formal thinking demanded in 'contrived' contexts such as a classroom and the real world considerations required when problem-solving in natural settings. For example, the archetypal maths question posed to children along the lines: 'If it takes 3 men 6 hours to dig a certain sized hole, how long would it take 2 men?', suspends the ordinary kind of pragmatic concerns with issues such as how soft the ground was, what kind of tools were available, or how the men would be paid, which would be explored in real life. In the contrived context of the classroom, most pupils recognise that this as a special kind of problem-solving with a defined outcome, the ground rules for which are typically required only in school.

Bruner also makes a strong case for studying children's behaviour in authentic social contexts as they collaborate with adults, rather than examining children working alone at their problem-solving. None of these criticisms have much of a bearing on Piaget's views of the nature of logic, although they do highlight distinct differences in relation to the nature of children's learning and how that may be supported, and they do have important implications for our understanding of the impact of a visual impairment on cognitive growth.

Visual impairment and Piagetian theory

Children with visual impairments depend to some extent on others to bring the environment within reach, or to provide explanations about what is happening elsewhere. A child without clear vision may be unaware of many of the interesting things around them, and may not reach out or grasp objects in exploratory play. All children will reach towards objects in response to sound. However, auditory stimuli are not so powerful as visual cues in stimulating reaching, and ear–hand prehension occurs later in development. Many objects do not actually emit sounds, whilst many that do, such as doorbells, televisions and washing machines, are not graspable. So a child's early attempts to explore sound sources may be unrewarding and not repeated.

Early intervention programmes always emphasise the importance of sustaining children's motivation to explore their immediate physical and social environments, using whatever evidence sources are meaningful. However, in many situations there are risks for young children with visual impairments allowed unrestricted crawling, head first. Early contacts with objects and surfaces that are sharp, cold or abrasive may have produced an anxiety in both parents and children about the free exploration of surroundings. There is a danger of some parents reducing the child's experience by being over-protective or moving interesting objects out of their way.

There may be a chain of consequences if children do not explore. Motor development may be affected, including the co-ordination of hands and eyes in partially sighted infants, or hands and ears in blind infants. Children with visual impairments cannot easily monitor their own body movements, leading to immaturities in the awareness of self in relation to the surroundings. Children who do not actively explore will also be immature in their concep-tual development: understanding what things are, how they work, differences and similarities between objects, how they may be categorised and classified. Instead of perceptual impressions based on the appearance of things, a child with a severe visual impairment must come to know objects and their inter-relationships in terms of tactile, auditory and kinaesthetic experiences, together with the commentary and explanations that adults supply, all of which may be more time consuming and demanding.

Understanding the physical world

The research evidence collated by Warren (1994) suggests that, in the absence of visual information, there are likely to be delays in a wide range of under-standings about the physical world: object permanence (that objects continue to exist even when the sensory evidence has disappeared); causality (the effects of given actions on objects); time (ordering of events in sequence); proper-ties of matter (continuity of properties such as number or volume despite changes to the appearance of things); space (how physical spaces are struc-tured and occupied by objects, including the relationships between objects).

Since cognitive development may be delayed in children with visual impairments, particularly the shifts into more logical thinking whereby children can weigh conflicting evidence, ignore appearances and recognise alternative viewpoints, research has also shown extended timescales for children with visual impairments in related areas such as the growth of social cognition (understanding other people's roles, relationships and perspec-tives) and moral judgements (taking account of intentions and circumstances when judging behaviour). As children with visual losses cope with the increas-ingly abstract curriculum of the secondary school, they may be less well equipped and informed to distinguish between the ground rules of contrived contexts, such as the classroom or science laboratory, and real world problem-solving.

We have spent some time on Piaget's work because of its significance for understanding conceptual development in relation to vision. Warren's (1994) review summarises most of the data that have been derived from the application of Piagetian tests to individuals with visual impairments. Typical tasks for young children include the presentation of materials, such as clay balls of equal sizes, subjecting them to transformations by dividing them into smaller pieces, and then questioning the child to probe understanding of conservation. A wide range of research has been carried out, using subjects with varying degrees of visual impairment, adapting tasks so that materials can be handled. Few consistent conclusions overall have been drawn from this body of work, except that cognitive development depends closely on experience, but generally follows the 'normal' path, albeit sometimes delayed. In other words, the stages of cognitive development outlined by Piaget tend to have longer time scales in visually impaired populations, but are attained in the expected sequence. Most importantly, there is substantial variation among individuals in the timetable of acquisition of Piaget's developmental milestones, depending on degree of visual function, the quality of interactive relationships with caregivers, opportunity and experience.

It would be more surprising if the acquisition of many of the concepts assessed by Piaget, dependent as they are on properties of shape, size, movement or transformation of objects, did not show some delays in children with visual impairments. The establishment of concepts such as cause and effect is arguably much more easily derived from the cumulative store of perceptual evidence that the sighted child can draw on. Delays on Piagetian tasks reflect the salience of visual experience to the concepts under test, rather than indicating any inherent conceptual inabilities in children with restricted vision.

As with much of Piaget's work, adjusting experimental conditions often allows children to display the real levels of their intellectual development. Demonstrations of conservation using salt or sand in containers, rather than liquid, is one example of how teaching can be planned to promote concepts in terms that are more readily apparent to children with visual impairments. Appropriately designed training and assessment procedures generally show that the presence of a severe visual impairment or blindness is not a barrier to the acquisition of cognitive skills, according to the stages and time scales defined by Piaget for sighted individuals (Stephens and Grube, 1982).

VISUAL EXPERIENCE AND THE EXTENSION OF CONCEPTS

All of the previous examples drawn from Piaget's work show the close interweaving of conceptual growth with certain kinds of perceptual experience and the language that encapsulates it. If children construct word meanings and conceptual categories based on their own unique experiences, one would expect to find differences in the ways in which all children abstract information, make classifications and extend word meanings from one situation to another.

Plate 3.1 Practical experience and conceptual development. For children with visual impairments practical experiences are important for understanding events often learned visually – for example, that plants grow in the earth

Some very interesting work, reported in Dunlea (1989), shows that the ways in which most children and adults tend to organise their thinking often depends on certain physical properties. Typically, categorisation is based on properties such as shape, movement and size. From cross-cultural studies, there appears to be a human predisposition to exploit features such as roundness, flatness or length, in constructing sets and defining classes of objects, which is reflected in language. This process is central in helping the child move from using a word as a name, learned in one context to denote one particular instance or event, towards using words more widely to apply to other referents that share similar perceptual features.

A large proportion of most sighted children's first 50 or so words refer to the 'here and now' of their daily lives: items of food, clothing, body parts, animals, vehicles, toys, people. There are also terms that relate to familiar routines, or social events, such as greetings. We would expect, since children with severe visual impairments must come to know many objects in terms of tactile, auditory or kinaesthetic experiences, rather than on the appearance of things, that this would be reflected in vocabulary growth, yet researchers who have studied the first 50 words of blind children highlight differences in content rather than rate of word acquisition (Bigelow, 1987). Children with visual impairments tend to use more words referring to their own actions, have fewer general names for classes of objects (cat, fish), but more specific names for individual toys, pets and people. Their word sets tend to have fewer modifiers (qualities of objects such as cold, hard) and function words ('what's this?'), but more words for use in social interaction ('excuse me', 'thank you'). Not surprisingly, contrasts between groups in early word sets are assumed to reflect differences in experience.

Word meanings

Perhaps the most interesting contrasts between children are those that have been highlighted in the development of word meanings. Early word meanings tend to be very fluid, as shown by the diary records of linguists who have documented the words children use along with their referents: what the child uses them to denote. For example, one child used the word 'bird' to refer to sparrows as well as all other moving objects. Another child used the word 'scissors' to refer to all metal objects, only later applying the word specifically to implements that cut. This process is usually described as overextension. What seems to happen is that the child associates the meaning of a word with a particular property, such as size, colour or shape, and then applies it to other objects that share the property. Development proceeds as the child redefines the important semantic features in line with the adult range of meanings.

Linguists also describe a process of underextension: the child's use of a word with a narrower meaning than it has in the adult system. For example, one sighted child described by Clark and Clark (1977) used 'car' to refer to vehicles moving on the street below as she looked out of the window. However, she did not use the word for cars standing still, pictures of cars, or cars she rode in herself. This child seems to have identified a highly specific property associated with car – observed from a height – and with growth in experience and interaction with adults the critical semantic features are eventually redefined.

Underextension and overextension in blind children

Much of the work on blind children suggests that there is a frequent occurrence of underextension in word meanings and a corresponding lack of overextension (Dunlea, 1989; Mills, 1993). Terms are used to refer to one specific object only, as a name, for an unusually long time and do not generalise. Where overextension does occur this is likely to be on the basis of perceptual features such as sound, texture, taste or weight, rather than shape or movement. For example, 'bear' was used by one child to refer to a particular toy bear, but not for any other furry bear.

Plate 3.2 Bridging 'word/world' differences. It is important for children with visual impairments to explore the world through available sensory modalities and for adults to provide explanations with the detail and precision to mediate rich understanding

The criterial attributes adopted by blind children – those features of objects that determine how words are applied – are different from those used by sighted children, reflecting the salience of non-visual information. Dunlea cites the example of a blind child who used the word 'cookie' to refer to eating a cracker, when feeling small rough surfaces such as a piece of paper, and whilst sniffing a pine tree. The more limited extensions of children with visual impairment reflect more limited experience of those features of the world through which objects tend to be classified. Blind children, with more limited stores of information about objects and events in their environment, find it more difficult to identify the common elements shared by different things, with the result that words associated with one context are not so easily applied to another (Dunlea, 1989).

Vocabulary fallout and idiosyncracies

Apart from the fixing of word meanings as names learned in one context but not applied to others, Dunlea also highlights some other contrasts between subjects. For example, no words acquired by the blind children were dropped from their vocabularies, whereas sighted children frequently discarded terms that no longer served their needs. Another process observed in sighted children only was the creation of idiosyncratic expressions, which also disappeared when no longer required. A child of one of the authors, for example, at about 4 years of age, briefly used the expression 'oppositting' to describe the position of people sitting across from him at the dining table, a term that later fell out of use.

Words may also be used in more egocentric ways by blind children. In Dunlea's research, for example, action words were used by the experimental subjects to refer exclusively to themselves (e.g. 'dance' while dancing, 'walk' while walking, 'rock' whilst being rocked). Sighted control subjects not only had expressions for their own actions, but these were also applied to other objects, people and animals (e.g. 'milk' to refer to own and another's drink).

Taken together, these findings regarding word inventions, fallout of redundant terms, egocentric references, and the more restricted extension of word meanings, seem to indicate that visual impairment disrupts the processes in early childhood that enable children to recognise and extract information as a basis for the spontaneous construction and generalisation of word meanings. This, too, has important implications for the strategies adopted by adults – how the world is mediated for the child in ways that link existing concepts to other points of reference – in order to amplify the child's constructs.

LANGUAGE COMPETENCE AND VISUAL IMPAIRMENT

As we have indicated, until recently most researchers concerned with the impact of a sensory impairment have focused on the evaluation of products rather than on co-operative social processes and the learning that is promoted through them. However, it is important to be aware of some widely agreed findings from this work in order to highlight the importance of more recent research concerned with how, rather than what, children learn.

Babbling

Some very early observations of babies with severe visual impairments show that they do vocalise, coo and cry at about the same time as infants with good vision. At the babble stage, when the child begins to produce the significant sound contrasts that are used around them, blind children have been reported to vocalise less than sighted children (Fraiberg, 1977). However, this may be because the infant is listening more intently. In terms of triggering babbling, watching a human face talking is apparently not so important as hearing the voice. Deaf babies, at this stage, for example, begin to produce a reduced range of babble sounds, in less quantity and with flatter tones (Webster and Wood, 1989).

Speech sounds

A number of studies have investigated the production of speech sounds in children with severe visual impairments. It has been argued that children watch mouth shapes and copy lip movements from adults. There is some evidence that children who cannot see clearly may have problems in using some speech sounds, particularly those that have a visible lip pattern, such as 'm', 'b' or 'f' (Mills, 1983).

One interpretation is that the speech sounds of some children are delayed as part of a general language immaturity. However, the fact that blind children show no differences in their production of speech sounds that are invisible on the lips, such as 'j', 'k' and 't', indicates that there is no general delay in sound acquisition. The visible information about speech articulation does seem to provide children who have good vision with clues to their own sound production. If children with severe visual impairments are felt to be delayed in reaching mature speech phonology, as some researchers suggest, then this is unlikely to be noticeable beyond the age of about 5 years (Mills, 1993).

Vocabulary

The vocabularies of children with severe visual impairments and blindness have also been studied in contrast to sighted peers. It is possible that some children with reduced play and sensory experience begin to say words at a later date than is usually reported. However, there do not seem to be major differences between children in the number of words acquired by the age of about 3 years. Simple word counts may, of course, obscure qualitative differences in the use of words. As suggested in the previous section, where we examined studies of the emergence of early language patterns, severe visual impairment does seem to be associated with thematic differences in the way in which vocabulary is categorised, created and extended.

Various studies (summarised, for example, in Mills, 1993) have been carried out on the use of spatial terms (this, here, that, there), locational terms (in, on, under), use of pronouns and gender terms. Where confusions do arise, for example, in a blind child's use of gender terms, these seem directly related to aspects of visual experience, such as the problem of determining the sex of the referent in the absence of visual clues.

Similarly, appropriate use of pronouns such as 'I' and 'you' requires an awareness of role relationships: 'I' must always refer to the speaker and 'you' to the hearer; and whilst children are always addressed by 'you', they must not call themselves that. However, many children at 6 and 7 years of age in ordinary circumstances continue to develop their awareness of different layers of meaning in words and phrases. Terms like 'ask'/'tell', 'here'/'there', 'bring'/'take', 'before'/'after', depend on understanding changes in reference points, which may be more difficult in the absence of spatial or context clues. In any case, as we have said, many sighted 7 year olds have considerable problems sorting out some of these distinctions (Webster and McConnell, 1987).

Grammar

Another aspect that has been given attention is the grammatical competence of children with visual impairments, displayed in aspects such as the length, type or construction of sentences. Again, the available research evidence suggests that any early delays in acquiring syntactic structures are made up for over time. Studies of the use of specific sentence forms or grammatical constructions, summarised, for example, in Mills (1993) or Dunlea (1989), show few significant delays that cannot be explained in terms of differences in exposure, i.e. the language being used around the child. Where any differences have been noted, children with multiple handicaps in addition to visual loss are likely to be involved.

Function

Differences have also been reported in the frequencies and types of speech functions in the language of children with visual impairments, i.e. the kinds of messages that young children attempt to convey. Interactive play between adults and children is an important activity where functions such as greeting, asserting, refusing, requesting, questioning, protesting, teasing, confronting, challenging, pretending and negotiating are likely to be observed.

Dunlea's case studies show remarkably similar patterns of development in both sighted children and individuals with severe visual impairments.

Differences tend to reflect the availability of visual information, and so blind children use many more attention-seeking strategies, requests for objects, actions and activities; they want to join ongoing games and play, or to involve others in what they are doing; they signal their displeasure at the actions of others, comment on events and ask questions, or simply use language to sustain social contact.

Since questioning figures highly in the language repertoires of children with visual impairments, strategies for questioning have been studied in some detail. Erin (1986), for example, in a study of 36 children with and without visual impairments between the ages of 4 and 10 years, showed that significantly fewer questions were asked spontaneously by sighted individuals. Questions serve a range of functions: soliciting information ('What happens at lunchtime?'), requesting action or permission ('Can I bend this?'), seeking confirmation ('That's hailstone, isn't it?'), or simply sustaining social contact with a partner ('Do you know what?'). Most children come to know that one way to get an adult to respond is to ask a question. For the child with a visual impairment, questioning develops as a specialised way of gathering information about the environment and, more importantly, keeping the adult source of useful information near to hand.

Sighted terms

Much has been made of the differences in word meanings between contrasting groups of children. An issue sometimes raised by mainstream teachers is whether they should avoid reference to visual imagery, colour names or 'look' and 'see' expressions such as 'Look at this'. Talking about things or processes that have not been directly experienced is termed 'verbalism'. The use of concepts and phrases that are associated with the visual world used to be condemned in the education of children with visual impairments on the grounds that it would lead to incoherent or 'loose' thinking (Cutsforth, 1932).

When a child with limited vision is asked to 'look', more than likely this is interpreted in terms of 'exploring', with no more sinister connotations than that. The meaning of sighted terms will be deduced in accordance with the child's growing understanding of the world, through the sensory modalities that are available, and the verbal interpretations from adults that accompany them.

Tobin (1993) considers these arguments about 'word/world' differences at some length, concluding that language serves a number of purposes other than the identification and labelling of objects. To prevent children from using terms that are not underpinned by direct experience, such as restricting blind children to the language of touch, taste, smell and hearing, would seem to be an unwarranted social imposition, even if it were feasible. Furthermore, there are many instances of verbal usage in fully sighted individuals where meanings are not derived from direct experience. In any case, Tobin argues (op. cit.), in line with our own thinking, that language itself can serve as a bridge between the child's current representation of experience and any new linguistic usage that extends that. For parents and teachers this view has strong practical implications: using language to take on some of the characteristics of vision by directing the child's attention to new objects, identifying similarities and differences, and providing explanations with the detail and precision to mediate richer understanding.

LANGUAGE DEVIANCE

Some researchers have also been interested in ways in which the language of children with visual impairments may be deviant, i.e. not part of the typical developmental route taken by most children. The use of stereotypic speech is felt to be one area that serves a specific purpose for children with restricted visual experience.

Frozen phrases

Stereotypic speech is the picking up of phrases used by caregivers in certain situations, which are then reproduced in similar contexts. The child may reproduce the exact rhythms, vocabulary and tones of voice heard previously, although the utterances are used by the child in a non-instrumental, non-interactive way. The chunks of language that are reproduced seem to be single, undigested, 'frozen' units that are closely associated with a given context. In fact, stereotypic speech has been reported in studies of sighted children and may be one of the mechanisms for language acquisition available to every language-learner. Clark (1974) provides several illustrations from her son's speech, where segments from the mother's utterances are reproduced in a familiar, recurring situation. The phrase 'Wait for it to cool', for example, was used by the child whenever a hot meal was brought to the dining room table.

In her case studies of blind children, Dunlea (1989) finds many examples of stereotypic speech. In some instances, a whole chunk of their mother's speech is reproduced in its appropriate context. Examples include: 'was that fun?' (sliding down a ladder); 'did you have a nice nap?' (on waking); 'I carry you' (wanting to be carried). What can also be noticed in these examples is that stereotypic speech contributes to the misuse of pronouns. Pronouns are reversed simply because they are recalled as part of a whole segment, without deconstruction. Interestingly, these utterances are reproduced by children at a time when other aspects of syntax structure are being acquired and used creatively, including appropriate use of pronouns.

Dunlea suggests that the use of stereotypic speech is unique to children with severe visual impairments and serves a special purpose. The sequences of utterances reproduced help to 'fix' a familiar or routine event. Chunks of language are an integral part of the available sensory information which represent an event in the child's imagination. They are more likely to occur when speech is difficult to map on to external referents. Reproducing speech patterns, albeit undigested, helps the child to recreate familiar situations in the absence of clear visual images.

Echolalia

Use of stereotypic speech or 'frozen phrases' is distinguishable from another frequently documented irregularity in the language development of children with visual impairment: echolalia. In fact, echolalia – the inappropriate parroting of words or phrases – can be observed in many young children, and may serve the purpose of rehearsal or wordplay.

The persistence of echolalia into later childhood in some blind children has invited comparisons with autism (Mills, 1993). Some autistic children repeat whole phrases heard previously, in a new but wholly inappropriate context, without understanding. Some autistic children, like blind children, also have persistent difficulties with personal pronouns in their speech, perhaps reversing 'you' and 'I'. These features are part of a range of cognitive and communicative difficulties associated with autism that no one has yet been able to account for satisfactorily. This has led to much speculation about the cause of the autistic syndrome, including damage to areas of the brain that deal with the use and understanding of language (Webster and McConnell, 1987). What is clear is that, when echolalia arises within a context of social interaction, individuals demonstrate their lack of understanding of how or what to communicate by repeating samples of language with little relevance or meaning.

To summarise this body of research on the impact of blindness, severe or mild visual impairment on the language development of children, there is little agreement on the nature and persistence of effects. Obviously, a child's use of language reflects individual differences in experience, sensitivity to varying forms of perceptual information, and the strategies adopted to explore the world. It would be highly surprising if these differences did not produce individual variations in language use. But there is no conclusive data that demonstrate that delays or differences in children's acquisition of a wide range of language competences are an inevitable consequence of a visual impairment. Obviously, vision is an important component of many aspects of cognitive and linguistic growth. The fact that most children do overcome the obstacles to learning and interaction that a visual impairment presents tells us much about the flexibility of language-learning processes and the social systems that support them.

LANGUAGE AND THINKING AT HOME

One of the ways in which research over the last 20 or 30 years has begun to examine processes of language development, as opposed to measuring outcomes or products, is by studying aspects of the language environment.

At the beginning of this chapter we considered some of the features that characterise very early interactions, as children are introduced to the social and linguistic conventions that underpin learning. These early features of adult speech to children, which seem specially dependent on vision, serve to capture the child's attention and promote understanding in relation to immediate objects and events, subsequently decentring from the child and involving aspects of the distal environment. Many of these processes, which adults intuitively adopt, operate before the onset of first words. However, researchers have also tried to uncover those aspects of adults' speech to older children that have a powerful impact on development.

Issues in the study of input and interaction in language acquisition are complex. Linguists refer to this domain of research as child-directed speech (CDS), or speech directed to young children. (For reviews of CDS, see Snow, 1995 or Gallaway and Richards, 1994). We shall be considering some of these issues in detail because of the central importance of language in the development and education of children with visual impairment. Knowing the processes that facilitate conversation provides important clues for intervention when atypical circumstances arise.

As might be expected, much of this work on the ecology of children's language-learning has been carried out within the framework of socioconstructivism. This is a term we introduced in Chapter 1 to denote a new emphasis in studying learning as 'guided participation'. Unlike Piaget, for example, whose method was to provide the child with materials or controlled situations as a basis for observation and questioning, more recent researchers have guarded against this view of the child as an independent little scientist or problem-solver. Instead, subjects are observed in normally complex circumstances, such as at home or in school, and the focus of interest lies with the collaborative problem-solving of caregivers and children. Perhaps the central tenet of these more recent accounts is that adults frequently assist children to accomplish things, through a wide range of sensitive 'moves' or strategies, that they could not do for themselves.

Main findings from CDS research

In the first instance, researchers were keen to denote ways in which speech addressed to young sighted children constituted a distinct register from adult–adult talk. Often-noted characteristics include using higher pitch, exaggerated intonation patterns and relatively simple grammatical structures, and providing commentaries on children's play that include naming objects, giving information and explanations (Webster and McConnell, 1987).

After the first demonstrations of the nature of the CDS register, researchers have been more circumspect. What might facilitate the acquisition of an object name in a 15 month old engaged in toy play may be very different during other kinds of activity and at other ages. The effects of adult inputs are likely to be

Attention-getting	High pitch or nursery tone
	Exaggerated intonation or rhythm
	Whispering in child's ear
	Making use of child's name to start a sentence
	Special vocabulary or nicknames for child
	Touching, eye-level contact, gesturing and pointing
Simplifying	Using shorter sentences
	Using relatively simple syntactic structures
	Avoiding pronouns
	Selecting familiar vocabulary
Clarifying	Providing commentary on child's play
	Pausing between sentences, slowing down delivery
	Enhanced clarity of vowel sounds
	Full production of consonants that are usually reduced
	'Here and now' topics of conversation in familiar settings
	Use of present tense
	Using more content words, fewer function words
	Repetition of key words

Figure 3.2 Features of adult speech to young sighted children

very specific. The number of words used by the mother influences the first words acquired by the child, but cannot be related to more global measures of language maturity. There may also be wide individual variations in these effects, with some children exposed to less than optimal input. In following sections of this chapter we shall return to the point that children with developmental delays or disabilities may be exposed to the *least* facilitating of adult strategies.

Bristol child language studies

An important source of data on how young sighted children interact with their parents at home, how they co-operate in conversation, and the strategies they use to negotiate meaning has been provided by the Bristol child language studies (Wells, 1981; 1985; 1987). In this series of research projects, a total of 128 pre-school children were selected from a random sample of more than 1,000 resident in Bristol and observed at intervals until they entered school. Equal numbers of boys and girls were chosen, and the sample was taken to represent a range of socio-economic backgrounds and seasons of birth. However, children with special needs, whose parents were not both native speakers of English, or from one-parent or 'unwaged' families were excluded.

The aim of the research was to obtain regular and representative samples of naturally occurring conversations in a group of 'normal' children in their home environments. The data were used to describe the sequence of emergence of aspects of the language system, including those features that predict rapid or slow development and that are associated with subsequent academic achievement in the first two years of schooling. Observations were made in every family involved in the study at three-month intervals. Using a radio-microphone attached to a child's clothing, all that was said by the child or in the child's presence was picked up by the microphone and transmitted to a receiver, where the speech signals were recorded, later transcribed and analysed.

The Bristol research provides some important evidence on how adults enable children to become more mature language-users, whilst also highlighting factors that may hinder or promote development. Although not specifically concerned with learning difficulties or sensory impairment, this work has major implications for children with individual needs, and the contribution that adults can make to all children's learning through their conversations with them. The Bristol studies emphasise the marked degree of consistency across samples in the devices and strategies used in dialogue, the kinds of things talked about, and the characteristic active involvement of children and adults as conversation partners. There was a general absence of deliberate instruction, apart from a few polite expressions, such as 'please' and 'thank you', and occasional vocabulary teaching with 2 year olds at the labelling stage. However, the focus of effort is on reaching understanding between adults and children, not teaching, correcting or drilling.

Despite the absence of a 'curriculum' at home, there were no children in the study who were non-verbal, who were not engaged as active meaning-makers. In family after family, conversations centred around mundane, recurrent events like mealtimes, dressing and undressing, what could be seen in the garden, how things work, television programmes, toys, pets, objects and artefacts that constitute the fabric of day-to-day life. Much of children's learning at home occurs in the context of purposeful practical activity, usually tied to the immediate context and jointly pursued with an adult. On average, about three utterances a minute were addressed to children, hour by hour, day after day. Sheer amount of conversation is important, in that the children who received the most language tended to make the most rapid progress. The amount of speech addressed to different children varied widely: children addressed the least received on average one utterance per minute, whereas those addressed the most often received on average 10 utterances per minute. The relationship between quantity of exposure and rapid progress is, however, not quite so straightforward as these figures suggest.

What promotes rapid development?

Some of the most rapid developers were not amongst the group of children who received the largest amount of speech. Bathing a child in language, on the principle of 'talk, talk, talk', does not guarantee progress: quality of interaction is also significant. Family background was much less important in accounting for variation in language development between the subjects in the study than the quality of interactive experience. According to Wells, the ideal kind of conversational experience for a pre-schooler involves the child as an equal conversational partner, with something important to contribute. Adults are more effective in sustaining conversation when they show an active interest in the child's view of the world, taking up opportunities for talk related to the child's play and activity.

Some of the more salient factors of adult–child conversations are highlighted in this example:

Child: Ot, Mummy?
Adult: Hot? Yes, that's the radiator.
Child: Been – burn?
Adult: Burn?
Child: Yeh.
Adult: Yes, you know it'll burn don't you?
Child: Oh! Ooh!
Adult: Take your hand off it.

(Wells, 1987, page 46)

In this extract it is the child who introduces the topic, which is then 'agreed' by the adult who confirms the appropriateness of the child's comment: 'Hot? Yes . . .', and adds useful vocabulary and information. The two participants alternate in taking turns to speak, with the adult encouraging the child to contribute, accepting the child as an equal partner with something important to say, however limited the means. What is said in each turn of the dialogue, despite the child's fairly limited repertoire, relates in part to what was said by the previous speaker. The adult includes in her utterances elements of the child's preceeding offering. The adult checks out the child's intended meaning: 'Burn?', allowing room for re-negotiation if the child wanted to convey something different. The dialogue is sustained and elaborated around an issue of mutual interest, showing how, with adult help, a sequence of ideas can be jointly put together to interpret an event that the child would be unable to achieve alone. This adult's strategies introduce the child to appropriate language and understanding, without overcontrolling. They reach beyond the child's words to the intentions they realise, in order to draw some useful conclusions. This is a good example of what we referred to earlier as adult 'scaffolding'.

The Bristol studies provide many other examples of co-operatively achieved success. Many parents read books with their children, introducing them to the power that written language has for creating imaginary, alternative worlds. They played word games such as 'I spy', watched television and shared everyday household chores, such as doing the laundry, vacuuming and dusting, baking, changing the bedclothes, making jellies, gardening or painting. All of these mundane activities provided the stimulus for discussion, questioning and clarification, as children sought to find things out.

In the following example, a 4 year old is watching her mother shovel wood ash from the grate into a bucket:

Child: What are you doing that for?

Adult: I'm gathering it up and putting it outside so that Daddy can put it on the garden.

Child: Why does he have to put it in the garden?

Adult: To make the compost right.

Child: Does that make the grass grow?

Adult: Yes.

Child: Why does it?

Adult: You know how I tell you that you need to eat different things like eggs and cabbage and rice pudding to make you grow into a big girl?

Child: Yes.

Adult: Well, plants need different food too. And ash is one of the things that's good for them.

(Wells, 1987, page 59)

It is the child who instigates this discussion around a shared, everyday event, and the adult takes the opportunity to clarify the activity in terms the child understands. Through the medium of language, the adult bridges from the child's current experience and understanding to make wider points about nourishment and growth. However, the child is not simply exposed to adult ways of managing and reasoning, although these are important. There are also covert messages about sex roles, cultural expectations and valued behaviour.

Some of the most important aspects of adult scaffolding of language interaction include the use of expansions and paraphrase, whereby adults build on children's comments with more complex descriptions and explanations, clarifying and restating the child's intended meaning. Each of the responsive adults in the extracts given above takes note of the child's focus of attention and interest, puts the child's gestures and exclamations into words, expands a single word utterance into a complete sentence, and builds ideas across turns. Incorporating the child's comments within the adult's responses each time ensures topical continuity across turns. Each adult listens to what the child has to say, hands conversation back to the child and allows time for a reply, without overdominating the exchange. Wells (1981) has described these processes in terms of parents 'leading from behind'.

Talking and thinking at home

Many of the Bristol findings are supported by the work of Tizard and Hughes (1984) who also made radio-microphone recordings of sighted 4 year olds at home and in nursery school. One striking finding was the sheer amount of talk between children and their mothers. On average the children in this study held 27 conversations an hour. If the 'turns' in conversation are counted, when first one person contributes, then another, each conversation lasted on average 16 turns. Half of these conversations were started by the children. As in the Wells study, there were few distinctions between working-class or middle-class families in the amount, frequency or nature of conversations. In all families there was a richness of talk, an endless asking and answering of questions whereby the adult would supply commentary, new possibilities, information and ideas to the child's play or activity, which both extended and developed the child's thinking and enquiry.

The range of talk covered topics as diverse as family relationships, science, time, geography, plants, history, together with the size, colour, number and shape of objects. In the course of simply chatting together, 150 turns per hour on average imparted information. Typically, the child requested answers to questions that arose out of current activities. On few occasions did adults use language specifically to direct or manage. Fewer than 28 turns per hour were concerned with control: 'Don't touch that!', 'Mind you don't spill it!'. Adults and children drew pictures together, played 'hunt the thimble', cards or tickling games, wrote shopping lists, changed babies, planned holidays, or argued irritably. Interactions were generally sustained over a long stretch of time. Even when primarily engaged in a job such as ironing, parents have the time to respond to children's questions. Almost every activity, including reading stories, seemed to be punctuated by the child asking for clarification or more detailed information. Since the adults and children knew each other intimately, talk was free-ranging, referring to events and activities out of the immediate context, centred around things of significance to the participants.

The following example, taken from Tizard and Hughes, illustrates what these researchers have called 'passages of intellectual search':

Child: Is our roof a sloping roof?
Adult: Mmm. We've got two sloping roofs, and they sort of meet in the middle.
Child: Why have we?
Adult: Oh, it's just the way our house is built. Most people have sloping roofs so that the rain can run off them. Otherwise, if you have a flat roof, the rain would sit in the middle of the roof and make a big puddle, and then it would start coming through.
Child: Our school has a flat roof, you know?
Adult: Yes it does actually, doesn't it?
Child: And the rain sits there and goes through?

(Tizard and Hughes, 1984, page 124)

Episodes like this show adults and children puzzling over inconsistencies and asking further questions to resolve them. They provide compelling evidence of the pre-school child's logical power in pursuit of relatively abstract knowledge. Visual imagery suffuses all of the examples we have cited here, demonstrating the salience of the physical parameters that serve to define the environment for these conversational partners.

One further point we need to make is that for most children, even where there are no obstacles to communication or perceptual experience to overcome, transfer from the culture of the home to the learning context of the school inevitably means a reduction in the quality and quantity of conversational interaction. Encouraging purposeful conversation with groups of children in classrooms is an altogether more formidable task.

FAMILY COMMUNICATION STYLES AND VISUAL IMPAIRMENT

Adult responsiveness to the child's interests and communicative attempts is especially important for cognitive and linguistic growth, as the studies reported above have shown. Of course, parents are not alike in their responsiveness to children: there are differences in the parents' skills as conversation partners, as well as differences in children's abilities to elicit effective behaviour from their caregivers. A point made when we examined recent thinking in CDS research is that children who are less active and effective communicators may elicit more directive and less facilitative speech from caregivers.

Some adults are particularly good at listening to children and talking with them at just the right pitch of interest and understanding, whilst some children are intrinsically more rewarding to spend time with. It is not yet clear from research whether adults intuitively shape their language input to levels just beyond the child's current competence (the 'fine-tuning' or 'teaching' view) or whether changes in adult speech reflect the child's growing understanding (the 'accommodative' or 'child-elicited' view) and are determined more by what the child evokes. Either way, the important point is that adult sensitivity to children's attempts to converse does play an important facilitatory role, and is reciprocal, depending on contributions from both parties.

Children who are hard to scaffold

A number of studies show that the language environments of children who are 'atypical' in some way may compound their difficulties in learning language. These findings have been confirmed for children with Down's syndrome, specific language impairments and learning disabilities (Conti-Ramsden, 1994). The research reported by Webster and Wood (1989), involving deaf children and their families, shows that adults tend to be much more didactic and controlling in their conversations with deaf children. For example, parents often attempted to elicit and rehearse vocabulary. Rather than words emerging from a natural context of interaction, reflecting expe-

101

riences shared, vocabulary was often deliberately taught and performed: 'We're working on names for animals at the moment.' Parents often insisted on better pronunciation or grammar, interrogated through questions, or asked the child to repeat a correct sentence.

These more directive, intrusive parenting styles seem to reflect a concern to work on language, to command the child's attention so that important language experiences are seized and practised. One of the consequences of these more controlling, managerial styles is that children may be inhibited, rather than facilitated, in their language development. To rework Wells' phrase, parents direct their child's learning from the front.

In a recent study of social interaction, Meadows (1996) suggests that we do not have enough evidence to know exactly what the components of good scaffolding are. However, this is not to deny the importance of parent–child interactions as a determining factor in children's learning and development. What Meadows also draws attention to are those situations in which adults find children hard to scaffold. The presence of a sensory impairment affecting hearing or vision is cited as creating a condition that frequently leads to difficulties for adults in supporting a child's language and thinking.

Speech directed to children with visual impairments

How, then, do adults speak differently to children with visual impairments, and to what effect? Adults may initiate many more topics, request more actions from a child, and ask many more questions than is usual. Parents may also respond to a child with highly directive interventions, reflected, for example, in a much lower ratio of declaratives ('You're eating a biscuit') to imperatives ('Eat your biscuit') in the adult's speech. Although blind children need many more descriptions and explanations than sighted children, it appears that they receive far fewer (Andersen *et al.*, 1993).

Paradoxically, given the importance of information about the environment, adults may offer children with visual impairments relatively few descriptions, and many of these may be limited in scope. Instead of providing children with rich, interpretive descriptions of functions and attributes ('That's the slippery fish that lives on the bottom of the pond but comes up for food . . . you can't hold it'), adults tend just to label ('That's a fish'). In the previous section we referred to 'passages of intellectual search' whereby children and adults puzzle over inconsistencies and make sense of their environment. This kind of interrogation of surroundings seems not to be characteristic of all families, especially where there are children with sensory impairments.

The study by Kekelis and Andersen (1984) examined these effects in six families whose children had varying degrees of visual impairment. Monthly visits were made to families with pre-school children, which were videotaped and later analysed. Parents were told that the researchers were interested in observing 'chunks of everyday life'. Analyses were focused on aspects such as the distribution of sentence types in the children's input, ratio of labels to attributions, and presentation of topics. Imperatives were the most frequent type of sentence that the subjects with severe visual impairments received. It might be expected that parents would provide children with the kind of information that is inaccessible without vision, such as descriptions of the immediate environment. In fact, children with visual impairments were given significantly more bald labels for things than were sighted children. They received fewer statements describing the persons, objects or events in their 'here and now'. In place of 'real world' information, as the following example shows, children with visual impairments were given many more questions, together with names for objects and actions that remained unelaborated:

Child: (pats belly) Belly.
Adult: Yeah, that's your belly. That's your belly.
Child: (hand on tub) Water.
Adult: Water. Mm hm.
Child: (touches toilet)
Adult: What's that?

(Kekelis and Andersen, 1984, page 60)

Parents also spent a lot of their conversational time requesting labels of objects or the identification of events. They encouraged children to respond by answering questions about their actions and possessions. Adults determined the majority of the topics of conversation, whilst few of these topics linked current interests to distant persons or events. Kekelis and Andersen explain these findings by suggesting that parents use directives to stimulate movement and exploration ('Stand up like a big girl ... put your hand up'). Ironically, bombarding children with directives tends to inhibit rather than stimulate the child's involvement. Without visual cues, such as eye gaze, these authors suggest, it is often much harder for parents to read their child's focus of interest and to supply commentary that is relevant. There are problems in both establishing and maintaining topics of conversation, in producing coherent and cohesive dialogue. Hence, adults frequently change topic, request objects or actions, and ask more questions.

One of the themes we have drawn attention to at various points through this chapter is the importance of contingency in the adult's behaviour and responsiveness. Contingency refers to adults pacing and timing the help they offer to children by taking cues from the child's moment-to-moment perception and understanding. Contingency requires sensitivity to the needs and perspectives of the individual. The child is allowed to take the initiative, whilst the adult's role is to structure the task by prompting, reminding, making connections, suggesting, thinking things through with the child, providing information and feedback. Contingent reactions to the initiatives of children are part of co-operative partnerships where the adult facilitates, rather than manages or controls. In many of the interactions reported by researchers involving children with

103

visual impairments, adults tend not to make their responses contingent on what the child does, or is currently interested in. When adults do home in on the child's focus of attention there may be a closing down of the child's thinking, rather than links forged with surrounding activities and events, so that the child has a sense of their own place in the wider scheme of things.

We shall be returning to some of these issues again in later chapters when we discuss how adults can engage in more enriching and satisfying interactions with children. An important issue is how far conversations may be jointly constructed with children so that language might substitute for missing visual information, whilst also taking account of the child's focus of interest.

LANGUAGE AND THINKING IN SCHOOL

By the time most sighted children attend school they are already competent communicators with an accumulated store of knowledge about the world in which they live. For many children, however, the transition from home to school marks a turning point in the nature and purpose of learning, reflected, for example, in a different kind of adult responsiveness from that experienced at home. Home and school present contrasting opportunities for learning. At home, adult–child interactions may be more intense, intimate, prolonged and wide-ranging. At school, children spend more time in groups, whether working alone or at shared tasks. On the other hand, children do make demands on peers in school and learn to co-operate with others. They are brought into contact with a wider set of values and experiences, especially in multi-cultural communities. Teachers have to divide their energies between distributing resources, paperwork, discipline and classroom organisation, as well as guiding the activities of large numbers of pupils. For many reasons, adult interactions with children in school are likely to be reduced in depth, frequency and scope, whilst the majority of teachers across phases appear to be management- rather than learning-driven (Webster *et al.*, 1996a).

We make these points here because it is sometimes assumed that a group of children playing or working together in a school environment is a natural setting for busy, purposeful enquiry, rich in meaningful talk. In fact, as we shall see, research shows that schools are not places where children can easily develop their basic linguistic or conceptual skills, and do not always provide contexts for intensive adult–child interaction. This is the case for all children; the presence of a visual loss may serve to exacerbate these factors. Although most children with severe visual impairments entering ordinary nursery groups or mainstream school settings will have extra adult help, it cannot always be assumed that they will encounter other highly responsive adults or the stimulation and excitement of joint enterprise involving peers. It is important to highlight, from the available research evidence, what seem to be the most productive ways of enhancing learning interactions in school. How this can be achieved, in principal, is an issue we shall be returning to in the later chapters of this book when we consider optimal learning environments and how adults, when motivated, can modify their practice.

Transition from home to school

In the Bristol child language studies referred to earlier, 32 of the sample of 128 children who had been observed in their homes were subsequently followed up at school. The intention was to compare children's experience of the quality and purpose of language use in the two settings. Apart from speaking much less in school, children initiated a much smaller proportion of conversations and got fewer turns to speak, asked fewer questions and made fewer requests. In school, children used grammatically less complex sentences and expressed a narrower range of meanings. Conversely, teachers initiated a much higher proportion of exchanges than parents at home, made more requests for action, and asked far more questions about the children's activities, particularly display questions. Unlike parents, teachers tended not to take up children's utterances in order to extend meaning. Rather than taking account of a child's actions, current interests or focus of attention, they were much more likely to develop the topics that they themselves had introduced.

The overall picture conveyed by the Bristol research is that, for many children, school requires them to take a passive respondent role, carrying out adult requests or answering questions. Teachers often engender a sense of purposefulness, but provide few opportunities for children to share in the planning of activities or to reflect on what they are doing in the sort of exploratory talk that typifies recordings made at home. For no child was the language interaction of the classroom richer than that of the home, regardless of factors such as social class. However, there were some family background differences, for example in the frequency with which children were read to at home. Many children started off at a disadvantage in terms of the competences and experiences they brought with them into school, which the school was unlikely to compensate for.

These findings are supported by the Tizard and Hughes (1984) study, which continued to monitor the children who had originally been observed at home in school. Some children appeared to come off worse than others in moving from the context of the home to that of the school. Particular children from working-class families were seen as persistent questioners at home, but became very subdued in school. Teachers were felt to make fewer intellectual demands on certain children, involved them less in discussion and fostered a respondent kind of interaction, where the child's role was to answer but not ask questions. For all of these children, too, there was much less talk recorded in school than at home, with fewer examples of language used to recall past events, to reflect on experience or to organise activities. On average, children took part in 10 conversations per hour with teachers, compared with 27 per hour with their mothers. The average length of conversation was 16 turns at home, compared with 8 at school. Talk was largely initiated and dominated by teachers.

How to enrich dialogue

The collective evidence of these studies provides a blueprint for the most facilitating conversation partner. We have made the point that language may serve to compensate for some aspects of experience that are missing or less well defined for a child with a visual impairment. It is therefore highly important to be aware of those strategies for interaction that we know to be associated with promoting learning in sighted children: the adult 'moves' in conversation that lead to a deeper engagement of children and more productive interaction.

A central issue is the concept of control. High-control moves include the adult asking questions, particularly closed questions that require a limited response, such as display questions aimed at testing the child ('What's that called? . . . Where does it live?'). Other high-control moves include correcting or instructing the child, asking for repetition of a better model. They are high control in the sense that they limit what the child does in the following turn: they do not lead the child's thinking or understanding on, for example, by linking or extending concepts. In contrast, adult moves that are low in control are more often followed by a response from the child. These include taking cues from the child's focus of interest, avoiding over-dominating, giving comments from personal experience and 'phatic' responses or social oil ('Ooh, lovely'), all of which sustain the child to say more.

The following extract, taken from the Bristol studies, identifies some important principles for enriching dialogue:

Child: Carol got a bed and Kelvin . . . and Carol.
Teacher: Um hum. What about Donna?
Child: Donna – we're sharing it.
Teacher: You're sharing with Donna are you?
Child: (nods emphatically)
Teacher: Do you have a cuddle at night?
Child: Yeh an I – when I gets up I creeps in Mummy's bed.
Teacher: For another cuddle? Ooh that's nice. It's nice in the morning when you cuddle.

(Wells, 1985, page 24)

The child has introduced the topic of sleeping arrangements at home, a topic of some importance to her. The teacher listens and shows a genuine interest in what the child has to say, picking up the child's topic focus and some of her vocabulary at each turn. The teacher's questions reveal more information, which the adult interprets, restates and expands. The conversation is handed back to the child each time and the adult waits for a reply. Comments are given from personal experience ('It's nice in the morning when you cuddle') and a little social oil is added to sustain the dialogue ('Ooh, that's nice'). There is no effort to correct the child's linguistic mistakes or to enforce correct responses. Essentially, the adult is trying to share the child's perspective, to help think around her experience, to explore and extend her understanding. We know that this kind of adult responsiveness is associated with accelerated language-learning (Barnes *et al.*, 1983).

There are important implications of this work for all children, when a programme of intervention is planned. We shall be returning to many of these conversation strategies when we consider how to design favourable learning environments for children with visual impairments.

PLAY

Play used to be thought of as nothing more than the purposeless release of surplus energy. We now view the child's play repertoire as both an important means to foster language, concepts and social competence, and as a useful indicator of the child's relative maturity. There is a small but important literature that has identified some of the salient characteristics of the play of children with visual impairments. In Chapter 6 we shall be revisiting some of the factors that determine effective play environments for these children, drawing on data from recent studies.

Play provides yet another example of how some of the important tasks of childhood are closely interwoven and cannot be understood without reference to one another. Play provides formats through which the child adapts to the physical world, exploring the properties of objects and space. Play

Plate 3.3 Sharing a story as a basis for conversation. The shared enjoyment of a story provides a context for exploring and extending both children's perspectives

activities also foster language and cognition: the intellectual tools for ordering and categorising experience. As play develops, children also acquire the strategies that sustain appropriate social relationships and promote understanding of the needs and perspectives of others. Play is a universal example of a vehicle for practising social and linguistic conventions, using the objects, tools and weapons of the host society, and where adults frequently take a facilitative role.

When studies have been carried out on the inter-relationships between complexity of play, levels of language, cognition and social behaviour, all of these areas have been shown to be strongly correlated. It also seems to be the case that the frequency and duration of different kinds of play, such as role play, are very highly correlated with the child's receptive and expressive language, irrespective of degree of visual impairment (Fewell and Rich, 1987). The sample of children with visual impairments (aged between 16 months and 6 years) observed by Ferguson and Buultjens (1995) showed the same wide range of play behaviours as sighted peers, although fantasy play occurred more often and for longer in children with good verbal comprehension. Interestingly, in this study peers and siblings were much more effective in promoting play than adults, a point we shall return to in considering our own research reported in Chapter 6.

The importance of vision in play

Visual information is important in enabling play. Familiarity with the physical context in which play may take place, including its boundaries, features and spaces, is important in group activities such as 'follow my leader', or 'hide and seek', where good distance vision will be necessary. The ability to model and imitate others in role play is also facilitated by vision. An important shift in the child's thinking, which Piaget draws attention to, is when the child is able to represent the world in other symbols. When plastic building bricks are used to play cars, the pretend objects are assimilated into existing ideas about the world, with the important development that one thing can now symbolise another in the child's imaginative play. Here, too, play may be stimulated by the physical properties of objects, their visual similarities and differences, and the abstracted criteria that link real objects to their play symbols (so that a red container, for example, can be adopted as a 'fire extinguisher').

Very few studies have, in fact, examined the play behaviour of children with visual impairments in everyday settings, for example with siblings or peers, in playgroups, at nursery or in school. Experimental studies tend to focus on children alone, playing with toys in the presence of adults, who remain distant from them. The evidence we have points to some interesting contrasts between play patterns in different groups and amongst individuals. In some studies, children with severe visual impairments have been characterised as being more inward and isolated in their play, less creative or imaginative, predisposed to spend more time in repetitive or manipulative activities, but less inclined to assign symbolic roles to the objects of play (Parsons, 1986a).

Parsons' (1986b) experimental study involved 36 children between 2 and 4 years of age, 18 of whom had a degree of visual loss but no other identified impairment. A protocol was used to code the play behaviour of the children, who were video taped alone, focusing specifically on the frequency and variety of ideas generated for play with a given set of toys. In this experimental setting, children with visual impairments spent a high proportion of time in non-functional play, mouthing, waving or handling toys. Sighted children, in contrast, spent most of their time using objects in pretend play: stirring tea, talking on the telephone, dressing dolls, loading up lorries. Children with visual impairments were more dependant on adult caregivers, frequently wandering away from the toys in order to engage adults in conversation. There was also more time spent by this group simply holding or inspecting toys, rather than exploring different ways of using objects.

Earlier in this chapter we referred to the notion of 'systematicity', whereby the infant tries out routines, repeats a narrow range of actions on similar objects, imposes rules and generates categories (Bruner, 1983). In play, as in many language activities, children are geared to generate and combine a small set of elements, in order to create a larger set of possibilities. Here, too, the salient underlying features that propel the child's strategies for organising and stimulating play are mainly visual. Parsons (1986b) recommends that children with visual impairments are directly taught appropriate use of toys in order to extend their repertoire of play behaviour. However, there are good reasons to believe that modifying the play environment itself will facilitate an increase in functional play.

A number of recent research studies have highlighted organisational factors that influence play. For example, Preisler (1993) observed the social interactions of blind children in mainstream nursery settings. Free play activities posed particular problems since toys could not be located, or were considered inappropriate. The blind children spent most of their time in the company of adults or moved to quiet areas where they could be on their own. Kekelis and Sacks (1992) observed blind children within mainstream settings at school entry. Key factors that promoted interactive play in this study were these: blind children's social and linguistic abilities; strategies for initiating conversation and play; careful choice of toys and activities; clear play rules; careful selection of small but compatible social groups; consistency of play groupings; layout and management of the play setting. In the final chapter, when we consider data from natural play settings, factors that have an impact on play patterns in visually impaired groups will be revisited.

It has generally been concluded that children with visual impairments spend much less time than their sighted peers (particularly during pre-school years) actively engaged in play, and when they do play, this tends to involve their own bodies rather than other objects or people. The reasons for some of these differences in play patterns may be due to the lack of appropriately designed and organised play environments, rather than to any inherent predisposition of such children towards more self-contained play.

Designing play environments

Design principles for play environments have been developed by Schneekloth (1989) from a study of 36 children, including subjects with a wide range of visual impairments, aged 7 to 13 years. The study considered those factors in play areas that were instrumental in promoting environmental interactions as opposed to self-manipulative play. These include exploring the wider boundaries; use of the environment as props for fantasy play; gross movement, orientation and social interaction. All of the children in the study preferred equipment, rather than open spaces, and used objects in the environment as activity organisers. Boundaries were frequently integrated into play by all the children in the study, but for children with visual impairments, physical edges and boundaries needed to be created within the play space, and not simply used to mark the periphery.

Complex equipment promoted the most complex motor behaviour and exploratory play in all children, regardless of age, sex or vision. Schneekloth suggests that few of the play environments in our schools or communities are suited to the needs of children, much less to the needs of children with visual impairments. The least inspiring play areas are static swings and slides in expanses of asphalt. Real world things permit children to build play around daily environmental hardware, such as doors with latches, knobs and locks; windows that open and close; turnstiles and revolving doors; kitchen equipment and machinery; old tractors, boats and cars.

In design terms, complexity refers to the number and kinds of elements: the number of pieces that can be linked together; options for access and the range of occupiable spaces; the presence of well-defined interior boundaries, districts and continuous links; together with cues to inform children where they are, such as sounds, textures, materials, colours, planes. For maximum effect, children with visual impairments will need very careful introduction, even to the best-designed play area. Children need to be shown how to understand the structure of the environment and the cues to locate themselves within it. They also need to know that the area is safe, so that they interact freely with equipment. Most importantly, they need to feel that the environment is exciting and holds many possibilities. Here, too, the adult has an important facilitative role.

MOBILITY AND VISUAL IMPAIRMENT

There is a wealth of evidence on the motor development of children with visual impairments (summarised, for example, by Warren, 1994), most of which points to delays in the attainment of developmental milestones in fine and gross motor skills. In an earlier section of this chapter we made the point that visual information is an important stimulus to children for investigating the immediate physical context. Caregivers may have discouraged active adventurous play, involving running, throwing or climbing, steering a child towards more passive, sedentary activities. Evidence such as that provided by Schneekloth (1989) indicates that environments differ in the effect they have on children's motivation to explore and engage in active play.

There may be a chain of consequences if children do not interact freely and actively with the environment. Children may be immature in their development of body awareness, sense of physical separateness from their surroundings, position of their limbs in space. Motor development may be affected, including the co-ordination of hands and eyes (or hands and ears in blind infants). Children who do not actively interrogate the environment may also be immature in their conceptual development, i.e. organising and categorising their surroundings. Warren suggests that the most compelling explanation for the research evidence that children with visual impairments are slower to crawl, walk or find their way around independently, compared with sighted infants, is one of opportunity.

Motor proficiency, posture and fitness

In older children with visual impairments, restricting the opportunities to enjoy physical activities can also limit motor proficiency, co-ordination, general fitness, together with confidence, self-esteem and general mobility. Posture may also be a concern. Some children adopt unusual head or body postures because of their visual condition, such as a nystagmus. Sighted individuals observe how others hold themselves erect, and catch sight of reflections of their own body images in mirrors or shop windows. A visual impairment obviously impinges on a child's ability to observe patterns of movement in others, or displays of skill and co-ordination. These factors reduce incentives to join in, as well as the potential to watch a demonstration or imitate a model. Sense of distance and movement across spaces may be difficult, as may be the integration of sensory information and musculature required, for example, to catch or strike a ball.

When studies of the relative fitness of pupils with visual impairments have been carried out (see, for example, Short and Winnick, 1986), evidence shows that many pupils have lower grip strength, less body flexibility, poorer static and dynamic balance and are more likely to be overweight than sighted peers. Many pupils with visual impairment do not take part in physical activity programmes, or spend less time, if any, on activities such as swimming, cycling, games, dance or gymnastics. This is partly to do with parental support (which is true for all children), but also because the inclusion of pupils with visual impairments in athletics and outdoor pursuits requires some ingenuity and confidence on the part of teachers. Many mainstream school contexts where children with visual impairments are integrated are simply not geared up for including these pupils in activities such as swimming or games.

Within the framework of the National Curriculum, PE is not just about fitness and body strength. It is also concerned with experiences that promote language and conceptual development; with the terminology and logic of mathematics, physics and biology; with the social dimensions of groupwork and competition; with the fostering of independence, self-esteem and enjoyment. In terms of lifelong learning, a concept that has come to national prominence recently, some key issues for older pupils with visual impairment include awareness of safe procedures around equipment, knowledge of environmental hazards, ability to travel confidently over different kinds of terrain, and strategies for familiarising oneself with unfamiliar situations. Mobility for many individuals with visual impairments is synonymous with personal independence.

SOCIAL DEVELOPMENT

The development of appropriate social competence is yet another area that has frequently been cited as vulnerable to the impact of a visual impairment (Warren, 1994). Here, too, it may be difficult to dissociate the growth of social skills from other areas of learning and adaptation. Social behaviour is shaped in various ways, across a range of social contexts, through the day-to-day processes of living and learning together with other people at different stages of maturity. Earlier in this chapter we saw that in the course of mundane conversational exchanges with others, where children are learning much about their surroundings, how things work, and the linguistic conventions that help to organise events, children are also exposed to cultural expectations about gender roles and 'good' behaviour. So the inter-relationship of social, linguistic and cognitive development is a complex one. However, social development is much more than simply acquiring skills and competences in the context of relationships with peers, siblings or caregivers. Importantly, children are also establishing who they are.

Social development is often distinguished from social adjustment. The former is usually concerned with progress in acquiring the behaviours that permit appropriate social relationships and entry into the surrounding culture, with a range of expectations regarding age-appropriateness. The latter refers to how well the individual adapts to the demands of the social environment, regardless of age. This distinction is important in reviewing studies conducted with children who have visual impairments, because research on social development will tend to provide only normative characteristics, whereas studies of adjustment take account of the challenges and opportunities for learning that are offered.

In his review of the data available on social development, Warren (1994) points to the very wide range of individual variation between children in their attainment of developmental milestones. A number of studies have examined factors such as self-help skills, dressing, washing, toileting, eating, sleeping patterns, use of everyday objects such as scissors, tableware and domestic equipment. There were few overall differences between samples of blind children and groups with less severe visual impairments, when age was taken into account.

Family reactions and opportunities for learning

A factor commonly noted in children making good progress in social skills was that the family encouraged, not so much by direct teaching, but by providing opportunities to learn. Many of the previous sections of this chapter have documented the important early interactive processes that occur within the family unit where young children spend much of their time. A number of research studies have documented the spectrum of parental reactions to the presence of a visual impairment in a child, and how this influences the child's progress (Jan et al., 1977).

More than a third of the mothers and fathers in the study by Jan et al. had reacted with shock and disbelief at the diagnosis of their child's visual impairment. Half of the parents did not want to have more children. Reflecting back, many parents reported positive effects on family life of having a child with a visual impairment, whereas others felt their marriages had been stressed. One possible source of distress was the unusual appearance of a child with a disfiguring visual condition, or unusual mannerisms, such as eye-poking. Parents were often aware of the difficulties in establishing emotional bonding in the absence of smiling or eye contact, or when a child spent long periods in hospital. Many were aware of their tendency to overprotect the child. A quarter said that their children had no friends. Problems were also reported in relation to brothers or sisters, including their wariness of competing or challenging a child with a visual impairment, or feeling embarrassed about their sibling in public.

The extent to which parents can achieve a realistic understanding of their child's needs within a positive family atmosphere is closely related to the child's general social adjustment. It is for this reason that parent support groups, LEA advisory services and family support networks have an important role to play.

A general conclusion drawn in the literature is that many children with visual impairments tend to be delayed in their development of social independence and personal organisation, with a higher degree of helplessness. This is more likely to be the case where children have more severe visual losses or additional handicapping factors. Critical factors include how far a visual impairment limits social experience, reduces the range of social interactions with peers, sighted individuals and wider social groups, or evokes overprotectiveness in some adult caregivers. Families react in different ways and childhood visual impairment inevitably puts additional pressures on a family unit. However, there is abundant evidence that otherwise well-adjusted and resourceful people can adapt positively and constructively to the challenges posed when a child is discovered to have a visual impairment.

SOCIAL INTEGRATION

In all families, social contacts usually increase significantly when children go to nursery or school. A wider social network provides opportunities for social interactions with sighted peers and other adults. The child's ability to cope with the intellectual demands of school depends to a large extent on social acceptance and participation. However, a different set of adaptive demands may be experienced as the child enters the more complex social system of school, which is geared to different kinds of learning activity and adult responsiveness.

In a previous section we considered the quality of conversational experience in the contrasting settings of the family and school. For all children this transition marks a dramatic reduction in the nature, purpose and intensity of linguistic encounters. Teachers are often preoccupied with the organisational demands of managing large group settings. They bear the continuous pressure of working towards planned work schemes within the National Curriculum framework and related assessment targets. They may share little of the children's social world outside of the classroom. These are some of the reasons why adult sensitivity to the personal needs of individual children are frequently subjugated to the broader, externally prescribed, more formal curriculum objectives of the school.

At school entry, adults other than the child's parents take on a significant role. Teachers have an important influence on the frequency and quality of social interactions between the children in their groups, for example by intervening to open up new opportunities, suggesting partnerships, resolving conflicts, prompting ways of extending play or investigations. Obviously, teachers may be less than confident in fostering positive social interactions where they feel anxiety, resentment, under-resourced, unsupported, or where they feel they lack appropriate knowledge of a child's capabilities and needs, and the strategies for intervening.

Children's perceptions about themselves

When a child with a visual impairment joins a mainstream class group for the first time, the reactions of peers are also important. There is the possibility of overprotection, of teasing, of social ostracism or of bullying. It may be difficult for some sighted children to understand how or what people see, leading to some confusion when attempts are made to involve a child with reduced vision in activities dependent on clear sight. One important factor is the child's own ability to understand the social behaviour of others, to 'read' social contexts and to behave in a way that promotes acceptance. To some extent, these aspects of social cognition follow on from children's perceptions about themselves: the functional implications of their visual condition; their own personal strengths and weaknesses; situations in which difficulties may be encountered; and attitudes and beliefs about themselves as persons.

Very little attention has been given in the research literature to those strategies that children can adopt to facilitate their own social integration. We might presume, for example, that a child with a visual impairment who is able to initiate interactions with peers and has the skills to sustain relationships and resolve conflicts, would be more quickly accepted on entering school and enjoy more positive interactions. There is a similar lack of knowledge about how the different characteristics of children with visual impairments affect the behaviour of sighted children in integrated settings. We shall address these issues directly in Chapter 6, from our own research.

Locus of control

An important psychological component of a positive self-concept relates to locus of control. Individuals with an inner locus of control assume responsibility for their own behaviour; they are more confident and active in their planning or decision-making, ready to believe that success follows on from their own efforts. Individuals with an outer locus of control tend to blame events on outside forces and see themselves as powerless; things happen to them and are beyond influence. When studies have been carried out on resilient children – those who survive and achieve well against the odds – a strong inner sense of being in control is a determining factor (Fonagy *et al.*, 1994).

Many individuals with visual impairments have been described in terms of low self-esteem, passivity, learned helplessness or limited assertiveness. Lack of control over events can be traced back to early learning transactions, according to some (Harrell and Strauss, 1986). This may arise from an accumulation of experiences where difficult tasks are avoided, where there have been few instances of coping with anxiety or frustration, where caregivers are over-ready to step into situations to avoid failure, and where general expectations are lowered. Adolescence is frequently cited as a challenging period of transition for youngsters with visual impairments, when there may be heightened feelings of anxiety and insecurity occasioned, perhaps, by evidence of the growing independence of peers (for example, learning to drive).

Social maturation

Knowledge about sex is an area of growing up that many researchers feel typifies the specific obstacles to social maturation that a visual impairment presents (Warren, 1994). Young people with severe visual impairments know about their own bodies, which they can explore freely, but may be completely uninformed about the bodily characteristics, particularly adult features, of the opposite sex. Adults may be reluctant or embarrassed to discuss issues of sexuality, as part of their tendency to overprotect.

All young people, in due course, sense the prevailing emphasis on sexual issues in popular culture. This is the point at which they are vulnerable to misinformation or the making light of issues such as AIDS or HIV. For the young person with a visual impairment, inadequate information and misunderstanding contribute to the individual's sense of being unprepared for, or out of step with, the demands of the adult world. Lifetime learning, a term we considered in the introductory chapter of this book, is a concept that requires all those involved in planning educational provision for children with individual learning needs to address issues such as personal effectiveness, independence, self-awareness and self-advocacy.

Mannerisms

To end this review of developmental processes and the impact of visual impairment, we consider briefly some aspects of behaviour that appear to reduce personal effectiveness and opportunities for social integration. The term 'mannerisms' (sometimes referred to as 'blindisms') covers a wide range of behaviour, many examples of which inhibit normal social interactions or interfere with the child's attention to important information or events. They include rocking, eye-poking, headshaking, bouncing, clapping or handshaking.

Not all children with severe visual impairments exhibit mannerisms; by contrast, they may be observed in some sighted children. They are more likely to occur in young children with multiple handicaps, particularly if this involves cognitive functioning. Some of these activities may be injurious, such as headbanging and eye-gouging, and efforts have to be made to control them, such as by encouraging competing activities (for example, by occupying the child's hands).

Various explanations have been attempted for these behaviours. Body-rocking, hand-flapping, spinning and twirling are often interpreted as self-stimulating activities in children who lack social contact or who cannot cope with an overstimulating environment. Eye-poking has been thought to produce visual 'sparks' through pressure on the eyes in children who have very low levels of sensory perception. Mannerisms have been associated with different conditions: very low levels of sensory stimulation; overstimulation or stress; constraints on environmental exploration or interaction. Thus, mannerisms, if they occur, may be a response to either boredom, arousal or overwhelming social demands (Warren, 1994).

SUMMARY

Considering the development of children with visual impairment takes us to the heart of some complex (and mainly unresolved) issues to do with the

116

nature of language acquisition and its relationship with experience and cognition. Children do not all learn in the same way. However, there seems to be a special place for vision in many processes of learning. Ways into language depend to a large extent on visual information in the immediate context and on visually based strategies for gaining and shaping attention. Vision is also implicated in processes of concept formation and the generalisation of language from one context to another. Many of the processes of learning that a visual impairment interferes with are interactive, involving other children, adults or environments. In our view, aspects of exploration, play, language and thinking cannot be understood without reference to the social interactive frameworks that support them.

At the beginning of this chapter we identified some of the important tasks of childhood that all individuals are concerned with. These include adapting to the physical world of objects in space; acquiring the intellectual tools of language and cognition, used for ordering and categorising experience; and developing a repertoire of social skills. The interdependence of all of these areas of learning and adaptation is evident. Most of the infant's early understanding of the physical world, such as everyday objects, for example, takes place within a framework of social interaction suffused with relevant language. The effects of a visual impairment are also interdependent and cumulative. Restrictions on vision limit the range and variety of an individual's experience, have an impact on the child's mobility and exploration of the environment, and affect the quality of the child's meaning-making and conceptual growth.

However, the literature shows that most children do eventually overcome the limiting effects of their visual impairment to develop language, concepts and effective representations of the world. We must speculate to some extent about how this is achieved. A key issue, in our view, is adult sensitivity, or contingency, to the child's perceptual world, and how this shapes the quality of the adult's interventions or 'scaffolding'. Our current understanding suggests that it is within the context of social relationships that adults guide and scaffold young children's development, and this is particularly important for understanding ways in which children are initiated into using language as a tool for learning. Arguably, it is through the co-operative use of language as a 'bridge' that some of the most limiting aspects of visual impairment can be overcome.

Over and above all of the findings that we have cited regarding areas of social, linguistic or cognitive maturity in different groups is the important issue of opportunity. There are very few barriers to learning, if any, that cannot be tackled. What is evident, however, is that learning progresses most effectively in social interactive contexts where individuals are prepared to be flexible, to 'read' the intentions and perspectives of their partners, and to share meaning. In Chapters 5 and 6 of this book we shall be returning to some of these issues when we examine how environments can be designed to maximise learning.

4

EDUCATIONAL POLICY, PROVISION AND THE CODE OF PRACTICE

In many respects the educational needs of all children, whatever their differences, have important common elements, and this thinking has informed the concept of 'entitlement' within the framework of the National Curriculum. However, it is clear that a visual impairment shapes the child's adaptation to the world and has an impact on the individual's ability to learn from different kinds of experience.

In this chapter, we examine the range of educational settings across phases of the educational system for children with visual impairments, and pose questions such as 'In which type of provision do which children tend to do best?'. Decision-making processes currently follow a Code of Practice, intended to promote what the DfEE considers to be exemplary ways of working. The Code has not escaped criticism, although its intentions are constructive. We look at how the Code may contribute towards the raising of individual achievement and the realisation of lifetime learning within the context of visual impairment. We also consider some of the issues involved in securing the most appropriate educational support for children with visual impairments under current legislation and guidance.

Approaches to the education of children with individual needs are influenced by changing policies, legislation and professional practice. For families and teachers concerned with children who have visual impairments, the most enduring questions relate to how decisions will be made about educational placement, the kind of support services available to help, and the respective strengths of different forms of provision. All parents of children with a visual loss will naturally be apprehensive about securing the most effective arrangements for schooling. The question of whether a child's needs are likely to be best met by being an ordinary member of a special school, in contrast to having special status in a mainstream school, will need careful consideration. In a climate of professional opinion that advocates the integration of children with very severe visual impairments and blindness into ordinary school contexts, teachers and families also require reassurance that this is a valuable, rather than makeshift, experience for those involved.

118

Educational provision varies widely from one local education authority to another. Many LEA services have their origins in systems where pupils with severe visual impairments were placed in segregated special schools. A growing trend is the blurring of distinctions between groups (such as 'blind' or 'partially sighted') and the tailoring of provision much more closely to individual needs. However, in some areas there is only minimal specialist teacher support for pupils attending their local or neighbourhood schools. In some LEAs, particularly at secondary level, resources are focused on a named school that serves a whole area and to which pupils travel. In the recent review of current practice across a wide span of LEAs undertaken by the RNIB, the pattern of provision was found to be very uneven: the quality of education that a child with a visual impairment receives depends to a great extent on where the family happens to live (Dawkins, 1991). The appropriateness and implications of different forms of provision can only really be weighed in relation to the specific circumstances of a family, which also vary over time.

In this chapter we explore some of the current policy and legislative issues that are likely to have a profound impact on how special educational provision is resourced, allocated and evaluated in the next decade. All schools and education services have recently come under public scrutiny from a number of stakeholders, and there are pressures to increase accountability for the spending of public money and to emphasise consumer rights through 'charters'. Schools and services that support pupils with visual impairments are also having to account for what they do, to demonstrate value for money and to highlight ways in which they are strategic in raising pupils' achievement.

THE CODE OF PRACTICE FOR SPECIAL EDUCATIONAL NEEDS

When the Code was announced in the House of Commons in the autumn of 1993, government ministers described it as 'setting a whole new framework for special education in the future'. The Code came into force in September 1994 and has major implications for all LEA and grant-maintained schools. The Code of Practice is part of regulations required under the Education Act 1993, governing policy and provision for identifying, assessing and meeting special educational needs (although the guidance is non-statutory). Circular 6/94: 'The Organisation of Special Educational Provision' offers guidance to schools on how SEN provision should be managed. Together, the 1993 Act, the Code of Practice and Circular 6/94 lay the foundations for policy and practice in meeting special education needs for the next five years.

Basic principles of the Code

The Code reaffirms such principles as the continuum of special needs and provision, with the greatest possible access for all pupils to a broad and balanced curriculum, including access to the National Curriculum. It envisages that the special needs of the majority of pupils will be met in mainstream schools without statements, and that many other pupils with statements will also receive their education in ordinary schools. Early action, close inter-agency collaboration, partnership with parents and children, with the views of the pupil taken into account, are also intrinsic to the thinking behind the Code. Schools will be obliged to follow procedures that pay due regard to the Code, designed 'to help schools make decisions'.

The precise way in which the Code is interpreted will be left to schools to determine, but this must be set out in a published policy. All schools will have to keep a register of pupils with SEN, and steps taken to meet pupils needs must be recorded. All mainstream schools must have a designated teacher who co-ordinates SEN policy and practice.

Stages of the Code

The Code sets out guidelines to be followed by LEAs for identifying and assessing individuals with special educational needs. It also clarifies the role of the school in five stages leading up to formal assessments and statementing. During the first three stages, as pupils' learning difficulties emerge, schools must take the lead and respond quickly; make detailed observations and keep careful records; explore the nature of the difficulty by involving parents and other professionals; and keep the effectiveness of whatever approaches are adopted under review. At Stages 4 and 5, LEAs will share responsibilities with schools. All of the stages are much more rigorous than many teachers will have followed previously, with all teachers required to be skilled at making close observations, setting specific targets and making detailed individual plans.

One of the criticisms that has been levelled at the Code of Practice is that it is written from a primary school standpoint, in terms of how teachers operate, how schools and resources are organised, and how information about individuals is communicated within and outside the school. The Code is built on key notions such as the progression of children through stages, the drawing up of individual learning plans, and differentiation of teaching within main-stream classes. For secondary schools, many of these critical aspects of the Code must be adapted to the much more complex structures of curriculum organisation, staffing and management that characterise the secondary phase.

Stage 1 of the school-based stages of the Code includes the initial identi-fication and registration of a pupil's needs, the gathering of relevant information, and increased differentiation in the child's normal classroom work. During Stage 2 there is a continuation of the arrangements made previ-ously, but an Individual Education Plan (IEP) is created, based on the information gathered. At this stage the school SEN co-ordinator takes the lead in assessing the pupil's learning difficulty, planning, monitoring and reviewing arrangements made. An IEP should be drawn up in consultation with parents and pupil, setting out the nature of the pupil's difficulties and specific learning targets. The plan should make use, wherever possible, of existing programmes, materials and resources and take place within the normal classroom setting.

At Stage 3 the school calls on outside specialist help. At this stage, responsibility for pupils with special needs is shared between the school SEN co-ordinator, class or subject teachers, and relevant outside support services, such as visiting teachers or educational psychologists. A new IEP may be drawn up including input from support services. A specialist teacher, for example, may advise that further investigation is required, such as a vision test. Advisory teachers may be involved in a range of tasks at this stage, such as direct teaching of the pupil, giving advice to the class or subject teacher, recommending appropriate materials, technology or classroom management, and monitoring the child's progress.

Stage 4 focuses on statutory assessment which may be requested by parents, school referral or another agency. Schools will need to demonstrate, following action taken and documented at Stages 1 to 3, that the pupil's needs remain so substantial that they cannot be met from the resources 'ordinarily available'. Exceptionally, pupils may show such acute difficulties that the school finds it impossible to carry through the first three stages. For example, diagnosis of a major sensory impairment may lead immediately to referral to the LEA for a multi-disciplinary assessment.

The new Code sets out criteria for making statutory assessments, a timetable of 26 weeks for carrying out the whole process from start to finish, and the procedures that should be followed. In the case of a visual impairment, evidence will need to be presented relating to a wide spectrum of academic, social and emotional factors: degree of functional vision from vision tests; recorded discrepancies between a pupil's actual attainment and levels expected; evidence that a visual condition significantly impairs mobility and participation in school activities; and signs of stress or underperforming to those who have taught the pupil in different areas of the curriculum and in other areas of school life.

Statementing at Stage 5 of the Code proceeds when the LEA is satisfied that the pupil's learning difficulties are significant and/or complex; have not been met by measures taken by the school; or may call for resources that cannot 'reasonably be provided' within the budgets of mainstream schools in the area. A statement will fulfil two main functions. First, it will be the means of access to extra resources, and second, it will provide a precise educational prescription for the pupil, based on an accurate and detailed account of needs. When the LEA sends the final version of a statement to the parents, it must include the name of an individual who can give them further information and advice ('named person').

Statements will be maintained by LEAs only when necessary, or until the pupil moves into further or higher education, or into provision made by

Stage 1: gathering of information, initial identification and registration of a pupil's SEN, and increased differentiation in the ordinary classroom

- responsibility for assessing pupils, differentiating teaching and devising appropriate plans remains with the class or subject teachers
- trigger for Stage 1 is when a teacher, parent or other professional gives evidence of concern
- class or subject teacher must inform the headteacher, parents and SEN co-ordinator, who registers the pupil's SEN
- parents' and pupil's own views on their difficulties must be sought
- any known health or social problems are detailed, together with profiles of achievement, National Curriculum Attainments and any other test data
- class or subject teacher can ask for help from school SEN co-ordinator, school doctor, other professional agency
- support services (such as teacher of the deaf) can be called in from Stage 1 onwards, and always at Stage 3
- record must be kept of nature of concern, action taken, targets set and when progress will be reviewed (within a term or six months, with parents kept informed)
- Stage 2 is reached if, after two reviews at Stage 1, special help has not resulted in satisfactory progress

Stage 2: seeking further advice and/or the creation of an Individual Education Plan (IEP)

- school SEN co-ordinator takes the lead in assessing the pupil's learning difficulty, planning, monitoring and reviewing arrangements made
- SEN co-ordinator seeks additional data from health, Social Services or other agencies and agrees appropriate action with parents and the pupil's teachers
- IEP drawn up, setting out specific learning targets, using materials and resources within the normal classroom setting
- IEP sets out nature of the pupil's difficulties, any special provision, staff involved including frequency of support, help from parents at home, targets to be achieved in a given time, monitoring and assessment arrangements, arrangements and date for review
- parents should be invited to a review of Stage 2, which might take place within a term; talk to parents in person if considering moving a pupil to Stage 3

Stage 3: school calls on outside specialist help

- responsibility for pupils with special needs is shared between the school SEN co-ordinator, class or subject teachers and outside support services (such as visiting teachers or educational psychologists)

Figure 4.1 Summary of stages in the new Code of Practice

- new IEP drawn up including input from support services, detailing new targets and teaching strategies, monitoring and review arrangements
- external agencies (such as teacher of visually impaired) may offer classroom support, advice on materials, technology or classroom management, or direct teaching
- review organised by the SEN co-ordinator within a term, including parents, focusing on progress made, effectiveness of the IEP, any updated information and future plans
- after review the headteacher considers referring the pupil to the LEA for a statutory assessment
- LEA will require a range of written information and evidence to support the referral (educational and other developmental profiles, views of the parent and pupil, health and social factors)

Stage 4: statutory assessment

- needs of the great majority of pupils should be met under the first three stages, with perhaps only 2 per cent of pupils being put forward for statementing
- pupils may be brought to the LEA's attention for formal assessment by a number of routes, such as parental request, school referral or request from another agency
- schools must demonstrate that pupil's needs remain so substantial that they cannot be met from the resources 'ordinarily available'
- exceptionally, e.g. diagnosis of a major sensory impairment, may lead immediately to referral to the LEA for a multi-disciplinary assessment
- new Code sets out criteria for making statutory assessments, a timetable of 26 weeks for carrying out the whole process from start to finish, and the procedures that should be followed
- local moderation groups may be set up to ensure consistency and fairness within an LEA
- evidence required for statementing includes a wide spectrum of academic, social and emotional factors

Stage 5: statementing

- statementing proceeds when the LEA is satisfied that the pupil's needs are significant and/or complex; have not been met by measures taken by the school; or may call for resources that cannot 'reasonably be provided' within the budgets of mainstream schools in the area
- statement is a means of access to extra resources
- provides a precise educational prescription for the pupil, based on an accurate and detailed account of needs
- parental preferences must be taken into account and arrangements made for reviews

Figure 4.1 Continued

another agency such as Social Services. Explanations must be given to the parents in writing when an LEA is considering changing or ceasing to maintain a statement, and parents must be informed of their rights of appeal. The first annual review of a statement after a pupil's 14th birthday, and any subsequent annual reviews until the pupil leaves school, should include a 'Transition Plan'. This draws together information from a range of agencies within and beyond school in order to plan coherently for the young person's transition to adult life.

WORKING WITH PARENTS

Throughout the Code of Practice the importance of establishing good working relationships with parents is emphasised. An important aspect of the partnership envisaged in the Code is that it should be based on mutual respect. Both parents and teachers have a voice, and should be able to listen and give due consideration to one another's views. The main reason for building partnerships with parents is to fulfil their need for information and participation, and to acknowledge their valuable contribution to the work of the school. Inevitably, pupils make greater progress when there is a positive sense of collaboration between family and school.

Positive partnership

Parents and other carers can be a reliable source of valuable information about pupils' intellectual strengths and weaknesses, as well as their social, emotional and physical development. This will range from factual details regarding address, GP or social worker, to information about medical treatment or other significant stresses that might have an impact on a pupil's schooling.

Making full use of parents' insights not only leads to more effective professional practice, it also helps parents to feel valued and that an active interest has been taken in their family concerns. Parents and carers who feel that a school listens to them will be more positive and consistent in their support of the work and life of the school. Most but not all parents will be able to collaborate with teachers by reinforcing school programmes at home. Some schools operate volunteer schemes whereby parents can come into school to work with pupils. This may be as reading or writing partners, or to offer special skills, such as in design or technology activities, preparing an exhibition, publishing a magazine or leading a business venture.

All parents have a right to be kept in touch with the day-to-day workings of a school, particularly as this affects their own children. The Code of Practice lays down minimum requirements for what information should be offered to parents. However, there may be situations that require close working relationships between some families and schools, through home–school diaries, weekly written updates or telephone calls on behaviour and progress.

In some instances schools may be successful in raising achievements of individual pupils by working through the parents. One strand of such an approach may be to skill parents to take a more encouraging role in reading or writing with their children. Parent groups for families with youngsters experiencing social, emotional or learning difficulties are an important way of allowing parents to share their concerns with others, to exchange information and practical advice. It is important that parents and carers do not simply consider themselves to be on the receiving end of advice, information or decisions, but are allowed to take a constructive role.

One issue raised in the RNIB's (1995a) booklet for parents, which details the precise way in which assessments are carried out and provision made, is that whilst LEAs have a legal duty to provide adequately for children, they do not have to offer the best possible provision. If disagreements arise between parents and LEAs over the level and quality of provision, there is the right of appeal to the SEN Tribunal, a body that decides on the best course of future action on the basis of the evidence before it. Many of the cases heard by the SEN Tribunal concern descriptions made by professionals of a child, refusals by LEAs to make statements, or appeals against the schools named. As well as independent assessment advice, the RNIB offers an advocacy service for parents who are considering making an appeal, and can arrange for witnesses or representation at hearings.

INDIVIDUAL EDUCATION PLANS

The IEP is a key component of the 'language of accounts' that the DfEE expects schools to adopt (and which it has also promised in the parents' charter), as a means of ensuring that the school is setting appropriate teaching targets for pupils with individual needs, checking the 'delivery of the goods' within stated time limits through progress reviews. Individual Education Plans are required at Stages 2 and 3 of the Code of Practice as a means of setting out the nature of a pupil's individual needs, drawing up actionable teaching targets and a timescale for review. We use the term 'plan' to indicate a longer-term strategic intent, whilst a 'programme' is generally concerned with day-to-day tactical delivery. Following a number of reviews of SEN provision in England and Wales (carried out, for example, by the Audit Commission), the specification of teaching objectives was recommended as a solution to the problem of accountability by schools and LEAs for the progress made by pupils.

In view of the high costs incurred in giving additional teaching support to pupils in mainstream contexts, the Audit Commission wanted a 'new type' of statement that gave details about targets to be reached and the resources to be used, embedded within a system of performance indicators at school and LEA level. IEPs have been put forward as a visible means of checking out a school's *modus operandi* in SEN: how it identifies, assesses, records, reports, communicates, co-ordinates, designs, plans, costs, allocates, delivers, reviews, monitors and evaluates.

Programmes and plans

For the SEN co-ordinator, the IEP has an important management function. The IEP identifies who is doing what to meet a pupil's needs, how success will be evaluated, and when progress will be reported to parents and any other interested parties, within the school's cycle of assessment, reporting and review meetings. Individual education programmes are focused on the immediate conditions in the teaching and learning environment. They may be drawn up for a pupil across core areas of the curriculum or reflect a specific requirement in science, design or technology. An individual education plan, by contrast, sets out the needs of a pupil in relation to the resources available within the school, across a time span.

Some schools have adopted a spreadsheet format for such plans which identify areas of the curriculum where specific kinds of teaching support are required, staff involved, resources allocated, dates for review, involvement of outside agencies and meetings with parents (see, for example, Came *et al.*, 1996). As a management tool, the IEP allows calculations to be made for individuals, year groups or specific sections of the school population on amount of contact time or classroom assistance required over a term or year. Out of the broader education plan the SEN co-ordinator can develop more detailed teaching programmes that specify activities, resources, materials, equipment, teaching and learning methods, including additional classroom assistance. The programme is thus a more focused working document that grows out of the master plan.

It is the drawing up of appropriate and manageable IEPs that has caused much consternation amongst mainstream teachers, particularly at the secondary level. Primary teachers are often flagging concerns about children as they first come to light, building up a child's profile over time as different approaches are tried and remodelled, building on strengths to create a positive approach, maintaining a close relationship between teachers and carers, assessment and teaching (Figure 4.2). Expectations at this stage are that the majority of children will progress towards 'normal' patterns of social behaviour and maturity, achieve basic self-help, language and academic benchmarks, reflected, for example, in the core skill areas of the National Curriculum.

IEPs in secondary schools

At the secondary level, a great deal of information on pupils is often already known and inherited, but may be difficult to use in relation to fragmented learning contexts. Decisions and predictions about pupils are being made by teachers who are not then responsible for their implementation. It may also

Name: Ben Marshall
Date of birth: 21.7.86
Year group: Yr5
Class teacher: ST
Previous reviews: Stage 1: 24.3.96 & 18.7.96. Stage 2: 30.9.96 Stage 3 . . .
Date of this Action Plan: 5.10.96

NATURE OF CURRENT CONCERN
Visual difficulties limiting access to curriculum

Evidence for concern (test results, observation, etc):
Eye tests show 6/18 vision. Ben has great difficulty working from visual displays in class (blackboard, OHP), even when sitting close to them.
Ben's pace of work is now very slow when the task involves gathering information visually and producing written work.
Ben is worried about his progressive loss of sight and his difficulties coping with school work that he once found easy. He is no longer confident in PE and playtimes. His parents report that he hates having to depend on others and ask for help. He often pretends he can see or understand when he can't.

Relevant background information (physical, social, emotional) to date:
Deterioration in vision monitored over the previous 18 months. Medical investigation suggests this is untreatable, and may deteriorate further.

Relevant information from school records (NC levels, previous reports):
Past reports show Ben had high attainments before his sight deteriorated: NC level 3/4 in all Core Subjects. No noticeable progress has been made in the past two terms.

Current performance in area of concern (level of skill or attainment):
Sometimes indicates to teachers when he cannot see something or read a text.
Negotiates known routes through classroom and around school without problems.
Handwriting is slow (10 words per minute) and large, but legible.
Looks for things in the right place, although often unable to discriminate them from others or from background.
Ben can read large print fluently, but cannot see the print in the stories, books and comics that interest him.

Figure 4.2 Sample IEP for a primary school child with a visual impairment

ACTION

Provision: teaching/learning environment (small group, frequency of support, staff involved):

Any new material to be presented in small group setting, in quiet environment, with checking of comprehension.

Keep resources, equipment and materials in consistent layout.

Non-teaching assistant or volunteer parent to be attached to Ben's working group to encourage Ben to use strategies from teacher of the visually impaired, and to facilitate group discussion (introducing speakers, indicating objects under discussion, etc).

Explain to other children in group that Ben needs verbal explanation of activities and has difficulty seeing things clearly.

External support (SEN service, Ed Psych, peripatetic teacher):

Peripatetic teacher of the visually impaired to be asked for specific strategies to help Ben with a) organisation and discrimination of his work and possessions; b) confidence in PE and playtimes.

Specific programmes, activities, equipment, resources:

Magnification aids and task-lighting for Ben's workbase. Use taped instructions and information where reading is not the essential part of an activity. Diagrams and other visual resources to be high in contrast and use large print. Limited amount of information on each diagram, OHP or worksheet. Verbal explanations and instructions to be given, backed up with large print 'job sheet' for reference.

Large print books from RNIB for use with curriculum content and for leisure reading.

Coloured strips to identify edges of desks; desk organiser to hold books and equipment; typist's copy-holder to hold job-sheet.

Teaching targets and timescale (include steps leading up to this where necessary):

Ben will indicate to a known adult or peer whenever he cannot see something or read a text.

Ben will tackle new routes to different classrooms around the school. At first he will be accompanied, and then go alone.

Handwriting will become more fluent (15 words per minute) and of more normal size with the use of lighting and magnification aids.

Ben will implement strategies to improve organisation of work and workspace.

Ben will choose from a selection of large print books for his leisure reading and provide information on the books he would like to have available in large print. He will read a book each week.

Figure 4.2 Continued

Targets to be achieved by next review:
Parents' role: Meet teacher of the visually impaired with the classteacher to see the strategies demonstrated and the lighting and magnifiers in use. Encourage Ben in his reading at home; read to him from texts he would like to read himself, or provide taped stories.
Talk about everything with Ben, providing as rich a verbal environment as possible.

Pastoral or medical arrangements:
Conferencing with his classteacher should include finding possible role models amongst blind and partially-sighted people, and praise for finding ways of coping. He needs to know that he can be independent once he learns how, and that he is making progress.

Monitoring and assessment:
Weekly updates on all targets to be kept by classteacher.

Date of review:
12.12.96

REVIEW
Progress made:
Indicates when cannot see or read something, usually to peer. Has been to 7 of the 12 classrooms unaccompanied. Handwriting reached 15 w.p.m. for some tasks. Using strategies to locate objects. Discrimination between similar objects still difficult. Reading a book a week of own choice from large-print library.

Effectiveness of plan:
Plan largely successful in producing academic progress and improved mobility and confidence. Level of support and kind of information needed for progress has been identified. Other children still need reminding to give verbal explanations and not assume Ben can see everything they show him.

Parental help:
Parents kept record of books read at home. Taped story library used.

Any updated information (from outside agencies, medical reports, etc):

Future action: (new IEP, referral for statutory assessment)
New IEP. Now at Stage 3.

Figure 4.2 Continued

be much more difficult (and inappropriate) to set tightly sequenced teaching objectives across different subject areas in the expectation that pupils will catch up with their peers. For secondary pupils, success of intervention cannot always be viewed in terms of 'removing a difficulty' or overcoming an area of weakness. An important shift in thinking, particularly at the secondary phase, is to look from the curriculum to pupils' needs, rather than the other way around. There is a strong case to be made for focusing on how targets are going to be reached through teaching and learning processes, rather than on what the targets themselves might be.

So what could an IEP look like in secondary schools? Rather than starting from a detailed catalogue of the pupil's difficulties, it may be prudent to begin with a brief description of need alongside the demands of the school timetable, indicating where additional help may be available and offered in certain subject areas, the precise contribution of mainstream staff, what home–school liaison hopes to achieve, and the role that external agencies, such as a sensory support team, have to play. The co-ordinator's plan for each pupil may overview three terms' development, identifying key components such as *who* will be helping with *what*, for *how long*, and with *which resources*? Subject specialists may also require their own spur or branch of the plan, containing information that is relevant to them. There should also be a pupil component to the plan, so that whatever is drawn up between teachers and pupils has been negotiated and is shared.

The pupil's voice

The last but not least component of an IEP concerns a shift in ownership to the pupils themselves. The format and construction of IEPs can lead to pupils being simply on the receiving end. As pupils proceed through to secondary school there is an important sense in which education is preparing students for adulthood and growing independence. Pupils can be centrally involved in the planning process, helping to articulate strengths and areas for development. The pupil's version of the education plan deals with shorter-term, specific targets in 'pupil speak', negotiated and owned by the individual student as 'My Action Plan' (Figure 4.3). The pupil's spur of the action plan establishes strengths and weaknesses, steps along the route to mastery of a skill or curriculum area, and the nature of curriculum experiences that will promote learning.

A negotiated learning pathway such as this reflects an image of the learner as one of active partner, involved in taking decisions and responsibility for aspects of the learning process under adult guidance. If we are to endorse the view that schools are part of the continuum of lifetime learning, then the IEP has to be part generated and owned by pupils themselves. The process of constructing a plan thus becomes an important means of encouraging pupils to take responsibility for their own learning and to achieve independence.

My Action Plan

Name
What I am good at
What I want to improve on

My targets
How I will work to reach these targets
How I will know when I succeed
Evidence of my success
Meetings with my teachers

My review
What I have learnt
What I would like to work at next

Signed (pupil)
Signed (teacher)
Date
Date of next review

Figure 4.3 Pupil Action Plan

EDUCATIONAL PROVISION FOR CHILDREN WITH VISUAL IMPAIRMENTS

LEAs have a duty to inform parents about the different kinds of educational provision available, and professionals involved must give advice about the advantages and disadvantages of different placements for a particular child. Professional advice should take into account the child's needs and characteristics, determined, for example, by the child's visual difficulties, social and emotional maturity. A child who is very sociable, highly motivated and quick to learn may well be able to benefit from a mainstream educational setting. However, a child who is immature socially and experiences complex learning difficulties may cope better in an educational setting where there are specialist resources and children can be taught for most of the time in smaller groups.

By far the greatest proportion of children with visual impairments will be able to take part in mainstream school settings that have appropriate modifications to learning environments, some use of specialised equipment or technology, and a flexible approach to varying teaching and learning styles that is tailored to individual pupil differences. The low incidence of more severe visual handicaps, especially total blindness, in the population of school-aged children in the United Kingdom means that there is only ever likely to be a few children in each LEA who require highly specialised provision. This is the main reason why, in some areas, there may not be a full range of educational placements, and there may be little flexibility in the way in which pupils are supported in mainstream school contexts.

An LEA with a very low incidence of children with visual impairments may have had the policy of sending children to special schools out of the area. In a large rural district, children may tend to be integrated in their local school or sent away to residential special schools. By contrast, in an urban area with a high incidence of children with visual impairments, there may be a choice between integration in a local school, attending a school with a visual impairment unit, or placement in a special school.

A peripatetic support service may be spread very thinly over a geographical region and have a mainly advisory role, rather than offering direct teaching help. A resource base in a comprehensive school may have to serve a wide area, with most pupils travelling daily. For pupils with severe visual impairments or blindness, compromises may have to be made between optimal educational settings and continuity of contact with family and friends in the local community. If the most appropriate school setting involves lengthy travelling or residential placement, consequences for the quality of a child's social experience need to be weighed against educational benefits.

First steps towards schooling

Parents will naturally be concerned about the availability of nursery or playgroup provision, and how the transition to school can best be managed. Children with visual impairments often benefit from being in contact with same-age peers before starting school. An early educational placement can provide the opportunity to learn how to deal and play with other children; to become familiar with resources and materials that will continue being used during the early school years; to learn how to be part of a group, conforming to rules and routines; and to become more independent. For children with complex needs, an alternative first step is to attend a small special unit attached to a mainstream school, such as an 'opportunity playgroup', which can offer a quieter and more protective environment. Well-negotiated first experiences of school settings lay the foundations for successful future integration.

Mainstream school settings

Information on mainstream schools will be provided by an LEA, 'named person' or visiting teacher. For parents, it is important to feel that a school is interested and willing to make a commitment to meeting their child's individual needs. If a local school has no previous experience of working with children who have visual impairments, there will be issues to address such as the willingness of staff to receive additional training and to adapt their teaching. The RNIB (1995a) advises parents to look out for aspects in the physical environment when visiting schools, such as consistent lighting levels, corridors free of obstacles, and well-lit classrooms with quiet conditions. There are important social considerations, too, such as whether there are enough children of similar abilities to provide a peer group that will be sufficiently stimulating. (One social indicator of the success of a child's placement in an integrated setting is how far friendships have been established with local children and joint activities arranged at weekends or holidays.)

Classteachers are usually interested to know the nature of specific eye defects and the implications for teaching and learning. There may need to be discussions about the use of specialist equipment such as task lighting, white boards, large print, the best print/background colour combination for a computer screen, or text enlargers. For those teachers who have never worked with a child with a visual impairment before, there will need to be considerations about safety in using science laboratories, equipment in food technology, and workshop activities in other subject areas where potentially dangerous tools are used.

Demands on teachers

A number of studies (from pre-Code of Practice times) have identified what mainstream teachers generally want of visiting specialist support staff (Millar, 1986). This includes providing information on the nature of the child's visual impairment, assessing and monitoring visual functioning and residual vision, together with any other relevant background information. Teachers were often uncertain of the expectations they should hold for a particular child and the levels of achievement to expect in different areas of the curriculum. Advice was often looked for on obtaining appropriate equipment or services and how to modify environmental conditions. Mainstream teachers also valued formal and informal in-service training sessions on aspects such as curriculum development, with reference to the special needs associated with particular visual conditions.

In the post-Code of Practice era mainstream class and subject teachers have been given much more sharply defined responsibilities towards pupils with individual needs. In the early stages of the Code all teachers must be skilled at making observations of children, devising individual plans and adapting their teaching. The visiting specialist may be asked to work with the school's co-ordinator for special needs to set out specific targets, teaching strategies, monitoring and review arrangements. In some instances, for example where a child requires a specialised orientation, mobility, keyboard or braille programme, the adviser may work directly with the teacher and the child. Direct work on aspects of a child's literacy or mathematics could also be part of a visiting teacher's remit.

Children who are considered for educational purposes to be blind are often integrated in mainstream schools. They usually require a high level of extra support. At an early age most of this will be direct teaching aimed at safety awareness, encouraging and motivating the child, providing appropriate verbal input, and promoting access to the school curriculum. At a later stage, extra support becomes progressively less direct as the child develops more confidence and independence. Children who are blind may require a number of technological aids and specialised equipment. The adaptation and production of materials is also important. There are practical difficulties in accessing a large variety of braille books, even with subscription to a braille library. Always, the nature of the support provided depends on a number of factors, such as age and maturity of the child and the level of demand from particular tasks. It is extremely important that class or subject teachers work closely together with advisory teachers and plan ahead how they are going to intervene.

A balance must be found between pupils participating as much as possible in classgroup activities, and working on specific skills on an individual basis for some of the time. For example, it could be that a humanities group is watching a television programme as part of a lead lesson on Third World economics, which would be inaccessible to a child with a visual impairment. This time could be used to teach a specific skill, or to work over relevant vocabulary, technical language and new concepts, in support of the mainstream lesson.

Resource units

Pupils with visual impairments may attend a mainstream school with a resource base. This arrangement also gives the advantage of pupils being socially integrated in an ordinary school community. Collectively, pupils with visual impairments attending a resource base may not feel so isolated or special. However, there are some disadvantages to this kind of arrangement. Pupils who attend schools with resource bases are often detached from their own communities and it may be more difficult to keep contact with local friends near to home. They may have to spend time travelling to the school, making it impractical to participate in extra-school activities.

In schools with a resource unit, the extra support that pupils receive whilst in a mainstream classgroup may not be very different from that which might be provided in any school. There is the advantage of having more resources all in the same place, and having permanent staff attached to one school who are experienced in dealing with particular needs. Specialist support teachers may collect pupils together for specific purposes, such as a sex education lesson. Support teachers working from a base can take on the task of providing professional development input to colleagues, for example in moving towards more differentiated styles of teaching.

Special schools

In an era when children were categorised according to their disabilities, and educational provision was made accordingly, educational placements depended very largely on the assessment of a child's vision by an ophthalmologist. Blind children went to schools for the blind where they were taught braille or through other methods not dependent on vision, whilst children diagnosed as 'partially sighted' went to special schools specifically catering for this group. According to Best (1992), in the period before the 1981 Education Act more than 90 per cent of blind children and 75 per cent of 'partially sighted' children went to special schools. However, there are now just as many children with severe visual impairments or blindness in integrated settings as there are in special schools.

These distinctions on the basis of categories of vision have now given way to placement according to individual needs and circumstances, with the views and preferences of parents and pupils also taken into account. This has meant a general blurring of boundaries between what were previously considered to be distinct groups. Obviously, braille-using pupils require specialised resources and teaching, but pupils are not always exclusively braille- or print-users, and the teaching of braille is no longer associated with schools for the blind. One study into the factors that affect the success of pupils taking part in mainstream school settings, undertaken by Bishop (1986), identified 69 salient factors, of which 'amount of vision' was ranked 60th.

There are approximately 30 residential and day special schools for pupils with visual impairments across the United Kingdom. The majority of residential schools are run by independent organisations such as charitable trusts or the RNIB. The survey of provision by Dawkins (1991) shows a general move away from special school provision towards some form of integration for most pupils with visual impairments. In some areas, units that were originally set up for the 'partially sighted' have become resource bases for pupils with more severe visual impairments or blindness. In some instances, a special school may serve as the centre for an 'outreach' peripatetic service for children with visual impairments in a district. Almost all of the special schools for pupils with visual impairments serve large conurbations or regions, with some children travelling long distances every day and others boarding during the week. In a few LEAs, special schools share the same site as a mainstream primary or secondary school, with opportunities for integration into selected areas of the curriculum. Many special schools are all-age, or offer facilities for pupils with additional learning difficulties or dual handicaps, such as vision and hearing loss.

Special schools generally have come under attack from bodies such as the Audit Commission in recent reports. Some special schools are felt to offer too narrow a curriculum, insufficient challenges to pupils, limited expectations and a pace of teaching that is often too slow. Despite the amount of assessment information available on pupils placed in special schools, this may not always be utilised to inform teaching. An absence of planning and target-setting was also felt to be characteristic of special schools, with teaching sometimes poorly matched to pupils' needs. Special schools have been accused of failing to provide evidence of their effectiveness, quality or value, compared with mainstream schools.

The issue of how best to evaluate provision and the raising of achievement of both staff and pupils in special schools is a separate one from whether some pupils' needs are best met in highly specialised learning environments. Increasingly, severe visual impairments arise in children with a complex of medical factors and learning difficulties. In the current educational climate, expertise developed to meet the needs of individuals with multiple disabilities is likely to be focused on a few national centres of excellence.

Special schools are part of the continuum of educational response that should be available to families where circumstances indicate that a more protective, smaller scale environment would be best for the child and parents. Special schools usually have a generous adult–child ratio. They may be expected to be staffed by teachers who are well qualified and highly committed to working with children with more severe difficulties or additional disabilities. They should have a range of specialist equipment and information technology, such as CCTV, braille duplicators and talking computers. They are usually recommended on the basis that a child's personality, ability to learn, confidence in relating to other children, communication and mobility needs, together with specialised teaching requirements, could not be met within a mainstream school context, even with additional resources.

Children with complex needs

Young children with severe and complex needs may require the expertise of a multi-disciplinary staff, including educational and clinical psychologists, speech therapist, physiotherapist, medical or nursing care. Special schools often offer 'assessment' places which allow detailed consideration of the child's needs and how they might best be met, over a residential placement of several weeks. Children with a progressive condition who are gradually losing their sight may need a period of time in a highly supportive environment with very small classes of three or four pupils, and intensive teaching to acquire new skills in mobility or independence. Parents may also require access to sensitive and practical counselling in the traumatic period following the onset of a child's blindness.

In some families, parents may not feel equipped to deal adequately with a child at home, particularly if they are faced with stresses in other areas of their lives. We have mentioned the possibility, under the terms of the Children Act and the Education Act of 1993, that joint assessments of a family's needs can be made, with the possible sharing of placement costs by Social Services and education departments.

Many children who have complex disabilities that include a visual impairment receive their education in special schools for children with severe learning difficulties local to where they live. Teachers in these schools will be working to meet the needs of a very wide range of individuals. There is likely to be an emphasis on self-care, personal independence, mobility, communication and lifeskills. Advice on the specific needs associated with a child's visual difficulties may come from an LEA advisory teacher, where such expertise exists. Alternatively, organisations such as RNIB or SENSE, the national organisation for deaf-blind children, employ teams of advisers who visit schools at the invitation of an LEA. These advisory services work with families and teachers, offer short residential assessments at their regional centres, and are involved in professional development work. (For further information on voluntary organisations and advisory sources, see Appendix.)

A number of questions can be asked about all special schools, including those for children with visual impairments. Are they, in fact, centres of excellence and expertise? Is special school placement offered as a positively planned opportunity, or simply opted for when all else seems to have failed, or resources are difficult to secure to support a child in mainstream? When decisions are made about school placement, parents have a right to unbiased information and clear indications about the pros and cons of each particular course of action. Parents may more readily accept the reasons for recommending a residential placement at the secondary level, when the social and academic demands of school are greater, and the child is more mature. On the other hand, children placed in a special school at a young age may benefit from more intensive help early on, with the prospect of returning to mainstream schooling later. Always, the advantages for the child in a special school have to be weighed against the disadvantages, such as distance away from home, loss of contact with local children, and perhaps a more restricted educational curriculum. One of the principles underlying the Code of Practice is that the views and preferences of parents should be sought, within an active, positive, mutually informative partnership between carers and professionals. Whatever provision is made to meet a child's needs must be closely monitored and frequently evaluated.

ACADEMIC ACHIEVEMENT OF PUPILS WITH VISUAL IMPAIRMENTS

There can be no definitive answer to the question: 'In which kind of arrangements for schooling do children with visual impairments make better progress?'. Degree of vision is of limited predictive power in determining the success of a school placement. The demands of school environments will, of course, change in relation to different subject areas, teachers and classroom contexts, including the willingness of staff to adapt to the needs of a child and the availability of additional help.

The child's resilience, self-esteem and motivation, profile of abilities, and social and emotional maturity will also play an important part in determining the level of additional expert help required. Resilience in educational contexts generally means the ability to succeed against difficult odds. However, children may vary in their resilience in different situations, in contrasting areas of development, and over time.

There are many reasons to expect some pupils with visual impairments to be progressing at a slower rate than sighted children, although there are no inevitable barriers to learning associated with a visual loss. Most modifications to teaching methods or resources, such as print enlargement, slow down the pace of learning. A compensatory approach may rely more on speaking and listening, or the critical reflection on learning that can arise through well-scaffolded interaction. However, research suggests that for the majority of pupils, particularly at secondary school, very limited amounts of time are spent by teachers reviewing or reflecting on pupils' work (Webster *et al.*, 1996b). The study by Keys and Fernandes (1993) showed that some 40 per cent of sighted secondary pupils did not have the opportunity to discuss a single piece of work individually with their teachers over the course of a school year.

The purpose of early intervention, of integration programmes with additional teaching support, or of special school provision is to provide appropriate educational experiences that will help pupils to fulfil their potential. For many pupils with severe visual impairments, especially if these arise in association with other learning difficulties, academic attainments, as measured by formal tests or examination results, may be less important as indices of success than personal achievements that contribute towards independence. There are, however, comparative statistics that examine the academic performance of pupils with a range of visual impairments across educational settings.

In a study by Dunkerton (1995), results of 198 students sitting GCSEs and 97 sitting A levels were scrutinised. The sample included registered blind students as well as 'partially sighted', in both mainstream and special schools. In those students sitting examinations, results indicate no overall differences in the spread of GCSE results for visually impaired compared with sighted groups. Students placed in mainstream settings appear to do better than those in special schools, with a larger percentage obtaining grades A or B, and a smaller percentage obtaining E or F grades. This is not to say that a mainstream setting is inherently better for a pupil with a visual impairment, but more likely reflects the trend to place academically able students in mainstream rather than special schools. For blind students there was little difference in their performance at GCSE level in either school setting. At A level, results for students with visual impairments are actually better than for their sighted peers, whatever the educational setting. These data support the view that a severe visual impairment is not an insuperable barrier to good academic achievements, even when benchmarks derived from sighted students are applied.

FURTHER AND HIGHER EDUCATION

Schools are a central, but not exclusive, part of a continuum of provision that society makes for lifetime learning. The DfEE's objectives for lifetime learning include raising skills and achievements, promoting individual choice and enterprise, equipping young people for the responsibilities of adult life and employment, and encouraging people to take charge of their own learning and development. For pupils with visual impairments these objectives can be fully realised only through the provision of a diversity of routes into further and higher education, and access to opportunities for vocational training and updating. LEAs remain responsible for pupils who remain at school until they are 19. Other pupils, including those with statements, may leave school at 16 to attend a college within the FE sector. Whatever the intended future destination of the young person, there is particular significance attached to a review of an individual's special needs when they are approaching 16 years of age.

Transition Plans

The Code of Practice makes some very clear recommendations about Transition Plans, which should form a part of the first annual review after a youngster's 14th birthday, and any subsequent review until leaving school. A Transition Plan draws together information from a range of individuals within and beyond the school in order to plan coherently for the young person's transition to adult life. LEAs should consult with child health services, educational psychologists and any other professional agency, such as a teacher of the visually impaired, who may have a useful contribution to make. Information should be sought from Social Services to ascertain whether any provision will need to be made post-school. If not previously involved, contact may be appropriate with mobility and rehabilitation workers employed by Social Services. Careers officers with specialist responsibilities will be able to advise on future training and development needs, options in further or higher education, and the drawing up of a vocational profile.

The Transition Plan is intended to build on the conclusions and objectives of previous reviews, focusing on strengths and immaturities, and covering all aspects of an individual's educational and personal development. Effective arrangements are meant to include young people themselves, centrally, in addressing issues of personal autonomy and competence, the acquisition of independent living skills, self-advocacy and awareness of the long-term implications of a disability. The success of Transition Plans will depend as much on what has gone before as on what is approaching. Although schools are expected to encourage student involvement at transition, pupils will be confident enough to contribute only if there have been opportunities to make personal plans previously. For pupils with visual impairments, particularly at the secondary school stage, it is vital that the curriculum helps to shape assertiveness and personal independence. This includes engaging pupils in self-assessment, in recognising their own patterns of learning and achievement, in setting objectives and planning learning routes.

The RNIB survey of provision referred to earlier (Dawkins, 1991) shows that the extent to which LEA specialist support services include further education (FE) in their brief varies widely from one area to another. Despite its importance to youngsters with special needs, opportunities for training and continuing education across the life span are less than satisfactory. Most LEAs do, however, employ specialist careers officers who will be knowledgeable about placements in FE and appropriate vocational training. The RNIB Student Support Service offers advice about post-16 options, including information on grants for equipment and services such as 'readers'.

Issues for the young person

- information required to make choices for the future
- local arrangements for advice or advocacy
- how young person can be involved in contributing to own Transition Plan
- hopes and aspirations for future
- locations of services and advice if a residential placement away from home is recommended

Issues for the family

- expectation for their son's or daughter's adult life
- parental contributions to young person's ongoing social and practical competence
- care or support needs of the family as young person matures

Issues for the school

- young person's curriculum needs during transition
- role in the community
- ability to use leisure and recreational facilities
- role in the family
- new educational/vocational skills

Issues for professionals

- collaboration to arrive at a coherent plan
- involvement of new agencies, e.g. mobility or rehabilitation worker
- any special health, welfare or Social Services support
- appropriate training for technological aids
- opportunities in further or higher education
- transfer of information to adult services or FE college
- involvement of careers service, including specialist careers officers for advice on future training or employment

---

Figure 4.4 Transition Plans under the Code of Practice

SUMMARY

In this section we have been largely concerned with the new framework of legislation and guidance under which the individual needs of families and young children are currently identified, assessed and planned for. There is no straightforward answer to the question: 'What type of educational provision best meets the needs of children with visual impairments?'. What is important, however, is that parents and professionals share an open dialogue about their concerns. An important role of the advisory teacher is to offer information about prospective schools, how a child may be supported to participate in mainstream, and what the likely advantages and drawbacks of contrasting educational settings are likely to be. The Code of Practice intends a positive partnership between families and professionals within clear and systematic procedures. Not least, if the objectives of lifelong learning are to be realised, the young person whose needs are under consideration must take a central role, wherever possible, in decision-making processes.

5

ENHANCING LEARNING ENVIRONMENTS FOR CHILDREN WITH VISUAL IMPAIRMENTS

In this section our focus shifts to some of the practical strategies that can be adopted by parents and teachers to create optimal learning environments. For parents, some of the early concerns are with social interaction: tuning into the child's focus of attention and reading signals of interest; the development of body awareness and self-image; promoting exploration, language and conceptual growth. Ideas are also suggested for stimulating aspects of vision, such as tracking, fixation and eye–hand co-ordination, for fostering conversation and the effective sharing of reading and writing at home.

We also consider how to design purposeful school environments for play, literacy and wider access to the curriculum. In many instances, adaptations to conditions for listening, the physical organisation of classroom spaces and strategies for differentiation support more effective learning for all children. In other instances, such as use of low vision aids and information technology, we shall be giving examples of how specialised equipment can enable pupils to take part in a broad and balanced curriculum, and highlighting some of the implications for teachers' classroom practice.

Adults can generally exert much more control over learning environments, teaching resources and strategies than they can hope to over the qualities and characteristics of the individuals they teach. For pupils with visual impairments there will be important questions about how best to encourage mobility, exploration, play, language and learning. Many aspects of development are inter-related and depend to a greater or lesser degree on the integrating qualities of vision. When a child's vision is affected, there is a reduction in the information necessary for understanding how the world is organised and how it can be acted upon. To help overcome the isolating effects of a severe visual impairment, adults play a very important role in bridging between the child and the environment. A responsive caregiver can enable the child to build up a coherent picture of the world by providing more information through different sense modalities, making

142

links between areas of experience, and by giving more time to assimilate the new.

In the early stages, parents and teachers can enrich the child's experience by introducing a variety of sensory stimulation: sounds, smells, textures and shapes. Adults can accompany everything they do with carefully tailored interpretive descriptions. We have said that an important principle is to try and understand how the child is trying to make sense of the world from the information available, making connections between this inner world and relevant aspects of the world outside. Vision also plays a valuable role in incidental learning. Sighted children learn continuously about events, people and their actions by observing what is happening around them. Children with visual impairments have fewer ways of observing what others are doing, how individuals deal with situations and events, and what kinds of responses adults tend to give to peers who produce certain kinds of behaviour. Incidental learning is much more limited for the child with a visual impairment, and certainly has an influence on the child's progress in school.

The new Code of Practice for schools, which we considered in the previous chapter, makes it clear that all teachers are being asked to take on significant responsibilities for identifying, assessing, planning and meeting individual needs in the early stages of the Code. When children with visual impairments spend part, or the majority, of their school time in mainstream settings, it is important that all teachers are aware of the conditions and experiences that promote effective teaching and learning. It has often been said that teachers who can organise their teaching to include pupils with specific individual needs will thereby improve the learning environment for all children. Most of the practical suggestions in this chapter, such as differentiating methods of presentation or modes of working, have a positive effect on all children.

All pupils, including children with visual impairments, can be affected by environmental factors such as lighting, listening conditions, decor and room organisation. The sound environment is particularly important, since children with limited vision will need to use more auditory information. Quiet listening conditions with few sound distractions or competing sound sources are crucial. Some regular sounds, like a ticking clock, may help with orientation. Large, echoey spaces often prove unmanageable and children may function much better in small, well-defined areas with a familiar layout, where resources are stored and replaced consistently.

This kind of practical consideration for managing learning contexts we shall cover in some detail in the course of this chapter, drawn from tried and tested 'good practice'. Although the learning environment is highly important, access to the curriculum for a child with a visual impairment also depends on the skill of the teacher in communicating the concepts of different subject areas and in promoting understanding in terms to which the child can relate. This inevitably means more use of verbal commentary; use of 'hands on' experience; sensitive questioning, explanation and description; and bringing alive the abstract material of some subject areas through a range of sensory modalities. Small group settings and additional classroom support may often be necessary.

Teaching typically starts by considering the content of a scheme or module of work, programme of activities or topic, bearing in mind how children will learn. At the very outset it helps to identify those parts that might prove difficult, require alternative means of presentation, or constitute a greater challenge for pupils with reduced vision. Designing contexts for learning includes providing a better match between pupils' starting points and the tasks that are set, based on careful observation in different settings and curriculum areas. It includes adapting tasks, teaching and learning styles to make the same programmes of study accessible, relevant and meaningful to pupils of different backgrounds, abilities and learning needs. It means shaping adult–pupil interactions (such as dialogues around text, question and answer routines) towards more effective encounters. There is also the issue of how technology and special equipment can be harnessed to help meet specific needs, such as the use of low vision aids or computers for print recognition.

EARLY SOCIAL CONTEXTS

The very first exposure of an infant to the world takes place within a framework of intense social interactions with caregivers, usually mothers. However, the reciprocal processes involved in early interaction depend heavily on vision. In Chapter 3 we considered some of the special properties of vision that enable caregivers to establish a social framework of 'intersubjectivity' in which infant and parent enter dialogues where they read one another's behaviour. Later this mutual responding in familiar contexts makes possible increasingly linguistic exchanges, as shared experience is suffused with appropriate commentary. Obtaining an infant's attention, mutual eye contact, the imitation of gestures and movements, the reading of intentions and the use of language in a shared context can all be impeded by reductions in visual information.

Whilst vision helps the spontaneity and ease with which these early interactions take place, there are steps that adults can take to enhance early encounters when a child has reduced vision. A child with a severe visual impairment may 'still', rather than smile, as someone approaches or speaks. There may be slight vocalisations, head or limb movements that register the child's interest or pleasure. In the absence of eye contact, these signals may not appear to be addressed to anyone. However, parents can tune into the special signals their child makes, and respond in return by vocalising, cuddling and touching. Some parents report that their infants seem unresponsive in the early stages and do not smile or gurgle when picked up or when a familiar face comes into view. In time most parents find, from careful observation of reactions to sensory cues such as smells, sounds or touches, that they do begin to read their child's signals of interest or excitement more clearly.

Suggestions for how parents can help to establish reciprocal exchanges when first the child, then the adult, responds can be found in the RNIB handbook to parents on learning through play (RNIB, 1995b). These include playing games with a child on the adult's lap, using rhythmical movements such as swaying, rocking and bouncing to accompany songs and rhymes such as 'London Bridge is falling down', 'Ring a ring of roses' or 'Round and round the garden'. Play routines like this, with elements of touch, sound or movement, establish turn-taking and social interaction, helping the child to discover that communicative intentions produce anticipated responses. The adult fosters this discovery by providing opportunities for the child to listen and join in at the correct moment, and when the child does respond, this is the occasion for the adult to reciprocate with words, laughter or a tickle.

Play routines with music and movement continue to be an important opportunity for children to enjoy interactive sequences when they join a play group or nursery. Use of a resonance board, for example, is an effective way of enabling children with visual impairments to experience the rhythms, beats and cadences of songs, rhymes and more dramatic wordplays through vibration as well as hearing.

EXPLORATION AND THE CHILD'S AWARENESS OF SELF

One of the consequences of living in intense social relationships with others is that very young infants quickly become aware of themselves and their bodies in context. Inevitably, vision is the major source of information for most infants, which enables them to see relationships between things, and to make distinctions between the limits of their own bodies and those of other people, the spaces inhabited at home and the world beyond.

It is through a gradual accumulation of experiences that the child comes to be aware of a sense of self in a defined space, where the contours of objects 'out there' are distinguished from the child's own fingers, hands and limbs. This awareness arises to some extent vicariously, through watching the bodies and movements of other children or adults. However, researchers such as Piaget have argued that it is mainly through physical action that children reach these understandings. There is a very real sense in which, for children with limited vision, visual observation as a basis for early learning must be replaced by physical exploration.

In Chapter 3, when we considered the impact of a visual impairment on developmental processes, we highlighted some important factors that influence children's awareness of objects and events in the environment, including reaching and grasping, exploring spaces, and coming to know that objects exist outside oneself and are permanent, even though temporarily out of view. Visual and tactile exploration are the main ways through which the majority of children learn about their surroundings, distinguish the cause and effects of their actions on objects, and discriminate outside stimuli in the flow of

145

Plate 5.1 Using a resonance board. A group of children with visual impairments enjoy songs and the rhythmic vibrations played on a resonance board

events, from inner experiences. This distinction of self from other, and of cause from effect, marks the beginnings of thinking, as infants begin to anticipate the impact of their actions on the world.

There are many ordinary experiences that may enable a child with a visual impairment to be aware of body parts and their movements, of a sense of separateness and relationship to other objects, or to make distinctions between entities that exist out there and can be lost (such as toys) and items that are integral and always available (such as toes). These include rolling a child against different surfaces and other people; massaging, tickling, touching and brushing different body parts whilst naming them; sifting water, blowing air or 'raspberries'; or moving a soft object such as a ball over a child's body contours. Other suggestions for parents to help establish a child's body image, such as giving 'piggybacks', walking a child on the adult's toes, 'touch-and-show' games with body parts, are provided in the RNIB handbook referred to above (RNIB, 1995b).

EARLY VISUAL ENVIRONMENTS

In Chapter 3 we outlined the capacity that young sighted babies have to find visual stimuli and to keep them before their eyes and in focus. Three-month-old infants can already fixate on objects, make complex discriminations of features close to themselves (such as familiar/unfamiliar faces), as well as tracking distant objects. Because of its immediacy, and the ability of the visual system to make sense of complex visual information in a single glance, vision enables us to build a coherent map of our surroundings, effortlessly and without the need to remember where and what things are.

For children with some degree of residual vision it is important to stimulate looking from an early age by providing a visually interesting environment that is accessible to the child. An important part of any educational programme is to encourage children to make full use of residual vision and, eventually, for them to become more skilled at interpreting the visual information available.

For very young children, looking can be stimulated by objects and displays that contrast with the background. Even newborn infants prefer to look at colours, patterns and objects that move, rather than stationary, grey, uniform elements. Mobiles with bright and shiny objects and items that rotate or wobble or make interesting sounds can be hung in positions so that the child can reach out for them. Shiny Christmas decorations suspended from elastic serve as attention-getters when they catch the light. Mobiles can also be made using cutlery, jewellery, ribbons, rattles, beads, foil, shells, flowers or toys. Coloured acetate or cellophane squares over windows or door panels will encourage looking, and help to identify places around the house. Fibre optic lights, novelty night lights or brightly coloured toys that illuminate can also stimulate looking. To begin with, objects can be placed where the child can easily see them. As the child matures, objects can be placed in locations that demand more from the child in terms of moving eyes and head to search.

Everyday settings can easily be adapted to make them more visually interesting. Places frequently revisited by parents and young children include playpens, changing areas and bathrooms, and these can be useful places to stick pictures, mirrors and brightly coloured displays, or to keep a notice board where objects can be pinned and replaced. Mobiles, toys and objects can also be attached to the child's cot, car seat, buggy or highchair. Obviously, a balance has to be found between overloading a visual environment with too much information, so that it becomes confusing, and selecting interesting items that stimulate looking. It may be a matter of trial and error to find the things that appeal to individual children, depending on their response to glitter, contrast, movement, shimmer or colour.

Visual fixation and eye contact

There are many practical suggestions for helping to establish eye contact with young children who have some residual vision. These include wearing coloured spectacle frames, funny hats, face paint, make-up, lipstick or masks, all of which emphasise facial features, when playing with a child. The RNIB handbook for parents referred to earlier (RNIB, 1995b) suggests that encouraging eye contact with other people or objects is best achieved in the context of interactive games, such as using a 'Jack in the box' to attract a child's attention. Through touch and adult commentary ('Where is he, where's Jack gone? . . . here he comes!'), the game also promotes turn-taking and anticipation, interfused with relevant language.

Suggestions for encouraging a child to fixate an object include toys such as glowballs, neon laces or luminous star shapes fixed to the child's bedroom ceiling. Spinners, reflectors or holograms can be used in combination with a torch to produce intense, bright or sparkling patterns. Moving clockwork automata, toys with flashing lights and sounds, and puppets of all kinds provide opportunities for gaining and holding fixation.

One interesting point is that all children develop grasping and reaching towards objects in view, prior to reaching for objects on the basis of sound. The development of eye–hand before ear–hand co-ordination is a contributory factor to the later development of a co-ordinated reach, object permanence and related linguistic concepts in some children with impaired vision. Whilst a sighted child may be motivated to grasp for an object in proximity, the child with a visual impairment may not be motivated to grasp for an object on the basis of sound until sometime later. Many everyday objects do not produce sounds, whilst the presence of a sound does not always mean that there is an object out there to be grasped (train passing, dog barking in a neighbour's garden). These are good reasons for assisting children with residual vision to reach and grasp on the basis of looking.

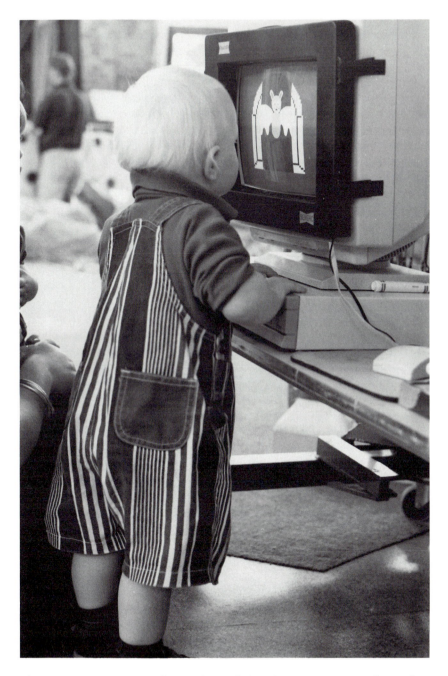

Plate 5.2 Using a computer for visual stimulation. An important part of any educational programme is to encourage children to make full use of residual vision

Tracking

Tracking can be stimulated by moving interesting objects horizontally or vertically, close to the child's line of vision. Variants of this include shining a coloured torchlight onto a pale wall or floor, and encouraging the child to track movements by placing hands or feet over the light. Brightly coloured toys can be held in front of the child's midline, then moved within the child's visual field and brought within touching range. Adult commentary about the toy during this game helps to bring language, visual and tactile experience together to make an integrated and meaningful whole. Tracking can also be developed by activities such as following coloured rolling balls or marbles on a 'helter skelter'; watching the progress of toy trains or racing cars around tracks; blowing and pursuing bubbles; and observing brightly coloured 'slime' toys as they make their way down a wall or window. Most toy stores stock a range of climbing toys with pull cords; wind-up frogs and fish that propel themselves in water; magnetic animals and insects that can be moved from beneath a tabletop; and radio-controlled objects or computer-programmable vehicles with light and sound effects.

Eye–hand co-ordination

Although our hands cannot provide such precise data as our eyes about objects and their positions in space, touch is still a very important source of environmental information for children with severe visual impairments. In Chapter 3 we considered some of the limitations of tactile exploration: objects have to be sought out to discover their characteristics; small fragments of information have to be put together serially to achieve an image of the whole; features of objects and their surroundings have to be remembered; whilst for many environmental phenomena, direct contact is impossible or inadvisable. Nevertheless, it is important for many children to use their hands effectively as part of a range of strategies for getting to know the world. Hand and tactile awareness can be stimulated by blowing, brushing, tickling and stroking, or by giving the opportunity to explore a range of materials, such as feathers, velvet, sponge, talcum powder, sand, silk, olive oil or treacle. Playing hand and finger games encourages looking at hands, such as finger or mitten puppets, 'Pat-a-cake', 'Fly away Peter', 'This little piggy went to market', or 'Three little mice came out to play'.

Objects grasped for detailed exploration need interesting stimuli that can be pulled, twisted, shaken or opened: music boxes, baby 'gyms', toys with lids and doors, containers within containers, and 'feely bags' with shells, beads, nuts, bells, buttons or keys. A selection of toys with different textures, sounds, shapes and functions will motivate children who may be reluctant to explore objects with their hands. Presenting objects from slightly different positions each time will introduce the idea that things do not always appear in the same place, in the same way.

Plate 5.3 Handling a variety of textures and materials. Tactile exploration is an important source of information about the world: providing opportunities for handling a variety of materials and textures stimulates hand and tactile awareness as well as conceptual growth. However, many children with visual impairments resist having their hands guided and avoid touching certain textures

151

Precision and strength in using fingers is important for children with severe visual impairments and underpins later teaching of braille. Tactile discrimination, power and accuracy in using fingers can be developed through activities involving squeezing, unscrewing, posting, cutting, threading, twisting, rotating, pulling and pushing. Useful materials for increasing the deftness and flexibility of fingers, wrists or hands include pegboards, keyboards, posting boxes, shapeboards, stacking rings, assembly toys, construction materials, and toys with push buttons, hinges, lids or winders. However, one of the points we draw attention to in Chapter 6, where we present research findings from social encounters including children with visual impairments, is that materials for manipulating, assembling or constructing tend to promote solitary, repetitive activities rather than imaginative or interactive play. It is preferable to use tactile materials in game formats with adults or peers to add a social dimension.

In order to understand the environment that surrounds them, children with visual impairments may have to be prompted initially to reach beyond themselves. To begin with, parents may supply interesting objects, such as a battery vehicle operated by a touch switch, just out of the child's arm reach. It is important that objects are located not only at floor level or on a tray in front of the child, but at different heights and in different directions. Noise-making toys can be placed at a child's feet, on a high shelf or at the back of a cupboard. Objects are often hard to recognise from unusual viewpoints and it is important that the child has opportunities to identify things in contrasting positions, different lighting conditions and whilst partially occluded.

Much has also been made, as we discussed in Chapter 3, of the shift in understanding that accompanies object permanence. Discovering that objects still exist, though not immediately in view, is much harder for a child with poor vision. Sighted children begin to look for objects they have dropped or that roll away. To help children with reduced vision over this conceptual hurdle, adults can play games such as dropping balls, blocks and other objects into a large bowl, helping the child to pick them out and hand them over. Caregivers can encourage the retrieving of dropped items in other everyday settings, such as mealtimes or bathtime, pursuing toys that float away or sink. Children can be taught tactile search strategies, whereby a surface is systematically explored using the fingertips, through increasing circles moving outwards from the body. Toys that emit sounds can be used to encourage the more demanding strategy of listening to discover the location of an object that has been moved out of reach.

SETTINGS FOR EARLY EXPLORATION AND MOBILITY

Sighted children are faced with panoramic views of locations for potential exploration. They see interesting things and seek them out. Motor development is a particular area of concern, since children with severe visual impairments cannot easily monitor their own movements or construct mental maps of their environments. Visual problems in very young children create difficulties in exploring and interacting with the world, linking words to objects and tying concepts and categories to the environment. Some of the literature we reviewed in Chapter 3 suggests that children with severe visual impairments may be passive and unmotivated, or lack confidence to explore or solve problems. We would prefer to think of this another way: that information motivates a child, and visual information is a particularly powerful stimulus for investigating things. The real question, looking through the child's eyes, is what kind of information is required to stimulate interest?

There are some fairly simple ways of encouraging a child to be more aware of things around them. Sighted children often explore spaces such as a laundry basket, large cardboard box, understairs cupboard, wardrobe or stairs. Parents of children with visual impairments can promote similar supervised explorations into containers, drawers, cupboards and through improvised play spaces, such as large cardboard tubes or tunnels made from packaging. Advisory teachers who work with families may suggest that parents move or carry young children around with them whilst they get on with everyday chores, such as washing dishes or unloading shopping. This is not always practicable, but it does give an opportunity for the child with a visual impairment to be more closely involved with familiar routines and to make connections between actions, events and relevant language. Instead of just hearing from a distance what a parent is doing in the kitchen, for example, the infant is assisted to feel the cold air as the fridge is opened and is given an explanation about why the milk needs to be stored there. The child can help by squeezing out the washing up detergent, noticing its smell and texture, and how it changes the water. One mother regularly gave her child rides on the vacuum cleaner as she did the housework, allowing him to switch the machine on, feel the sucking action and help to empty the bag in the dustbin. This was also an important opportunity for the child to explore the edges, entrances, routeways, objects and landmarks within and between rooms.

Early mobility, for a child with a severe visual impairment, is an important aspect of the development of a number of inter-related concepts about the physical world. These include how spaces are structured and occupied by objects, and the child's own relative position within a given space. Early numeracy is an aspect of development closely linked with the child's involvement with everyday moments such as counting fishfingers, biscuits, placemats or cutlery; weighing ingredients for cooking; making lists and shopping; using household equipment such as timers, washing machines and microwaves. There is some evidence, which we considered in Chapter 3, that children with reduced vision who do not actively explore may be immature in understanding processes such as causality (effects of actions on objects), time sequences and the properties of matter. Opportunities can be created that help to overcome these immaturities and establish a foundation for later mobility training and social independence. In the support service where one of the authors works, children with visual impairments are encouraged from a very early age to join family swimming, riding, skating and other activity sessions, in order to develop confidence, mobility and a positive orientation to new experiences.

Spatial maps

There are a number of games and activities that can stimulate children to move around in space and act on the physical world. For example, a child can be asked to move around the perimeter of a room in order to find particular points, such as marks on a wall. They may be taught simple routes from one wall to the next, anticipating what they will find along the way. For example, it may be that the wall has a cupboard on it and a floor-standing radiator, with a windchime to the left. When the child moves to a different starting point, these objects are in a different sequential position relative to the child's route across the room. Some objects can be moved, others stay put. Another game involves leaving objects in certain places around the room; the child then identifies and relocates them from different starting points.

The literature on spatial maps (see, for example, Spencer *et al.*, 1989), which we considered in Chapter 3, suggests that all children start out by representing spatial relations in terms of separate landmarks or a succession of points along a route. Integrated, survey-like spatial maps are not typical of children's thinking until school age, and even then complex routes may be constructed on the basis of a sequence of observed fragments.

In order to move around efficiently, children with visual impairments must start to gather experience from exposure to different environments at an early age. In the vicinity of home, parents can supervise children's exploration of environmental features such as garden fences, archways, low walls and verges, telegraph poles, lamp-posts, bus stops, post boxes, telephone kiosks, trees and shrubs. Surfaces with different textures and gradients can be noted, such as tarmac, paving stones, gravel, grass or cobblestones. Both visual and gross motor skills can be practised and refined outdoors whilst the child constructs routes to and from familiar places. On entry to nursery or playgroup, time can be spent learning the positions of gates, doors, passageways, windows, washbasins, television, home corner, books and equipment. It is important that children learn to use all their senses to know where they are and to get from one place to another, whilst also protecting themselves from harm. In some settings, young children with severe visual impairments are helped in their early mobility by using equipment such as hooples.

There are also important factors that adults control in the organisation of communal play and teaching spaces, such as removing dangerous obstacles and maintaining a certain continuity and predictability in the way in which some areas are laid out. Findings from our own study of social encounters between sighted and visually impaired groups, reported in Chapter 6, suggest that large play areas with scattered toys, frequent changes in layout and the groupings of children increase the amount of time children with limited vision spend locating things or familiarising themselves with their play partners.

Physical activity and orientation

For many children with visual impairments there is an ongoing need to sustain a programme of physical exercise, spatial awareness and mobility training. Paradoxically, as some children with visual impairments get older, there is a tendency to withdraw from physical exercise and to restrict opportunities for developing motor proficiency, co-ordination and general mobility. The evidence we reviewed in Chapter 3 suggests that young people with visual impairments may be less fit, have less body flexibility and poorer balance than their sighted peers, and do far less physical activity. A strong case has been made (see, for example, Stone, 1995) for the systematic teaching of mobility and orientation from early infancy onwards in order to promote the acquisition and extension of competences that are critical for later personal independence.

Whilst mobility training may be felt to be more the province of a specialist, there are many aspects of the ordinary school curriculum for physical education that contribute towards general fitness, mobility, co-ordination, spatial awareness and confidence. Participation in PE also provides opportunities for team work, challenge and competition. A handbook for teachers produced recently by the RNIB suggests that PE is not just about improving children's fitness and assurance to move through space independently, but is also useful for developing concepts in language and mathematics, and for enjoyment (RNIB, 1994). However, one of the reasons why some pupils with severe visual impairments do not take part in regular physical exercise or games activities is that teachers themselves lack confidence about how this should be managed.

For mainstream teachers, a first step is to establish any medical constraints, such as an eye condition, that might affect an individual taking part in PE, and to understand the implications of a visual loss for balance, movement or the use of equipment. When apparatus is being set up or demonstrated, thought will have to be given to the clarity of instructions and to keeping to systematic routines for layout and storage. Safety precautions will need to be gone over thoroughly with all pupils. Children with visual impairments will need time to become familiar with aspects such as changing rooms, as well as reference points within the activity space, such as lane markers or posts. Areas of play, balls, goal areas and team colours will need strong visual definition.

Some activities will be more straightforward to organise than others: small game situations using audible balls with bells, or velcro bat/balls, will be easier than fast-moving, full team games. With assistance and adaptations, such as brightly coloured balls and targets, children with severe visual impairments can learn to project with increasing accuracy. They can take part in a range of dance, athletic activities, swimming, gymnastics and outdoor pursuits. Some of the specific modifications that may be appropriate for these different areas of physical activity are provided in the RNIB guidelines for PE, which cover key stages 1 to 4 (RNIB, 1994).

PURPOSEFUL PLAY ENVIRONMENTS

When children are engaged creatively and imaginatively in play with others they are likely to be achieving a number of things. First, they will be enjoying social contacts, learning to share with others and to understand other people's requests, needs and perspectives. Second, they will be actively involved in exploring some aspects of the physical world, learning about the properties of everyday spaces and the objects and materials that occupy them. Third, they will be using language for communicating, organising and reflecting on their play. Lastly, play provides a vehicle for children to enter imagined worlds and to practise using the symbols, roles, tools and weapons of wider society.

Vision is an important dimension in young children's play. Modelling and imitating the actions of others requires their behaviour to be witnessed. Using objects to symbolise real world artefacts, such as building a moonbuggy with a scientific building kit or a rocket out of a metal construction kit, draws on perceptual similarities recognised through vision. Active play, such as 'tag' or 'hide and seek', is also enabled by seeing the boundaries and physical structures of play spaces. The literature on play, which we discussed briefly in Chapter 3, suggests that children with visual impairments spend much less time than their sighted peers, particularly at the pre-school stage, actively engaged in purposeful play. When they do play, children with visual impairments may be more inclined to inspect or manipulate objects, rather than using them symbolically. They may be more self-contained in their play, involved with their own bodies rather than with other children. We shall be revisiting these assumptions about play patterns in the final chapter, in relation to our own research data.

Some of the reasons for these play differences are to be found in the nature of toys and equipment provided, the attitudes and expectations of adults and peers, and how play is organised and facilitated. Sighted children are often attracted to toys because of their visual appeal and very quickly apprehend a toy's play possibilities, especially if it is representational rather than simply manipulative. In fact, many toys, particularly character dolls, are advertised on the basis that to play with the materials or equipment is to enter into a virtual reality. But for the child with limited vision, the appeal of such materials may be on a different basis from that of sighted peers. The possibilities for imaginative play may become apparent only after a considerable time simply exploring the components, textures and structure of a toy. It is worth trying to anticipate, from the cue sources available to an individual, what the likely appeal (colour, sound, movement, function) of a toy will be.

Many toys are designed to reinforce concepts of shape, colour, pattern and size, or to establish fine manipulative skills (pegboards, post boxes, formboards, shape puzzles). Imaginative, interactive play is more likely to be promoted using toys that can be played with representationally and in partnership. There are many kinds of materials available commercially that can be fitted together to build vehicles, racetracks, space stations, pirate ships, forts or marble mazes. Other toys provide a context for joint imaginative play, such as dolls' houses, kitchen sets, zoos, farmyards, military bases or science fiction replicas. Imitative play, which perhaps holds the greatest potential for stimulating social interaction, can be promoted by small 'stage sets' and 'props', such as a Post Office counter, toy gardening equipment, workbench and tools, kitchen range, grocery shop or take-away, dressing up clothes and hats, finger and glove puppets. It is important that representative toys look and feel like real objects. A child with a visual impairment will be helped to recognise toy kitchen equipment, such as pans, if they are made of metal and not plastic.

Outdoor play areas

Outdoor play settings are very important for schools with children who have some degree of visual impairment, since how these are equipped will influence free movement and adventurous play. Of the schools that took part in the observation studies reported in Chapter 6, none had installed the kind of 'designer' playgrounds advocated by Schneekloth (1989). However, many schools have now discarded potentially dangerous equipment such as swings, and installed more interesting play areas with shock-absorbent surfaces, ropes, cranes, bridges, ladders, walkways and tunnels. Soft play structures and ball parks are particularly good for encouraging boisterous activities and mobility in small children with severe visual losses.

In Schneekloth's study of the effects of play settings on exploration and social interaction, certain conditions promoted the most complex and adventurous play in all children across the ages of 7 to 13 years, regardless of sex or vision. These included the presence of real world objects, such as windows, doors, turnstiles, machinery and old vehicles such as tractors, trailers and boats. Spaces divided into a flexible range of occupiable units, accessed by tunnels, platforms and ladders, also inspired play. Boundaries, routeways, storage places and access points require careful definition through contrasting textures, sounds, materials and colours. For maximum effect, children need careful introduction to the environmental structure and its play possibilities, the cues to locate themselves within it, and reassurance about safety issues. It is important to note, however, that no play environment, albeit well-designed, is a sufficient stimulus of its own accord.

Although children interact more with each other in play sets such as the home corner, these areas also tend to generate more conflict. Resolving conflicts is an important part of learning how to deal with others, but many children, both sighted and visually impaired, will need adult help to negotiate and reach agreement. Adults have an important role in deciding which children will be socially compatible and will make a viable group. They may select materials and activities, bearing in mind how particular children will access them, if they depend on visual features to be understood. They can also 'scaffold' play by suggesting possibilities, providing resources, establishing rules, standing back when groups are playing successfully, but perhaps suggesting new directions when the activity appears to be flagging. The issue of how the adult's behaviour has an impact on the play of children with visual impairments is one we return to in the final chapter.

THE LANGUAGE ENVIRONMENT

A central issue in the development and education of children with visual impairments concerns the relationship between experience, language use and conceptual growth. An extensive literature, which we considered in Chapter 3, highlights some of the ways in which thinking is organised through language, leading to some assumed differences between sighted and visually impaired samples. Most of this published research is concerned with the impact of a visual impairment on the products, rather than the processes, of learning. So, for example, discrepancies have been shown between sighted and visually impaired groups in the development of speech sounds, use of vocabulary, grammar and language functions, such as questioning.

Much has been made of differences in word meanings between sighted and visually impaired groups, sometimes referred to as 'empty language' or 'verbalism'. These terms refer to concepts based on a limited experience of what they represent, such as the language of colours, space and movement, or of distant objects such as the horizon, ceilings, birds or rooftops. If children with reduced vision construct word meanings and conceptual categories based on their own unique patterning of perceptual experience, then one would expect to find differences in the ways in which individuals abstract information, make classifications and extend word meanings from one situation to another.

Most support teachers affirm that this is not an argument for avoiding 'sighted terms', such as references to 'see', 'look', or colour terms, although it may be necessary to be more precise and elaborate in explaining word meanings. However, the most interesting and practically useful ideas stem from a consideration of how these processes operate and how adults can intervene to make a difference. At a number of points in this text we have stressed the important role of adults in bridging between the child's inner world and the environment, helping them to make sense of things in terms they understand, with language as the medium for bringing this about.

Conversation

Some important insights into the most effective strategies for promoting language and conceptual development in all children has come from studies of child-directed speech, or CDS. The review of CDS research in Chapter 3

Helpful

Create a context for conversation

Share activities and experiences that are relevant and meaningful to children's lives

Give commentary on the child's play and activity, show an interest in what the child is doing, help to explore a topic further, make links with previous experiences

Talk with, not at, or for children, providing rich interpretations or descriptions of events

Remember that the key, at all levels, is to share meaning and understanding, taking into account the child's perspective

Encourage the child to question and initiate dialogue

Listen to what the child has to say, allow the child to introduce new topics, read signals of interest and attention

Provide social oil to sustain interaction: 'Hmm, that's really nice . . .'

Expand, clarify and restate the child's intended meaning

Make explicit the basis of adult concepts, explore similarities and differences in the way things are classified

Incorporate some aspect of the child's contribution in the adult's response to ensure topical continuity across turns

Hand conversation back to the child after 'turn', leave time to reply, avoid dominating the conversation

Give personal contributions: 'On our holidays we went . . .', 'I had a surprise today . . .'

Use low control moves to encourage contributions

Less helpful

Deliberate teaching of vocabulary or grammar out of context: 'Today we're going to learn the names of things you find in a bedroom'

Asking for information that the adult already possesses: 'What colour are your shoes?' (test or display questions)

Comments that manage, dominate or control

Overuse of 'open' questions, such as 'What did you do at the weekend?'

Enforced repetition: asking children to imitate a correct model ('Can you say "went", not "goed"?')

Avoid stepping in to improve pronunciation: 'Make a better "s" sound'

Responses that discourage children's exploration and confidence: the focus should be on sustaining engagement and interest in the the world around, making 'bridges' between the child's current understanding and external events

---

Figure 5.1 Key points in conversation strategies

suggests that there may be wide variations in the effects of different adult strategies, with some adult inputs more useful for promoting certain language aspects (but not others) at different ages. However, work such as the Bristol child language studies (Wells, 1987) indicate some generally propitious adult conversation moves. One significant point is that children with sensory impairments seem destined to evoke the least facilitative conversation strategies from adults. The data presented in Chapter 6 from our own research confirm that adult interactions with young children with more severe visual impairments are characterised by an increase in management and control, and a tendency to question or command.

Responsive adults, according to the CDS literature, pattern their encounters with children by responding to the child's apparent interests, providing them with rich, interpretive descriptions of events. They avoid trying to teach, drill or elicit new words. They rarely correct errors in grammar or faulty pronunciation. The adult reflects and develops the child's focus of interest, taking up opportunities for talk related to the child's play and activity, adding new information, interpreting events, making links with prior experiences, clarifying and extending the child's thinking and enquiry. Responsive adults listen with genuine interest to what the child has to say, handing conversation back to the child and inviting a reply. Sentences are tailored to the child's level of understanding, providing a more explicit and elaborate version, just beyond the child's in complexity. A number of examples of this kind of responsiveness were given in Chapter 3, showing how adults may successfully 'lead from behind'.

Strategies that are high in management or control (interrupting, talking for the child, not giving time for turns to be taken, and dominating dialogue) are avoided. Over-use of questions by adults is also inhibiting. Display questions that request information already possessed by the adult, such as names for objects ('What do you think that is?'), leads to a closing down of children's thinking and their engagement as conversation partners. Many children, quite rightly, interpret such questions as requests to speak. Questions are an important means of extending the child's enquiry into new possibilities. Importantly, in the 'passages of intellectual search' described earlier in most family contexts, a great deal of time is spent considering mundane issues, puzzling over inconsistencies and using questions to resolve them. But it is the child who is instrumental in raising queries and interrogating adults, not the other way around.

The family context and language interaction

More directive, intrusive styles of interaction seem to stem from the over-narrow concerns of parents or teachers to practise vocabulary, or the names of objects and actions. Studies of family contexts including blind children show that many parents find effective 'scaffolding' hard to achieve (Conti-Ramsden, 1994). Ideally, children with limited vision require full interpretive descriptions and explanations of surrounding events. They depend on a richness of real-world information to link current interests with prior experiences, more distant people and related occurrences.

Through dialogue, children can be informed about similarities and differences between environmental features and the basis on which adult concepts are constructed. Layers of meaning in vocabulary or phrases can be examined, to iron out any confusions. These processes of linguistic extension and refinement depend on adults helping children with restricted vision to think beyond the immediate focus of interest. Siblings and peers are also important data sources for children with visual impairments, enabling them to capitalise on what others already know about the environment, where things are located, which equipment is available and how it operates, together with aspects such as who could be recruited as play partners. In order to use other children to make sense of things, as an aid to exploration or play, children with visual impairments must be encouraged to take the initiative.

Available research on family contexts indicates that children with restricted vision are actually exposed to much more bald labelling of objects, questions, demands and requests than sighted children (Andersen *et al.*, 1993). They receive fewer descriptions, interpretations, links and explanations of surrounding events. Adults tend not to read the child's focus of interest in order to supply relevant commentary. They tend not to discuss the basis of concepts, such as similarities and differences between objects, animals, people, places or events. Discussions are not usually wide-ranging, but seem to be confined to the child's immediate activity. There are problems establishing topics and maintaining coherent dialogue around a theme of mutual interest. Children are discouraged from taking initiatives by being exposed to more imperatives and directives. Paradoxically, adult conversation strategies seem to inhibit, rather than enlarge, experience through language, requiring children to take passive, respondent roles.

There are a number of suggestions for improving the language and communication environments of family contexts. When introducing a new toy, for example, it will be more productive to describe and demonstrate its properties, rather than simply providing a label. Kekelis and Andersen (1984) suggest that families should risk some 'creative confusion' by engaging their child in elaborate conversations that are more wide-ranging than simply providing names and descriptions for current activities. The most useful input is detailed and takes account of the child's focus of attention, stimulates interest in what others are doing, creates play openings and social contacts, and enriches the terms through which the world is understood.

EXTENDING CONCEPTS

In one example of adult intervention (Harrison and Crow, 1993), a blind child had been told that the object that produced a distinctive noise in the kitchen was a blender. 'That's the blender', Laurie would say on hearing the noise, although she had no idea what a blender was. Much later, having been shown the equipment, put food into the receptacle, felt the vibration of the equipment working and touched the consistency of the blended food, Laurie was very angry at her previous superficial understanding of what the sound represented. The opportunity to explore an object functionally, and to discuss its properties in the context of real experience, brought about more exact understanding.

In another example, provided by Tobin (1993), a 14-year-old girl with very little residual vision was preparing for the school's Christmas party. Mary was asked by her teacher to put some loaves of bread on the dining room tables, but she complained that no bread had been given to her, despite the four unwrapped crusty loaves she was holding. For Mary, loaves were pre-sliced objects covered in greaseproof paper.

Occasions like the above, when mismatches are exposed between the child's concepts and those of other language-users, provide opportunities for the adult to supply further information and to extend the child's conceptual range. For sighted children, vision provides much of the information required for concept extension and class inclusion or exclusion. An apple, for instance, may take several forms: wrapped in plastic bags in supermarkets, toffee apples at a leisure park, windfalls on a garden path. There are sufficient visual features in common for the family resemblances of these apples to be quickly appreciated. However, reduce an apple to pulp in a blender and many sighted children will require connections to be made explicit. The principle at work here is enabling children, especially when visual information is reduced, to experience the notion of 'apple' in many different ways. For a child with a severe visual impairment, this might include picking, feeling, tasting, smelling, slicing and cooking apples, so that there is some awareness of the many attributes through which an apple is defined.

The data on conceptual development, reviewed in Chapter 3, suggest that the most vulnerable areas of experience for children with visual impairments are those pertaining to the physical world (object permanence, cause and effect, time and space); social cognition (roles, relationships and moral judgements); together with more abstract problem-solving (formal areas of the school curriculum). There are many creative ways in which adults can support a child's learning through concrete and direct experience in order to avoid gaps and confusions. If a child's only experience of zoo animals has come from handling plastic replicas, for example, it would not be surprising if there were serious misunderstandings about the respective size, sounds, temperament and skin textures of real animals.

We are not advocating that children must always find out about the nature and quality of things by being able to touch and manipulate them at close quarters, but it should be possible to plan first-hand encounters with lizards, worms, gerbils, cockerels, sheep and even elephants, so that aspects of size, shape, movement, texture, warmth and smell are made real.

In school contexts, particularly, language acts as a substitute for missing visual input. What this means for teachers and classroom assistants is the provision of detailed descriptions and explanations about what is happening and what other people are doing. Pupils with limited vision may be unable to see gestures or facial expressions clearly, which often clarify a speaker's intentions. Instructions that lack specificity ('Take this over there to the others') may be far less helpful than more precise directions ('Take the red metal stapler to the writing corner where Venus and Ashraf are fixing the notepads').

Adults can make explicit the basis on which sighted people construct categories and classify things, identifying similarities and differences. Practical, hands-on experiences enable children to supplement their understanding. For example, during one classroom activity where sighted pupils talked about animals that live in the sea, a blind child was provided with the skeleton of a fish to feel, together with shells, starfish and a live eel in a bowl. We shall be considering further examples of the use of 'hands-on' experience together with other ways of presenting and working over topics in differentiating the school curriculum later in this chapter.

TRANSITION FROM HOME TO SCHOOL

Potentially, the language environments of both the home and the school can be intensive, wide-ranging in scope, providing endless opportunities for adults and children to enjoy sustained interactions around shared issues. For all children, sighted and visually impaired, the move from family to school contexts may herald a reduction in the frequency, quality, duration and purpose of conversational interaction. Some children are more vulnerable to these changes as they move from one context to another. In Chapter 3, where we reviewed the research on home–school transition, we saw that persistent questioners at home sometimes became very subdued in school. Here, too, many of the key issues for promoting classroom language depend on management and control.

There are many strategies for easing transition from one context to another. In the support service for the visually impaired where one of the authors is employed, families meet together on a regular basis when children of all ages take part in activities such as horse-riding, tap-dancing, skating and trips to the theatre or museum. These activities not only help with children's mobility, independence, confidence and wider experience of new settings, but they also provide an opportunity for parents to share concerns about school placements, to exchange insights, and to meet informally with teachers.

Introductions to a new school can be gradually phased, with a number of visits before entry, when the physical layout of buildings and routeways can be explored. There may be an opportunity to join in the class routines of registration, breaktime or lunch in advance. Some schools encourage the 'adoption' of a child with impaired vision by an older and sympathetic pupil who is available in the first few months to 'show the ropes'. For younger children, keeping a scrapbook of interesting activities out of school, including photographs and artefacts such as tickets, brochures or souvenirs, can provide a stimulus for conversation and discussion with classmates and teachers. Similarly, a home–school diary that goes backwards and forwards with the child provides a basis for sharing main activities enjoyed during the school day, or impending events at home, and openings for less formal conversational interaction.

ENHANCING CLASSROOM LANGUAGE ENVIRONMENTS

Dialogue is put to many uses in the classroom. Teachers use their verbal interactions with pupils to present information, instruct, admonish, check out what children know, praise or review, and to develop children's thinking. When teachers deliberately shift their conversation styles to include more informal, low control strategies (personal contributions, interpretive commentary, phatic responses), there can be a dramatic increase in the spontaneous contributions made by the child.

Strategies that have an inhibitory effect include interrupting the flow of conversation to correct faulty pronunciation and grammar, and the extensive use of questions to check out children's retention of information. One commonly reported teacher-managed sequence of events is the classroom exchange structure known as I-R-F: Initiation of a question by the teacher, which elicits a Response by a pupil, followed by evaluative comments or Feedback from the teacher. 'Ground rules' such as these, which we considered briefly in Chapter 3, create expectations in both pupils and teachers about the constrained nature and prescribed form of classroom problem-solving.

Wood (1992) has recently taken up this theme of teacher language styles and the effect on all children's learning. Contrary to popular belief, he feels that most of the dialogues that teachers hold with pupils do not promote reflection, analysis and enquiry, or sustain interest and motivation. In fact, Wood argues, most verbal encounters in the classroom are low in intellectual challenge, and most questions asked by teachers are closed, factual questions with known, right answers. Teachers get to ask practically all the questions, whilst students strive to provide the answers. Typically, teachers usually give pupils around one second of 'wait' time in which to formulate and produce a reply. Simply increasing 'wait' time in itself promotes more effective classroom dialogue.

The features of classroom discourse that affect children's participation in classroom talk have been summarised in Figure 5.2. These apply to mainstream pupils generally, across the age range 3 to 17 years, but they also have important implications for pupils with visual impairments. Teachers whose interactions are high in 'power' or 'control' are those who pose most questions, who try to repair and improve on what children say, and who have a rapid 'turn rate'. What this last factor means is that each participant's contri-

Features of teachers' style

- Pose frequent questions (especially closed or display questions)
- Frequent repair (checking, asking for repetition or improvements)
- Frequent demands
- Fast turn rate or pace
- Low in sentence complexity

Effects on pupils' responses

- Few questions
- Few elaborations or additional comments
- Low take-up of opportunities to contribute
- Few interactions with peers
- Many misunderstandings
- Low initiative
- Short responses

Figure 5.2 Classroom discourse: features and effects

bution tends to be very short. Wood suggests some alternative strategies. These include teachers giving their own thoughts and ideas to children, speculating, suggesting, surmising, interpreting, illustrating, listening, planning with, sharing and acknowledging what children have to say. These features create an atmosphere in which classrooms are concerned with raising hypotheses and testing these out in a shared spirit of problem-solving, where 'showing' and 'telling' replace 'demanding' and 'asking'.

THE PHYSICAL ENVIRONMENT OF THE SCHOOL

At home, children learn to find their way around fairly quickly, to locate toys and other objects, especially if living and storage spaces are not changed around too much. Other environments, such as school buildings, may be much more demanding for a child with a visual impairment. Although it is unrealistic to think of entirely restructuring environments, there are some fairly straightforward measures that will help pupils to move around independently, improve safety and facilitate learning.

Safe, independent mobility requires individuals to learn how to act on the environment in a purposeful way, and to negotiate unexpected hazards. However, for children with severe visual impairments becoming familiar with new surroundings, an orderly and predictable physical environment helps to build confidence. Low-level objects can be a hazard to any pupil, but more so for individuals with restricted vision. Refuse bags left in corridors, fire extinguishers, briefcases or bags, extension leads and trailing flexes from electrical equipment are all potential dangers, especially in poor lighting conditions. Partly opened doors are difficult to detect by listening and feeling, whilst windows that open outwards at head level are especially dangerous. Other objects that can be hazardous include radiators, protruding notice-boards, milkcrates, wastepaper bins, sharp-edged pieces of furniture, and other objects left unexpectedly in thoroughfares.

Some visual impairments, such as poor peripheral vision or monocular vision, create more problems for environmental awareness than others. Imagine a blind child entering a room and the perceptual information that is likely to be attended to. Much of this will arise from what can be felt underfoot, together with tactile information from exploring with the hands. Anticipate what will be encountered as the child's routes around the school are negoti-ated. A radiator or fish tank with a gurgling pump may give useful information to the child along a route, whilst sharp edges, unmarked steps or wall-mounted objects at head height could prove dangerous.

Features can be added to walls and floor surfaces to help individuals with little or no sight to find their way about, especially through corridors and spaces that provide little continuity of hand or foot clues. Metal strips give visual and auditory clues to help locate entrances. Non-slip mats can be used to warn of doors across a corridor, junctions in a thoroughfare, or the top of a stairwell. A series of mats can mark a route across a large, open area such as a hall. Fixed floor matting can be installed at important points, such as steps, to provide permanent clues. Suitable surfaces that will not ruck or slip are rubberised flooring, cork tiles or nylon grass. Texture strips on walls and floors may be helpful, whilst other spaces may need to be kept clear and other objects moved. In outside areas, there may be other hazards at head height, such as tree branches, signs, brackets and building projections. Landmarks can be installed such as raised flowerbeds and borders. Advice from a specialist teacher will be important to create good working environments for a child with a visual impairment, and to examine the different areas of a school that the child will have access to.

IMPROVING THE VISUAL ENVIRONMENT

When trying to assess the visual demands made by different environments, it is useful to identify the clues that children may be able to use as they move around, and how the surroundings help or hinder people. The RNIB suggests using blindfolds or looking through 'bubblewrap' when assessing environ-ments for people with visual impairments (RNIB, 1995c). Lighting and decor are the two main considerations in improving the visual environment.

A point we made in Chapter 2 is that the effects of different visual impair-ments can be very specific. Some conditions affect vision in low lighting levels, over distances, or over certain parts of the visual field. Some children func-tion better in slightly lower light levels than normal; others require good overall levels of illumination and task-lighting for more visually demanding work. Photophobic, or light-sensitive children, for example, will find it difficult to work in bright light or glare, to listen to a teacher who is silhouetted against a light source, or to see displays and notices positioned against the bright light of windows.

Two functions of lighting are normally considered in school settings: environmental and task-lighting. Environmental illumination is often from a central source, such as a ceiling-mounted fluorescent strip, which provides a wide arc of light around much of the room. Insufficient central lighting, such as from a single ceiling bulb, creates hard shadows. The sun is another source of environmental light, but this can be difficult to control. Glare is created by sunlight being scattered through dirty windows, which can be avoided by keeping windows clean and by fitting blinds. Task-lighting is required for specific, more focused armchair or desktop activities, such as a spot lamp for reading.

In special schools for children with visual impairments, environmental lighting levels are usually slightly higher than normal, especially in areas that might cause problems, such as stairways. Overhead lighting is often recessed into sloping panels, and spotlights are used for illuminating specific areas. Windows in classrooms almost always have curtains and blinds. In mainstream school settings where it is not practical to adjust lighting, visual clarity can often be improved by increasing contrasts.

Most school environments are full of visual ambiguities: an aluminium door handle merges into a white door, light switches the same cream colour as the wall, print that does not stand out from the page on notices, steps with no distinct edge. Coloured doors in contrasting frames will be much easier to find than white doors in white frames. Border strips on walls or stairs provide both visual and tactile clues. A red light switch will serve to define both the switch and the wall. Colour contrasts in walls, carpets and doors provide outline and definition to objects and spaces for people relying on limited vision.

Task-lighting can be carefully tailored to individual pupil's needs using specialised desk lamps and spotlights. Good task-lighting has flexible mountings so that the light can be positioned to illuminate an activity in the best position for the user. The lamp should be designed to minimise glare from the bulb and so that the heat from the light is not uncomfortable. All lamps have to be plugged in somewhere, which limits the situations in which they can be used, although the hazard of trailing wires can be reduced through brightly coloured flex, plugs and sockets that children can locate.

When a child is working at a desk or table, it is important that the lamp is positioned so that light falls on the work surface without casting shadows from parts of the child's body and without creating glare by being tilted towards the child's face or reflected from a polished surface. Good positioning includes lamps placed just behind the child's left shoulder (for a right-handed child), or in front of and above the child, but tilted away from the face. The amount of light arriving at a work surface will also depend on the texture and colours of the walls, ceiling and floors in a room.

Glare, shadows and reflections from different surfaces also affect working conditions and may be more of a problem than insufficient light to people with reduced sight. Surfaces painted in white gloss will reflect most of the light falling on them. The texture of surfaces such as brick walls, tiled or formica worktops and wooden floors also affects the amount of reflected light. Shiny floors and worktops are not recommended. Blackboards should have a matt green or black finish and be angled slightly downwards so that light from the ceiling is not reflected; white or yellow chalk should be used.

Conditions for children with visual impairments will need to be checked out for each individual. However, providing visual environments that are clear and unambiguous, with flexible and appropriate lighting and contrasting decor that serves to define different areas, will enhance learning conditions for all children, both sighted and visually impaired.

CLASSROOM ORGANISATION

Good classroom organisation stems from an awareness of the ways in which children with visual impairments relate to and use their surroundings. The daily landscape of the curriculum depends on a certain amount of routine and pattern: balance of group work and individual learning activities, use of books and equipment, how resources are stored and accessed, areas for 'circle time' and review.

Children with visual impairments need to explore the classroom to find out where different activities take place, or where equipment is stored, and to become familiar with routines. Locating and using equipment without too much difficulty demands that materials are kept consistently in identified locations, with some thought given to how different work spaces are set out and equipped. It will be time-wasting and frustrating for a visually impaired child to be dependent on others to search jumbled drawers and cupboards on their behalf.

We have mentioned that decor, using strong colour contrasts, is a good way of emphasising different focal points in a room. Personal independence and a maximum use of children's residual vision are both encouraged in classrooms where there are clearly located areas, stimulating visual displays and explicit means of organisation. Noticeboards, classroom charters, alphabet friezes, montages of children's work, posters, murals and other visual material can be mounted at eye level for closer inspection. Resources, trays, cupboards, drawers and resource banks should be clearly labelled in large print, or in braille.

In primary classrooms, different activity areas can also be screened, decorated in contrasting colours and signposted, such as writing areas, computer or listening centres, library and references corners, areas for play equipment or construction toys. Colour coding may be useful for certain resources, and is widely used in many schools to denote the readability levels of books. How visual material is organised for display is of particular importance in busy teaching areas. We have already considered some of the factors that contribute towards improving the general visual environment, such as lighting, decor and glare. Here we are concerned with how a teaching context can be both visually accessible and stimulating, in ways that encourage all pupils to use visual information for learning. Overcrowding a wall space is often much less effective than a more limited amount of material, strikingly mounted. Wall-mounted material can include both tactile and visual interest. One group working on insects produced models of bees, dragonflies and their habitat, using a mixture of fabrics, egg-boxes and plastic bin-liners. Another class, following an enquiry into Egyptian culture, created large wall engravings using a range of tactile materials such as shells, beads, wooden offcuts, aluminium foil, container lids and bottletops.

Some of the equipment that may be required for children with visual impairments is bulky and requires space for storage, such as braillers, tape recorders, magnifiers, word processors and CCTV. The child's work position is also important. Working on material at desk height may produce a tiring, hunched position as the child strains to get close enough to see details. For near tasks, the surface of a worktop could be raised at an angle so that material is brought closer to the child, rather than the child having to bend over to see. Portable deskstands are available which can be adjusted for height and angle. With a sloping work surface, consideration then has to be given to how a pupil holds material to the surface and stores pens and other equipment. Some worktops have adjustable clips, bars or magnets to hold paper, whilst implements can be stored on a lip or tray. Work surfaces for many pupils may need to be much larger than usual, for example if tactile diagrams, large-print books or braille writing equipment are being used. Some worktops have a matt green covering to reduce glare and reflection.

A question many mainstream teachers ask is where a child with a visual impairment should be positioned within the classroom to facilitate learning. Several factors will need to be taken into account, depending on the physical constraints of a particular teaching area, and the curriculum demands on the pupil concerned. Some aspects will be fixed: use of CCTV, desk lamps or word processor requires access to electric sockets, which are frequently wall-mounted. Positions may also be dictated by the natural light from a window, which pupils may prefer to keep behind them. If task lighting is required, situations will need to be selected that avoid glare or reflected light from shiny surfaces. If the teacher's style of working involves writing on the blackboard or classroom discussion, when it would be helpful to see the blackboard and to hear the contributions made by other pupils, then positions near to the visual displays or speakers can be adopted.

VISUAL ENVIRONMENTS AND INDIVIDUAL NEEDS

Teachers who have pupils with visual impairments in their classes are sometimes uncertain about some basic issues, such as whether children wearing glasses should rest their eyes, and whether getting too close to printed material or reading in poor light can be harmful. There used to be the view, since discredited, that restricting the use of whatever residual vision a child had would thereby conserve it. In fact, children can be trained to make the most of their residual vision, and although this may be tiring, sight cannot be worn out through use.

Enhancing lighting conditions depends on the needs of the child concerned. For light-sensitive children, overall illumination levels may need to be reduced, though task-lighting and the elimination of glare can contribute markedly to the effective use of vision. Getting very close to visual material is one way of enlarging it. This practice is not harmful in itself, though there may be long-term consequences for body posture.

Not all children with visual impairments can derive benefit from wearing spectacles, but all those children who have been prescribed spectacles should be known to all relevant teachers. Obviously, glasses or contact lenses do not cure a visual condition but they do give appropriate correction whilst they are being worn. It is important to ensure that glasses are kept clean and worn at all appropriate times. Because levels of vision may change, it is important that appointments are kept for regular reviews.

There are some commonsense considerations with regard to eyecare and visual environments for all children. Wearing safety goggles is an imperative in workshops or laboratories involving activities such as drilling or sanding, or substances such as bleach, glue or ovencleaner.

THE AUDITORY ENVIRONMENT

Sounds are a valuable source of information for all individuals with visual impairments, enabling them to understand what is happening and to orientate to the surroundings. For example, a classroom door opens and a person enters, moving to a particular location in the room in order to carry out a task, before leaving. Sounds inform a child dependent on listening that a projector screen has been set up and extended, and an OHP plugged in and switched on. In other contexts, a blind child may clap whilst walking in order to receive information about obstacles through sound reflection.

The ability to attend to sound stimuli, ignore competing sound distractions and make sense of events involves a complex hierarchy of skills that depend on experience and training. Utilising sound information is made much easier in good conditions for listening with controlled noise levels. Both an over-noisy, reverberant environment, and an environment that absorbs too much sound, would prevent children with visual impairments from using their hearing to make sense of what is going on around them.

Good listening conditions are achieved in two main ways. The first is by keeping out unwanted sound. A room that is regularly invaded by noise from heavy road traffic, an upstairs workshop, adjoining dance studio or gymnasium, or voices and clattering feet from a busy corridor, will be much less conducive to listening. Whilst double-glazing and sound-proofing may be beyond the resources of many schools, some thought can be given to the siting of rooms and any likely noise sources, when the timetable is planned. The second consideration is the reduction of noise within a room. Concrete posts, hard floors, high ceilings, breezeblock walls and wooden cladding reflect sound and prolong sound interference. In a large space, room-dividers or large pieces of furniture can be used to create smaller 'sound areas'. If these are covered in contrasting colours for mobility clues, they will also help children to gain useful information about sound sources within the area.

Choice of seating position away from well-used noise sources such as sinks, cupboards or passageways also helps children to listen more attentively. Present-day classes are often grouped around tables, rather than set in rows, whilst the teacher may move around freely. Pupils with useful vision should be able to work in positions where they can see and hear easily. In order to follow a demon-stration or blackboard presentation, positions in close proximity to the speaker are necessary. Good classroom positions will need to take account of both listening and visual factors, such as lighting and decor, for individual pupils.

It is important for children to be involved in determining what, for them, appear to be conducive arrangements for looking and listening. Large, open-plan, busy classrooms may be very noisy and confusing places to children with visual impairments, where the origins of sound sources are difficult to locate. Well-designed spaces, screened or divided into areas, are more easily understood. An interesting sound environment provides discrete, identifiable sounds, and these are helpful for orientation by indicating the direction and distance of features.

A programme of listening activities can be introduced for young children to practise skills in locating and identifying sounds. Fixed sounds that recur in the same place help to establish reference points, such as a bead curtain in an entranceway, a wind-chime near a window or a ticking clock above a door. Children can practise locating themselves in an environment in rela-tion to sounds such as a hamster racing around its exercise wheel, a bubbling fishtank or the tinkling of a mobile. Attention can be drawn to naturally occurring environmental sounds, such as a passing siren, office telephone, or worker in the vicinity. Activities can be introduced such as identifying different objects and activities, using tape recordings of frying food, running water, photocopier, microwave, kitchen timer, telephone, washing machine, kettle coming to the boil, or alarm clock.

THE LITERACY ENVIRONMENT

Being able to access and manipulate information is important to all pupils, but for children with visual impairments, early mastery of written language is an important component of language and conceptual development, as well as the determining factor in terms of optimal educational achievement.

Current thinking views reading and writing as integrated processes that should not be taught in isolation from the child's wider experiences of language, communication or the curriculum (Webster *et al.*, 1996a). Early literacy helps children to think about the structure, organisation and function of language, and is a means of developing vocabulary and understanding. Literacy also embraces a set of skills that enable individuals to tackle subject-specific tasks in science, history, food technology and mathematics. Later on, literacy enables individuals to operate effectively at work and in the community, to access services and entitlements, and to be included in society's everyday transactions, information networks and cultural events.

Early exposure to written language may be much more fragmented and infrequent for children with limited vision than for the majority of their sighted peers, leading in some instances to children arriving in school with a very limited repertoire of literacy experience and behaviour, and perhaps only barely formed ideas about the relationship between speech and print. For most sighted children, exposure to a wide range of written signs, symbols and text formats begins in early infancy and is often incidental, as notices, labels and instructions are encountered in everyday settings. For example, one of the authors' pre-school children, noticing the engraving on a letter box, surmised: 'That says "letters".' In another context, the same child referred to a price tag, whilst queuing at a supermarket checkout, and remarked: 'Special offer'. Sighted children's growing awareness of print, how it works and what it signifies is intercalated with the 'here and now' of their daily lives. Enhancing the literacy environment for children with visual impairments starts at home.

Strong family environments for promoting literacy in children with limited vision include a wide selection of written resources, big-print signs and labels, 'feely books' and tactile materials. For story-reading with very young children, support teachers recommend 'book bags' containing objects from a picture-book which can be explored and used as props to act out the story as it unfolds. Other picture books can be given a tactile dimension by having objects stuck onto pages. Book-making around a child's interests and familiar world can include finger holes, 'pop-ups' and materials of contrasting textures.

In early shared reading activities, some attention can be given to book behaviour, such as handling books, turning pages, moving from left to right, and identifying headings and page numbers, areas of picture or of text. For children who have very severe visual impairments, pre-braille activities can be introduced at home, such as using a raised line drawing kit for drawing and scribbling. Children can also be introduced to braille writers and encouraged to make 'dotty pictures', to 'pretend write' letters or stories, in the same way that sighted children scribble. Practice can be given tracking along a line of braille, finding gaps in a line, locating and discriminating between lines. Braille letters and overlays can be incorporated into existing texts. Children can dictate picture captions or stories, which can then be produced in braille.

Some of the family's everyday occasions for using print can be shared with children in braille or enlarged text, such as shopping lists, notes, cards, thank you letters, recipes and invitations. For all children, however, it is the quality of interaction with reading partners around text that creates the most positive shared reading encounter.

To start with, the adult may want to read a story whilst the child tracks the braille, examines the tactile features or follows the print. There may be discussion of characters or plot, and predictions about what happens next, providing as many practical experiences or illustrations as possible to understand the events portrayed. Children very quickly want to identify parts of the text that carry meaning. Good reading partners respond to children's efforts to make sense of print, helping them to ask questions about text, drawing on their own experience of stories or of reality. In the early stages, reading errors are corrected only if the meaning is likely to miscarry. However, this may be a useful occasion for drawing attention to any conceptual anomalies, such as drawing distinctions between tigers in zoos and those that turn up for tea parties in children's storybooks!

We know from evidence such as the Bristol child language studies (Wells, 1987), referred to in Chapter 3, that growing up in a literate family environment in which reading and writing are daily occurrences, and where stories are frequently shared, is a factor highly associated with later academic success in school. Shared reading enables children with visual impairments to enter other possible worlds, to examine how stories represent events, to shape their feelings and organise their thoughts.

LITERACY AND THE PRIMARY CLASSROOM

For educationally blind children, braille is the most widely used means of reading and writing. Although braille activities can occur in the classroom whenever sighted children are involved in activities of reading or writing, the educationally blind child may need extra time to develop braille skills or even pre-braille skills, such as finger dexterity and fine tactile discrimination. An important role of classroom assistants, where these are provided for children with severe visual impairments in mainstream groups, is to support the use of braille. Some technical points for braille learners may need to be clarified with a specialist support teacher. For example, the sequence for acquiring braille letters may not follow the scheme drawn up for work on the alphabet or 'phonics' by an infant group. A child learning braille contractions for 'th' and 'the' (which are different) may be confused by a class lesson based around 'th' word structures for sighted children.

'Print-rich' environments are characterised by a diversity of resources and literacy events, which may also incorporate large print and braille. Book areas should be attractive, well stocked and well organised. Contrasts, textures, lighting and dual print/braille labelling can help to create book displays that inform and inspire children with visual impairments, highlighting authors, illustrators, themes and genres. A variety of scripts, text formats and community languages should be available, including books written and made by children. Books can be displayed with their front covers visible, whilst non-fiction can be extracted, labelled and displayed separately according to subject or topic, or current interest domains. Other aspects to consider include book-fairs, events with visiting authors, illustrators and professional storytellers, and times when parents can come into groups to read.

Book selection criteria should include intrinsic quality of text, presentation and cultural relevance to children's lives. However, one important consideration for children with limited sight is that books that rely heavily on illustrations for comprehension may limit accessibility. For example, a number of books in reading schemes finish with text such as 'Oh No!', where the meaning has to be deduced from the picture. For much of the 5 to 11 age range, some readability guidance will be necessary to ensure that children choose books that match their competence; this too can be coded in braille or large print.

Collections of favourite books, such as picture books with tactile features or braille captions, are useful for encouraging independence and enjoyment, even for the most immature readers. CD-ROMs, taped books and headsets are also valuable resources for children with visual impairments. Using 'big books' is a way of including children with limited vision in a whole class reading activity. Important, too, are opportunities for shared or paired reading between sighted pupils and their visually impaired peers, and activities such as re-drafting and reviewing one another's written work. The important point to convey, in every aspect of the literacy environment, is that the school is an inclusive community of readers and writers.

'Print-rich' environments also include the clear print/braille labelling of cupboards, trays, drawers and resource banks. Activity or play areas in infant classes often contain literacy materials and artefacts, such as telephone directories and Yellow Pages, notepads, calendars, pens, bills, junkmail, catalogues, magazines and newspapers, which also need clear labels.

Writing areas should contain suitable worktops and task-lighting, a variety of writing implements, a range of coloured paper, envelopes, cards, stapler, adhesive tape and paper clips, word processing facilities and concept keyboards and, where appropriate, a 'braille 'n' print' machine (produces a print version of whatever a child writes in braille). A bulletin board may mount children's messages, jokes, memos, stories, postcards, invitations or announcements. Younger children may also need access to alphabet friezes, magnetic letters and letter templates.

Handwriting and letter formation can be problematical for children with certain visual conditions, such as nystagmus or a narrow visual field, leading to difficulties in seeing whole words. Dark-lined paper may be a help for children in seeing the position of ascenders and descenders. Some children may also prefer to work with dark blue smudge-free pens on cream or matt white paper, avoiding pens or pencils that produce a shiny line. Some guidelines on the teaching of handwriting to children with visual impairments has recently been provided by Arter *et al.* (1996).

ACCESSING THE WIDER CURRICULUM

For many pupils with visual impairments, a careful balance has to be achieved in covering a broad academic curriculum, whilst also paying attention to more specialised curricular needs, such as social independence, mobility, and learning keyboard or computing skills, and possibly braille. How an individual plan is negotiated, implemented and reviewed will depend very much on the individual needs of the pupil concerned and the resources available to a school, in particular the amount of additional adult classroom assistance. These planning and resources issues, currently shaped by the Code of Practice, were discussed in some detail in Chapter 4.

In this section we highlight some of the adaptations that can be made for pupils with restricted vision in some important areas of the school curriculum. Flexible, multi-layered approaches to teaching, using a range of approaches to meet individual needs, lie at the heart of inclusive education. Differentiation means recognising the differences in learners and devising activities that enable pupils to learn at different rates, at different levels, using a range of strategies and resources for their support. However, differentiation of teaching is not easily achieved and requires a great deal of planning and organisation. A significant issue, intrinsic to realising the goals of lifelong learning referred to previously, is the degree to which pupils can be involved in determining their own learning needs.

Planning for differentiation

Differentiation can be planned for at both whole school level and at the level of the classroom. In the primary school, decisions will need to be made about the suitability of classgroups and working conditions for a child with a visual loss. At the secondary phase, a support teacher may work with department heads to make decisions about the appropriateness of courses for a pupil with a severe visual impairment in terms of relevance, examinations and vocational options.

In the classroom, there are a number of ways in which differentiation can be approached. In the first place, it can be considered in relation to teaching styles, i.e. the ways in which teachers present information to pupils, how tasks are set and the pace and complexity of concepts. In the second place, differentiation can be considered in relation to how pupils are asked to carry out their work, i.e. pupil groupings, classroom interactions, use of information technology and feedback and help during learning. Finally, differentiation is also achieved through outcomes or responses, i.e. the way in which students show the results of their learning, including different formats for presentation, recording and assessment.

Whole school issues
Suitability of classgroups (academic level, social mix)
Appropriate working conditions (physical layout, lighting, equipment)
Relevant course options (including examinations)
Balance of social, academic, vocational factors
Additional classroom support
Staff development and training

Teaching styles and presentation
Pre-tutoring
Study outlines and guides, supporting notes
'Hands-on' experience (visits, artefacts, music, tools and implements)
Low vision aids (magnifiers, reducers, exposure devices)
Print access (CCTV, Optical Character Recognition)
Use of language (clarity, specificity, technical jargon, interpretative
    description, conceptual links)
Visual presentation (blackboard/whiteboard, print size and contrasts)
Reprographics (print size and clarity, tactile diagrams, enlarging photo-
    copier)
Pace and information-load of lessons

Ways of working
Classroom organisation factors (layout, storage, working conditions,
    lighting)
Listening and viewing position
Technology (alternative keyboards, word processing, microwriters, dual
    print/braille machines)
Recording (variable speed tape machines, tone/voice indexing)
Paired work (study 'buddies', reading and writing partners)
Group work (writing/investigative crews)
Classroom assistance (voluntary/specialist)
Classroom dialogue (questioning, scaffolding)

Learning outcomes
Multi-media formats for displaying finished work
Using IT for presentation
Post-tutoring (concept clarification and reinforcement)
Portfolios of achievement (including self-assessment)

Figure 5.3 Planning for differentiation

TEACHING STYLES AND PRESENTATION

Many areas of the curriculum at primary and secondary level can be made more accessible by attending, in the first place, to presentation. Adaptations to subject areas such as English, humanities or RE will involve more elaborate verbal descriptions, explanations and instructions. When topics are planned, thought can be given to the demands that are likely to be made on pupils. What can be considered is the size of a task and the amount of a topic that can realistically be completed. Issues such as the level of language complexity, familiarity of vocabulary, concepts and any technical information can be discussed, so that any unnecessary jargon terms, unusual or confusing terminology can be modified.

Where pupils are able to utilise some information in written form, the way in which this is produced will have an impact on accessibility, accurate comprehension and speed of working. Typed material will be easier to read if enlarged and scanned into specialised equipment for automatic transcription of print. Print size and contrast are important for reading. Black on cream or white is usually best. Overprinting on pictures, diagrams or coloured paper is to be avoided, although many school texts, such as science coursebooks, are now produced like this. Zoom photocopiers or magnifying lenses are useful for enlarging print, which we consider later in this chapter. Small amounts of information, on diagrams for example, can be supplemented by taped commentary. Blackboard work is likely to be visible only if yellow or white chalk is used on a clean matt black or green surface. Whiteboards also give good contrast but suffer from glare. Many pupils will learn more effectively when lessons are supported with written summaries, lesson organisers, learning maps or concept posters. (For detailed examples, see Webster *et al.*, 1996b.)

Many pupils with visual impairments will prefer to explore information orally with a discussion component to their learning, perhaps working through tasks in pairs. At various points in this chapter we have emphasised the need for verbal descriptions to be specific, rich and interpretive, and to link concepts, wherever possible, to practical, hands-on experience. Every subject area in the secondary school introduces pupils to different technical terms, to specific ways of organising and analysing information, and to special forms of thinking and enquiry.

In mathematics and science, for example, early restrictions in experience may have led to gaps in understanding of terms such as 'equal to', 'more'/'less', 'increase'/'reduce', 'greater'/'fewer', 'same'/'different', 'true'/'false'. Language relating to science and maths concepts requires careful explanation and discussion, tying terms to practical experience, wherever possible, and requiring ongoing consistency in classroom usage. Technical terms, forms and functions of writing, and ways of accessing and recording data vary widely from the science laboratory to the design studio or technology workshop. The problems that people address, research and discuss in history are different to those addressed in drama, food technology or PSE.

Many pupils may not understand the language of instruction: 'Place in order of preference'; 'Transfer this diagram into your folder'; 'Identify the odd man out'; 'Evaluate the relative merits of . . .'. For many pupils with visual impairments, there may be misunderstandings about technical terms and unfamiliar vocabulary, as well as a general difficulty in dealing with abstract linguistic usage. All pupils will benefit from careful explanation of technical terms, unfamiliar vocabulary or subject usages, making bridges with pupils' previous experience or knowledge in other subject areas.

Pre- and post-tutoring

Many pupils with individual needs benefit greatly from pre-tutoring (preparing for a lesson beforehand) or post-tutoring (reviewing key points afterwards). This is often difficult to organise, given timetable constraints and resource limitations, and is probably most useful for older pupils following a subject-based curriculum who spend only a part of their time in mainstream groups with additional adult help.

Pre-tutoring can be invaluable for enabling a youngster to participate effectively in a key lesson in humanities or English, where there is a lot of written or verbal material to cover. This can be worked over in advance with a support teacher to give a preview of content, iron out any misunderstandings and provide a foundation for learning. A pre-tutoring session can also provide the opportunity to work on skills such as finding one's way around a textbook, including using index, contents, glossaries, pictures, captions, headings, subheadings and other forms of cross-reference. There may be a specific task ahead, such as constructing a pie chart or interpreting a bar diagram, that can be rehearsed, and any special materials, such as a tactile diagram, introduced. A pre-tutoring session is an important opportunity to think with pupils about their learning needs, how they plan to organise their work and tackle tasks effectively, in which sequence and at what pace.

A post-tutoring session gives an opportunity to go over key concepts and processes, discuss what went well or was particularly difficult, and examine the quality of any work produced. Any gaps or shaky areas of understanding can be covered in more detail and further explanations given. An important aspect of post-tutoring is that students identify for themselves what additional help they need and how to adjust their approach to learning. Self-evaluation and independence are therefore keynotes, although a teacher will obviously use these sessions to help make decisions about the degree of additional help indicated across the curriculum to foster confidence and success. In terms of lifetime learning, these occasions reinforce the sense in which pupils take responsibility for aspects of their own organisation, timekeeping, direction and motivation, i.e. learning how to learn.

'Hands-on' experience

The greatest impact on learners is often achieved by marking out a topic area through real-life or participatory experiences. It is important that pupils with restricted vision do not always have to rely on descriptions provided by others, which then have to be remembered. In any case, how a child constructs personal memories from evidence such as smells, tastes, shapes, textures and sounds may be very different from that of a fully sighted individual. Actual visits to farms, foundries, art galleries, airports, building sites, factories, docks and bus depots, excavations, museums, monuments, graveyards and studios will provide much more meaningful encounters as a basis for learning.

Some processes in a mathematics scheme of work may be difficult to illustrate for pupils with poor vision. Concepts of time, distance, quantity or estimation may require a practical element for full comprehension, such as estimating time to cover a prescribed route around the school and then pacing or timing it. Science processes such as conservation may require some ingenuity for demonstration, such as pouring sand (rather than liquid) from one shape of container to another.

Inevitably, there will be some areas of experience that cannot be accessed directly: one of the origins of conceptual confusions that we discussed in Chapter 3. It may be impossible for some pupils to experience many distant, fragile, transitory or dangerous phenomena and objects travelling at speed. A science experiment involving the close visual monitoring of chemical reactions may require close supervision, whilst projects involving dissection or use of a microscope may also prove difficult.

Remote or elusive subject matter can often be brought to life using enlarged photographs, sound recordings, videos, recorded music, artefacts, tapestries, tools, implements, archive materials, jewellery, stories and poems. A unit of study on the Second World War was developed by members of the class bringing in ration books, blackout cycle lamps, newspapers, gas masks, shellcases, helmets, bayonets and even a tin of bully beef! A key lesson on the conservation of natural habitats was recently kick-started by a teacher handing round a selection of pet spiders, reptiles and snakes! Teachers usually find that planning and presenting lessons in ways that add to clarity and excitement helps most other pupils as well as those with limited vision.

WAYS OF WORKING

Inevitably, pupils overcoming the impediments to learning associated with a visual condition are going to take longer at many tasks than sighted peers. Speed of working is affected by many aspects: the need to familiarise oneself with room layout, resources and equipment; finding one's place in a textbook; transforming text into a form in which it can be read. Additional

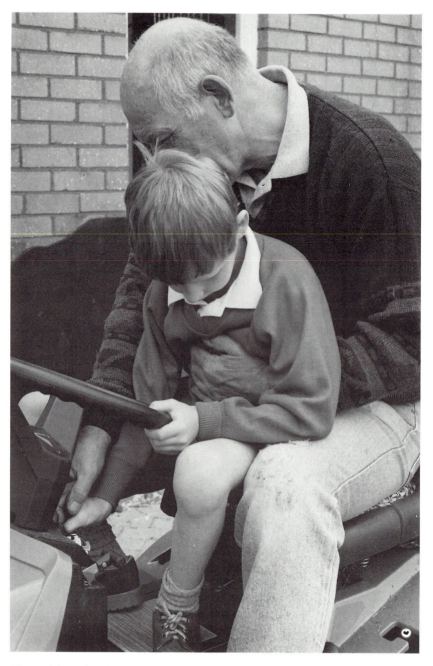

Plate 5.4 'Hands-on' experience of starting a tractor. Direct, participatory experiences promote understanding, helping a child with a visual impairment to construct events from evidence such as smells, textures and sounds

demands on pupils' powers of concentration, listening and the integration of information not readily accessible with poor vision, requires mainstream teachers to be realistic in their expectations. Another important aspect of differentiation, for all pupils who must work harder in order to keep pace with the rest of a group, concerns the flexible ways in which pupils are able to pursue tasks.

In some subject areas, special equipment can be used for pupils with restricted vision, so that individuals do not spend all their time trying to work with poor tools. Clearer visual or raised tactile markings may need to be added to rulers, protractors and other measuring instruments. Various pieces of equipment have been produced for work in maths, design or science, such as talking calculators, click measuring wheels, auditory timers, graphboards and light probes (used to measure light intensity which is indicated through pitch changes in an auditory signal). Full details of the specialist machines and equipment available for people with visual handicaps, including items for use in school (clocks, measures, timers, compasses, thermometers), are available from the RNIB at the address given in the Appendix.

There are many ways in which pupils can be guided towards exploring a given subject area, working over it to make the subject content, concepts and processes their own, in ways they can more easily access. All pupils benefit from co-operative groupwork for some of the time. However, co-operative groupwork is more than simply 'working in groups'. Few teachers, in fact, plan for class groupings with real collaborative learning, in which all pupils are given a role. Mostly, even when grouped by ability around a common task, pupils still work individually towards individual outcomes. True co-operative groupwork involves pupils working on a task that has been divided into elements for a joint outcome, or working jointly on one task for a shared finished product.

For example, pupils might allocate sub-tasks of compiling headlines, news, sports' results, pictures or an events' diary for a class newspaper. In science, an 'investigative crew' may work together to set up equipment, record data, collate and write up findings. Decisions have to be made about who does what, individuals take responsibility for one aspect and the whole has to be co-ordinated. When a single outcome is requested, such as a group working together to construct a bridge of a certain span, at a given cost, within certain time constraints and using specific materials, pupils must work together, but individual accountability is lower and some students 'coast' along in these situations. The danger of groupwork is that some pupils with low academic images will be assigned low-level roles and be carried by more dominant members. Some pupils do only what they are best at, whilst those whose contributions are rejected by the group may cease to try. Managed effectively, groups promote higher self-esteem and confidence, and can involve pupils with visual impairments in more positive interactions, negotiation and discussion.

'Buddy' system

One strategy that works well in both primary and secondary school contexts, however the pupils are grouped and taught, is for a pupil with individual needs, such as a youngster with a visual impairment, to be 'adopted' by a sympathetic class member, or 'study buddy'. Prior to any topic changes, important listening points, announcements, plans or instructions, the buddy gives a signal, such as a nudge or quiet word, which alerts the pupil. Study buddies can be equal partners tackling the same areas co-operatively. In this case the partners share problem-solving approaches and 'swap notes', test each other and reinforce one another's learning.

One form of this is for pupils to share reading or writing together. One listens whilst the other reads, monitoring meaning. At a pre-arranged signal, the roles are changed around. Alternatively, pupils can take turns to work over and extend one another's writing drafts. This form of shared reading or writing helps partners to sustain interest and engagement, and provides a check on the interpretation and construction of text.

Extra adults in the classroom

For most teachers in mainstream, the most welcome kind of additional help for a pupil with individual needs comes in the form of extra adults in the classroom. However, the collaboration of two adults in the same classroom must be carefully planned if it is to be effective, and to prevent misunderstandings arising. Despite what most teachers feel, there is no strong evidence that an adult working intensively with one pupil is a good investment of time. This argument has been made, for example, by the Audit Commission Reports referred to in Chapter 4, because reviews of support teaching show that this form of intervention is rarely planned or evaluated.

Supporting adults who do wish to work intensively with an individual pupil have to decide whether it may be more valuable for help to be given within the ordinary classroom setting, rather than for pupils to be taken out. The advantage of working within the classroom is that it is easier to incorporate any individual work with the mainstream curriculum, communication between staff is eased, and the stigma of removing pupils is avoided. A support teacher or classroom assistant can make an important contribution to effective differentiation.

Not all classrooms have the luxury of additional classroom help, but where this is available some thought needs to be given to how extra adults are used. Acceptable levels of noise or movement, who takes responsibility for discipline, the nature of record-keeping, who prepares what, and exactly which lessons will be supported across the timetable must be made explicit if extra help is to be used to maximum effect. Depending on the skills of the individuals concerned, the role of an extra adult or support teacher in the classroom could include:

- Adult works with one pupil (such as reading with) on lesson prepared and delivered by mainstream teacher
- Class work in groups whilst supporting adult provides help to other pupils with special needs
- Supporting adult circulates freely to help all pupils
- Supporting adult makes contribution to lesson and takes over responsibility from time to time
- Withdrawal by either teacher or adult
- One teaches while other observes for assessment
- Both plan and prepare materials and share teaching

In most secondary contexts the subject teacher will probably take the role of overall manager, maintaining discipline, presenting tasks to the group, organising resources and materials and taking charge of specific aspects such as the amount of movement around the room or noise generated. The supporting adult might work with individuals at breaking a task into more manageable steps, explaining and clarifying, introducing additional activities and materials and extending a pupil's understanding by supplying a useful illustration of a technical term or elaborating a concept.

There may be opportunities to check comprehension, prompting a pupil when failure is met, encouraging reflection and the relating of new concepts to old, discussing ways of tackling a problem, providing rapid feedback and praise and guiding pupils' problem-solving to the point where they are able to uncover solutions for themselves.

TECHNOLOGY IN THE LEARNING ENVIRONMENT

Differentiation for pupils with visual impairments, in terms of flexible ways of presenting, pursuing and showing the results of an enquiry, involves effective use of technology. Technology can enable many pupils with visual impairments to work at the speed of sighted peers and to present their finished work with a degree of polish. Some children may be able to use normal or large print, but take much longer, whilst their handwriting can be so untidy that it is very difficult for them to read back what they have just written. However, simply providing a piece of high-tech equipment is only a small part of the process of devising effective teaching and learning conditions for children with visual impairments. Using a CCTV to enlarge print will not help a pupil with limited vision to understand visually based concepts in humanities.

Technology is an important means of individual support, but requires expertise to capitalise fully upon it. A wide range of information input, memory and output facilities is available. In this section, we give some brief indication about the role of technology in supporting learning, although the possibilities are changing rapidly. Further sources of information where current technological advances can be pursued are given in the Appendix.

Access to print

Technology assists many pupils with limited vision by converting information from one medium to another, and allowing text to be transformed into a form where it becomes readable. Low vision aids, such as hand-held or stand-mounted magnifiers, can be used with existing print, maps, plans and diagrams. Exposure devices, such as an oblong window in dark card, can help some children attend to word shapes. Pupils with a peripheral field loss, or tunnel vision, may find that a 'reducer' assists reading by decreasing the size of print in the central areas of vision.

CCTV consists of a camera, a movable trolley on which printed material is placed, and a TV monitor. Some systems allow for the camera to focus on material at a distance, as well as print close to. The degree of enlargement of text, picture brightness and contrast can all be varied to suit individual preferences, including reversed images of white on black. CCTVs can also be linked to a typewriter or computer display. These systems permit access to print at high levels of magnification, but they are costly, difficult to move, and can lead to a sense of isolation in group settings.

Other approaches to accessing printed material include enlarging photocopiers. These are helpful when materials are being prepared or adapted for individuals with a visual loss, though their use requires advance planning. Large sheets of scaled-up text may also be difficult for some children to scan for information. Optical Character Recognition methods (such as the Kurzweil Reading Machine) use computers to read printed type-face (but not hand-writing or diagrams), which is then output as synthetic speech or braille. Viewscan is an electronic reading device that requires a pupil to scan a small camera across a line of print; the letters are then displayed on an electronic screen. Because it is portable and can produce images of different size and contrast, it is especially useful in a secondary school context. Optacon is another electronic camera system that reads print, converting it into a tactile image of the letters which can then be felt by the finger. The main drawback of this process is the speed limit on reading, since the display presents only one letter at a time.

One approach to accessing print at speed is to use tape-recorded material. Pupils in secondary or tertiary education may need to become adept at taping in order to cope with large volumes of information. Some special features are available on tape machines that make them particularly useful for students with severe visual impairments. Four-track and variable speed facilities allow more material to be recorded and to play back at speeds that enable rapid listening. Tone indexing is a technique that inserts tones to mark sections of a text as it is being replayed. Voice indexing inserts commentary onto the second track of a tape, along with an indexing tone. Both permit sections of taped material to be identified or annotated. Another feature is a pitch compensation device which adjusts the pitch of a taped voice played quickly to its natural register so that it becomes intelligible at high speeds.

Keyboard skills and computing

The use of most technological aids requires pupils to acquire keyboard skills and touch-typing. Many support teachers recommend that children learn to type as soon as possible, although blind children are usually taught basic braille first. Earlier in this chapter we suggested that children of pre-school age can be given a pre-braille programme to develop the finger strength and co-ordination necessary to operate a Perkins Braille Writer. They can enjoy making dot patterns and writing pretend messages whilst also developing finger strength and familiarising themselves with the braille keys.

By the time children with visual impairments start school they should also be familiar with computers. Computer keyboards now have a range of input options to meet the needs of the user. Examples include touch screens, alternative keyboards such as microwriter, 'concept' and 'adventure', or electronic braille key inputs. Depending on the individual needs of the user, output systems include large-character screen displays, tactile graphics, braille and synthetic speech.

In school contexts, word processing systems are much more useful if they are portable and flexible. The processing and storage power of portable systems is usually vastly increased when used in conjunction with a desk-top system. A microwriter is a rechargeable, lightweight piece of equipment that can be used at home, on the bus or in school, and is operated with one hand using a combination of keys. The letters produced can be viewed in a window through which the text scrolls by, 12 letters at a time. Designed to be used in conjunction with a desk-top for subsequent printing, the microwriter is an effective means of note-taking, but has scope for only limited text editing. Some training is required to master the letter codes.

The Versabraille system is a word processor with a braille input, and outputs in braille or print, capable of storing hundreds of pages of text on disk, with search and editing facilities. This is a more expensive but much more powerful system which enables blind individuals to use a full word processing system. Several computer programs are available that enable braille to be produced from a standard Qwerty keyboard. A braille printer is required, and whoever inputs will need a knowledge of braille.

There are also a number of systems that allow the simultaneous production of hardcopy print and braille, such as Braille 'n' print; these are indispensable in shared reading or writing activities involving blind and sighted children. The Vincent Workstation is another versatile system that allows

Plate 5.5 Joint construction of text using a brailler. Children take turns to re-draft and review one another's written work

blind students to produce written material that can be read by sighted people. The input is typed in braille, which is then converted into speech or print, allowing a student to review and check what has been drafted.

Reprographics

There are a number of ways to produce materials that support teaching and learning for pupils with limited vision. Tactile diagrams are made from a master copy using a vacuum-forming process. Symbols are drawn onto the master (usually aluminium foil) or constructed as a collage with materials such as textured cloths, string and plastic shapes. A plastic sheet is placed over the master copy and melted slightly, then it is sucked tightly into the shape of the master by a vacuum pump. Minolta manufacture a piece of equipment that converts line drawings into raised tactile images using heat sensitive paper in a stereo photocopier. It is usually not possible to produce intelligible diagrams straight from the pages of a textbook without selecting and redrawing. A great deal of thought has to be given to the information provided if it is to be meaningful to a child. Maps, graphs and flow-diagrams may be straightforward to transfer into tactile diagrams, although symbols, perspective and 3-D representations, for example, would be difficult to interpret.

SUMMARY

In this chapter we have indicated some of the possibilities for enabling pupils with visual impairments to learn more effectively, to use their visual capacities to the full, and to access the mainstream curriculum. For young children, the first concerns are with social contexts for interaction, and how adults can establish more satisfying and productive reciprocal exchanges. Children can also be stimulated to explore their surroundings visually and physically, and to develop competences in eye–hand co-ordination, tactile and motor skills. Exploring the environment is critical to the child's sense of space, for language and conceptual growth, but much depends on how adults encourage physical activity and how they organise spaces for enquiry and for play.

If we were to identify one area of development that seems central to the education and development of pupils with visual losses, this would be language. Here, too, language environments at home and in settings for learning can be enhanced by adopting strategies that enlarge, rather than inhibit, understanding. The most useful input provides rich descriptions and draws attention to similarities and differences, exposing how the world is categorised and defined. However, conversation is essentially a constructive process in which both partners have an active role. In classroom contexts, dialogue is put to more specific uses, but here, too, language environments can be more or less engaging.

Much of what we have identified in terms of good practice for pupils with restricted vision, such as classroom organisation, the literacy environment, working conditions with visual clarity and good listening, promote learning in all pupils. Strategies for differentiation, including flexible formats for presenting information, ways of working and showing the results of an enquiry, can also be tailored to some extent to meet the learning needs of a wide number of pupils.

Obviously, some of the adaptations to teaching styles, equipment and materials that enable pupils with visual impairments to work at the same speed as peers, and to produce finished work efficiently, require some specialist advice and assistance. We have provided an introduction to some of the technological resources that assist learning and participation, although this is a field characterised by rapid innovation.

6

RESEARCHING SOCIAL ENCOUNTERS

This chapter focuses on the importance of social interaction for promoting children's cognitive, social and linguistic development. Nowadays, it is widely accepted that learning and development always take place within a social context and that it is insufficient simply to consider individuals as solitary problem-solvers without taking account of how adults and peers shape, guide or 'scaffold' their behaviour.

Initially, we concentrate on a framework for examining adult–child encounters developed at Bristol University in a programme of research undertaken in specific social settings such as families and classrooms. Thereafter, the main part of this chapter focuses on a project that has analysed aspects of peer interactions, play, language and learning in children with visual impairments in mainstream settings. Finally, we analyse the implications of this study for designing an effective teaching and learning milieu.

All children grow up in the company of others. No child grows up in isolation, without human social contact. Every child's development is shaped and modified by the environments of home, school and wider social contexts. However, theories of development vary widely in the emphasis they place on contributions made by either individuals, or the environment, to patterns of learning and behaviour. This is a reflection of the respective value placed by researchers on the characteristics and capabilities that individuals bring to learning, in contrast to the processes through which one person helps another to develop their skills and understanding.

In Chapter 1 we discussed the commonly held view that a severe visual impairment has such a profound effect on children's perceptual experience that they must be bound to make sense of things in ways that are typically distinct from sighted children. This belief is the underlying reason why most research on children with visual impairments has focused on the impact of a visual loss on aspects of the child's individual functioning. In Chapter 3, for example, we reviewed some of the data derived from the application of Piagetian tasks to individuals with visual impairments, showing delays in understanding about the physical world. One problem with this approach is that it assumes that knowledge is built up inside the child's head from solitary exploration and problem-solving. What is largely ignored are the ways in which adults, often using the medium of language, share experiences with children and jointly make sense of them.

Rather than speculating on the nature and extent of any distinctions between typical and atypical groups, we have preferred to shift attention to the processes through which children and adults interact with one another in different learning environments. Instead of thinking of learning as essentially private or 'internal' processes, inside the individual, we prefer the view that adults use a wide range of strategies for helping children to develop their understanding. Learning that takes place in families, playgroups or schools can be thought of as a shared enterprise, jointly guided and constructed. Some writers (such as Rogoff, 1990) refer to children's development as a form of apprenticeship, occurring through guided participation in social activities that use the skills and tools of a specific culture. Amongst researchers there is a growing appreciation of the significance of social contexts, and the transactions that take place within them, for all children's learning and development.

For children with visual impairments, this view of learning embedded in social encounters raises many new and important questions. It brings us to the heart of the issue of how adults' talk and actions shape children's thinking and learning. How adults set up activities, how they group children together and how they intervene to promote the smooth progress of a game has an important influence on the social setting and dynamics for those involved. How language is used to recap events that happened earlier, to get things done in the present and to predict what might occur next influences how the child connects with the surrounding world. The adult's effectiveness in making these links and bridges, expanding on what the child already knows in terms that can be readily understood, structuring and supporting children's efforts to make sense of things, is the key to overcoming some of the limits that a visual impairment may impose.

Our final chapter in this book reports some recent developments in research with children across the primary age range, most of whom have severe visual impairments, some of whom experience additional learning difficulties, and all of whom receive the major part of their education within mainstream school settings. The intention here is to signal gaps in our current understanding of important developmental processes for children with visual losses, to describe current efforts that may provide answers to some of the questions raised, and to point up future issues for research.

THE IMPORTANCE OF SHARED ENCOUNTERS

The work reported in this chapter is part of a programme of research that has attempted to capture data in family and school settings, where adults are involved in joint enterprise with children, and in some instances are concerned to optimise children's progress towards some specific educational objectives, such as extending reading or writing competence (Webster and Wood, 1989; Webster *et al.*, 1996a). The specific data we report here have been gathered as part of research on the play and social interaction of children with visual impairments, in collaboration with peers or adults (Roe, 1997).

Effective teaching and learning, in our terms, is more than just the transmission of information from one individual to another. Rather, successful learning is constituted in certain styles of co-operation, negotiation and guided participation. In the early stages of development, which we discussed in Chapter 3, most sighted children are quickly and actively engaged in social encounters with immediate caregivers, who read the infant's intentions as meaningful, provide verbal commentary to interpret events, and use intimate encounters to create mutual communicative frameworks suffused with language. Infants come already equipped with a repertoire of behaviours, both to initiate and to respond to the social overtures of others. Sensitive adults assist children to make sense of things in terms they understand, guide efforts to solve problems without over-interference, and gradually hand over responsibility for learning to youngsters themselves. Through social interaction with the more mature, children are also exposed to practices and models of how others tackle tasks and manage their thinking.

This approach rejects the view that learning can be frequently reduced to small fragments or steps, building from smaller to larger skill sequences, acquired by rote or drill in isolation from genuine contexts. Learning is a complex and unpredictable process, more than just the sum of a number of small parts, and often occurring in social settings that also defy simplistic description or analysis. How new information becomes meaningful to the learner may be impossible to capture with any precision. However, effective learning often does require opportunities for children to take risks and make mistakes, to weigh alternative strategies and review consequences of different ways of proceeding, within supportive social partnerships involving others.

A theme that runs throughout this book, and which we shall be revisiting in this chapter, is that for a multitude of reasons, the presence of a visual loss changes the conditions and dynamics of social interaction between children, their peers and caregivers. So an important objective of our current work has been to apply what we know of ordinary social encounters between learning partners to situations where a visual loss must be taken into account.

A RESEARCH FRAMEWORK

The conceptual framework depicted in Figure 6.1 considers learning and development for all children in relation to two major dimensions, reflecting the degree of engagement of the learner in relation to a relatively active or passive environment. This is a simple but powerful framework that has been adopted in a number of studies (see, for example, Webster and Wood, 1989; Webster *et al.*, 1996a). The horizontal axis represents the degree of initiative, engagement and active involvement of the child in the learning process. The vertical axis is concerned with the nature of adults' management or control within the learning environment. Using these two continua, fundamental to all teaching and learning contexts, we can describe the nature of interactions between children and peers or caregivers, the way in which environmental inputs are structured and made accessible to children, and whether individuals are treated as passive recipients of information or are engaged as active learning partners. In effect, the model reflects different images of children and their learning accomplices, and the quality of transactions between individuals within the learning milieu.

The framework provided in Figure 6.1 is not intended to be a precision instrument, but is a way of looking, of gauging relative emphasis. Not all that transpires in a learning context can be 'measured' by this model. The intention is to identify predominant kinds of teaching and learning, how they overlap or emerge, and the possible consequences for children's development. It should also be noted that we expect individuals to interact with one another in different ways to suit different purposes. There are occasions when parents and teachers adopt more didactic styles, giving priority to managing learners, rather than learning, establishing order and setting rote tasks. Similarly, there are other occasions when adults encourage children to listen passively, to occupy themselves without help, to pursue their own learning pathways and to make their own discoveries and mistakes.

The point is that people are mostly adaptive to the conditions under which they operate, the characteristics of the individuals involved, the resources available and the nature of the tasks in hand. The framework presented in Figure 6.1 is descriptive rather than judgemental. It provides background reference points against which the data from our observational studies involving children with visual impairments can be interpreted.

Quadrant A

Quadrant A in the framework is characterised by high adult (or peer) management and control, where the child is assumed to make little contribution to learning but is merely a recipient of information or instructions handed over by others. Adults and teachers structure tasks for the child in terms of pace, sequence and repetition, without negotiation. A feature of this quadrant is that adult responses are not contingent upon the child's. Contingency requires sensitivity to the needs, starting points, interests and perspectives of the individual. Adults or peers in quadrant A demand that the child responds to their initiatives and interests, not the other way around.

Because it is high in adult or peer management, but low in child engagement or contingency, the kind of interactive behaviour described in this quadrant is termed 'adult- or peer-driven' and has important implications for understanding some of the social processes that affect children with sensori-impairments. In Chapter 3 we considered some of the consequences of a visual loss on processes of interaction, such as the nature of family conversation styles. A number of studies show that the language environments of children who are atypical in some way are characterised by highly directive, intrusive parenting

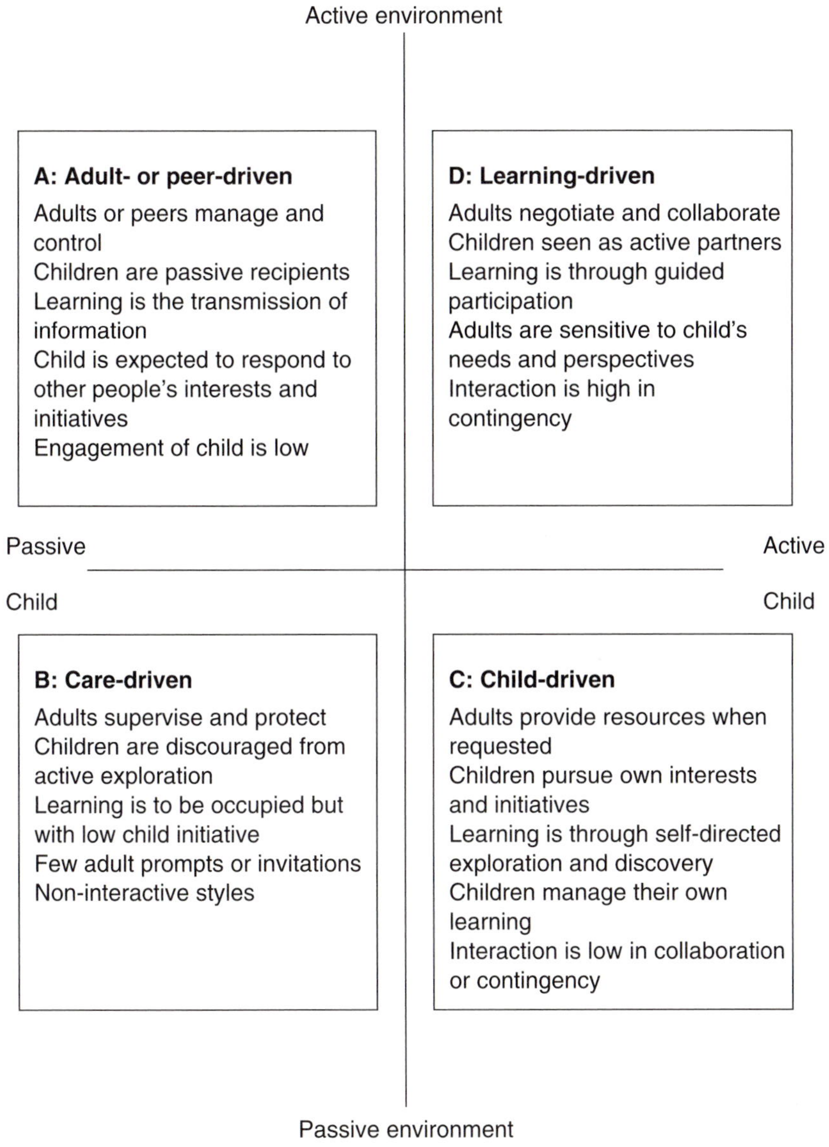

Active environment

A: Adult- or peer-driven

Adults or peers manage and control
Children are passive recipients
Learning is the transmission of information
Child is expected to respond to other people's interests and initiatives
Engagement of child is low

D: Learning-driven

Adults negotiate and collaborate
Children seen as active partners
Learning is through guided participation
Adults are sensitive to child's needs and perspectives
Interaction is high in contingency

Passive   Active

Child   Child

B: Care-driven

Adults supervise and protect
Children are discouraged from active exploration
Learning is to be occupied but with low child initiative
Few adult prompts or invitations
Non-interactive styles

C: Child-driven

Adults provide resources when requested
Children pursue own interests and initiatives
Learning is through self-directed exploration and discovery
Children manage their own learning
Interaction is low in collaboration or contingency

Passive environment

Figure 6.1 A framework of adult–child interaction

styles (Conti-Ramsden, 1994; Webster and Wood, 1989).

Research also summarised in Chapter 3 (Andersen *et al.*, 1993) suggests that adults in conversation with children who have a visual impairment initiate more topics, request more actions and ask more questions than usual. Although blind children, for example, require many more descriptions and explanations from caregivers than sighted children, in fact they receive far less. Instead of providing children with rich interpretative descriptions of environmental situations or events, adults tend to bombard blind children with requests for labels, or questions relating to the child's current activities and possessions. Rather than actively drawing children with severe visual impairments into active engagement with environmental contexts, adult responses tend to be restrictive and inhibitive.

Quadrant B

In contrast, quadrant B is marked by a lack of adult or child initiative, and a limited amount of management, direction or control. In this domain the adult's role may be seen as one of supervising, overseeing or protecting, with little interaction. The adult may give few signals, such as explanations or descriptions, prompts or invitations, that steer pupils towards interesting events or that evoke responses or engage pupils. The image of the child is a passive, recipient one. The adult's main concerns may be for the child's safety and care. Because it is low in child initiative and adult engagement, the kind of behaviour outlined in this quadrant is described as 'care-driven', which also has important implications for understanding social interaction and the role of vision.

In many ways, vision is centrally involved in stimulating early interaction and exploration, as has been considered in some detail in Chapter 3. Problems in establishing eye contact with a blind infant may lead some parents to feel that their child is unresponsive, and the normally intense social engagement of adult and child can be disturbed. Without eye gaze, it may be difficult for adults to read a child's attention focus, to establish topics of conversation and maintain a cohesive dialogue. Caregivers may discourage adventurous play, with a chain of consequences for language and conceptual development if children do not interact freely and actively with their surroundings. There is a danger that a visual impairment results in a reduction and dilution of the ordinary transactions between child and the environment that promote development. In other words, a possible outcome of a visual impairment is a passive individual in a passive context, with much reduced stimulation.

Quadrant C

Quadrant C draws on child-centred models of teaching and learning, and the view that children are basically architects of their own understanding. The image of the pupil is one of a self-motivated individual or little scientist, struggling to assemble a personal understanding of the physical world, its logical and mathematical properties. In contrast, the adult's or teacher's role is to provide a wealth of materials to furnish a rich and stimulating context. The child takes much of the initiative in constructing knowledge, based on experience with the environment. The environment is a necessary part of development, but has no active role in structuring thought or activity.

This quadrant is consistent with many interpretations of Piaget's work, which we considered in Chapter 3. At the heart of Piagetian theory is the view that learning arises out of the child's own action and problem-solving. What sets the pace in the child's thinking is the individual's exploration and discovery. Since it is the child's interaction with the physical world that provides the timing and motivation for change, social facilitation of development works only when the child is ready to move forward. Processes of social interaction involving teachers and adults thus have a low-key effect and are not really important in fostering development. Because it is low in adult contingency or peer collaboration, this quadrant is described as 'child-driven'.

Child-centred models have important implications for understanding processes of development in children with visual impairments. Child-initiated explorations – pointing, reaching, grasping, exploring spaces, coming to know objects and the effects of their actions upon them, weighing perceptual evidence to make logical judgements, abstracting features to form concepts – all of these processes are heavily dependent on vision. In order to mirror the natural and incidental ways in which most sighted children learn, the environment has to be brought within reach, or explanations provided about what is happening elsewhere. Quadrant C highlights the difficulties that are likely to be encountered by many children with visual impairments, in the absence of links between the child's inner world and the world outside.

Quadrant D

The emphasis in quadrant D is on learning that is facilitated through co-operation. Through close relationships with parents, teachers, siblings and peers, the child is guided in joint processes of problem-solving. Learning is a social and communicative enterprise, whereby knowledge is co-operatively constructed. Learners are not seen as isolated individuals who succeed or fail by their own efforts. Children participate with adults to interrogate events, negotiate tasks and solve problems together. Important here is the timing and pacing of adult intervention or contingency, gauging a child's moment-to-moment understanding of a situation or task, providing explanation and description where needed, but allowing initiative when the child succeeds. In this way the child is never held back by teaching that is over-directive, nor left alone when understanding is likely to miscarry. Both require an astute awareness of the learner's perspective. Over time the adult's guidance, prompting or support is reduced, as responsibility for problem-solving is handed over to the child.

Because it is concerned with adult sensitivity to the needs and perspectives of children, how learning takes place and the requirements for understanding, when to step in and when to step back, quadrant D is described as 'learning-driven'. In relation to visual impairment, it is the combination of active adult and active child that is most powerful in highlighting the transactional basis of learning and development.

Perhaps the most important way for adults and other learning partners to be facilitative involves the making of conceptual bridges for children with visual impairments. This requires tuning into the perceptual evidence available to the child and gauging current levels of understanding. Effective ways are found using direct experience, language and discussion, to make sense of objects and events, to clarify confusions, to shape concepts, to highlight similarities and differences, and gradually to bring the child's inner representation of the world into line with the adult's. For the child, developmental outcomes are not determined by the perceptual limitations imposed by a visual condition, or by the environment, or even by their combined effects. Learning arises from the complex interplay of all these elements, embedded in social relationships, to form a continuous dynamic and transactional process.

SOCIO-CONSTRUCTIVISM

The kind of experiences we have described in quadrant D draw on attempts to consider development in terms of adult–child proximation or 'guided participation'. At the heart of our research programme lie some important ideas that stem from a body of knowledge known as 'socio-constructivism'. There are some very compelling accounts of learning processes in this work that hold significant implications for parents and teachers involved with children with visual impairments.

The socio-constructive approach, represented in the work of writers such as Burgess (1993), Moll (1990), Rogoff (1990) or Wood (1988), dismisses the view that in order to learn more about how children think and learn, we must focus on individuals and their solitary problem-solving. Although physically distinct and separated off, children do not grow up in isolation. It is a mistaken assumption, these writers argue, to view children's development as driven from within the individual, according to the cognitive level already reached. Socio-constructivism sees children's achievements as being determined, at least in part, by the particular circumstances in which learning takes place and by the contributions of others involved. This does not mean that children do not differ in their innate potential for learning, or that if a learner fails, the responsibility is entirely the teacher's. What it does mean is that a learner's progress always reflects a joint achievement.

The family, for example, is a social context that operates within certain organisational constraints and practices. Children will quickly acquire modes of behaviour, roles, values and ways of dealing with the world that are specific to different family cultures and sections of society. The school is another example of a cultural institution that defines and constrains the nature of activities, relationships and behaviour, and the tools and artefacts available for people to use. Some of these constraints are more explicit than others, such as legal requirements for what must be taught, assessed, recorded and reported. Implicit rules govern how adults and children will address one another, form friendships and be grouped. There are characteristic resources to be found in classroom contexts, such as fiction and reference texts, computers or listening centres. How pupils use computers and books, and how adults will question, direct, discuss and reflect on issues with pupils, have a typical 'school' format that is different from that found in an office, library or at home. Obviously, even within similar societal contexts, there is much variation from one family to the next, and from one school setting to another.

Social constructivists argue that children's thinking and learning is bound to these specific contexts of social practice and that learning is based on the mastery of these. Forms of language, including types of text, writing and talk, are tightly linked with particular social institutions such as families or schools. In order to study teaching and learning, researchers must examine the detail of moments when adults interact with children in order to achieve certain goals, together with the tactics and tools that are used. In many family and school settings, it is through conversation around learning activities that children's thinking is constrained, supported or extended.

An important theme of socio-constructive accounts is that children are guided towards competence and independence in learning through interaction with the more mature. In other words, children's thinking develops as a result of 'borrowing' ways of speaking, acting and problem-solving that are first encountered in collaboration with adults or more capable peers. This borrowing, or 'appropriation', works both ways, in that parents and teachers have to think about children's prior experiences, ideas and starting points in order to adjust their interactions with individuals and plan relevant challenges. Appropriation underpins the process of conceptual bridging for parents and teachers of children with visual impairments: entering into the child's perceptual world; seeing things from the child's point of view; and making connections between the child's inner representations and the world outside, using language as a medium.

Scaffolding

One of the most important ideas in social-constructive theory is the notion of scaffolding. Scaffolding addresses what it is that adults do when they interact with children that actually promotes learning. It can be considered as a more detailed breakdown of roles characterised in quadrant D of our framework

197

in Figure 6.1. The term is a metaphor for the strategic quality of adult inter-ventions that move children on in their thinking, until they are fully ready to take over responsibility for their own enquiry.

For example, a parent introduces a 4 year old to a jigsaw puzzle, showing the child how to sort the pieces and the relevance of the picture on the box. The adult may need to offer a lot of encouragement to start with and model strategies such as finding all the pieces with a straight edge in order to assemble the frame first. Specific prompts might be given, such as finding a piece with a certain colour, turning it around, suggesting areas of the puzzle it might fit. Over time, the parent reduces the amount of help given, bearing in mind the child's competence in the task, until the child can eventually do the puzzle independently.

Scaffolding is a compelling way of understanding the active, sensitive and supportive involvement of an adult in a child's learning. In its original for-mulation, scaffolding described the nature of guidance or support during one-to-one tutoring, where the adult's appraisal of the growing competence of the learner determined whether assistance was withdrawn or increased (Wood *et al.*, 1976). One problem with the idea of scaffolding is that of applying it to large classroom contexts, where factors that have nothing to do with learn-ing *per se* often determine the teacher's priorities, and where teachers have to engage groups of learners, not just individuals. These issues are considered in some detail in relation to primary and secondary school contexts in Webster *et al.*, 1996a. In this account, the components of scaffolding are defined, including how the adults recruit, warm or inspire children to be interested in an activity, shifting the focus of attention from one aspect to another.

A second dimension of scaffolding consists of helping children to represent tasks in terms they understand, clarifying and affirming elements, reducing the complexity of steps involved to create manageable tasks. Reducing the degrees of freedom in carrying out a task ensures that children experience suc-cess by constraining a problem to smaller specifics, without losing sight of the whole. This restructuring or remaking of tasks with children includes helping to plan, drawing attention to key issues or points of information, reminding pupils about the problem in hand, giving prompts, suggestions and shortcuts.

A third component of scaffolding consists of assisting children to develop or adapt their concepts. This may entail fitting new information into existing conceptual frameworks, or adapting and reconstructing previous ways of thinking to accommodate new learning. This stage of 'elaboration' may involve the marking out of critical features, drawing attention to similarities and differences between current ideas and previous episodes, information or events, and finding analogies, parallels and links.

A fourth aspect is referred to as 'mediation': ways of organising and representing children's learning activities through conventions such as print. Mediation involves finding the right words, helping children to externalise their thinking, listening to the accounts made by children of their own learning, and selecting appropriate methods for recording.

The final component of scaffolding is concerned with drawing together the fruits of children's learning, reflecting on process and worth. An important distinction is drawn here between *closing in* on children's thinking and *closing down* children's thinking. How adults manage these transactions determines what children believe to be of value: amount of work completed correctly, or how resourceful the child was in setting out to solve a problem.

Although it is convenient to depict scaffolding as a series of steps, these

---

1. Recruitment
Recruiting interest
Gaining attention
Shifting interest from one activity to another
Drawing children into task
Directing to resources or events

2. Representation and clarification
Adding information
Restructuring tasks
Identifying key elements
Paraphrasing
Exploring current understanding

3. Elaboration
Developing or adapting concepts
Fitting new information to old
Marking critical features
Highlighting similarities and differences
Bridging: finding analogies, parallels and links

4. Mediation
Finding ways with words
Organising and externalising thinking
Representing learning, e.g. through print
Strategic listening to learners' accounts
Thinking dialogues

5. Finishing
Convening (drawing together)
Reflecting on process and worth
Celebrating, storing and displaying
Weighing and valuing
Closing in on children's learning

Figure 6.2 Components of scaffolding

199

components do not necessarily unfold in linear fashion. In the classrooms observed by Webster *et al.* (1996a) scaffolding was often recursive, with some aspects, such as recruitment and elaboration, overlapping. Teachers were often engaged in multi-faceted acts of discussion and elicitation, scaffolding various children in different ways at different times.

Scaffolding is closely linked to the idea that adults and other learning partners can frequently help children to accomplish things that they could not do by themselves. The gap between what children can do on their own and what they can achieve with the help of others more skilled than themselves is known as the 'zone of proximal development' (Vygotsky, 1978). In other words, adult sensitivity to the needs of the learner and the nature of the task in hand enables children to understand problems and find solutions in situations where, left to their own devices, they would be overstretched. Here, too, the notion of entering and exiting a singular physical space evoked by the term 'zone' must be reinterpreted in relation to classroom settings. Children and adults may construct multiple zones with different levels of intensity that are dependent not so much on spatial proximity as on the close sharing of working minds on tasks in common (Webster *et al.*, 1996a).

Scaffolding and visual impairment

Most of the processes of early social interaction that we considered in Chapter 3, including the mutual responding described as 'inter-subjectivity', depend to some extent on vision. Scaffolding accounts for the frameworks of joint reference that adults construct as a basis for shared attention and meaning-making, but these too require the reading of visual clues. Later, these prototypes for communication support conversational exchanges. In accounting for what promotes rapid development towards more mature language use, it is the quality and processes of adult scaffolding that are instrumental for most children.

There are some children, however, who are hard to scaffold (Conti-Ramsden, 1994; Meadows, 1996). Learning difficulties and sensori-impairments, in particular, seem to evoke more intrusive, managerial parenting styles. Children with visual impairments may be denied opportunities for exploration, collaborative play or risk-taking, due to adult overprotection. Some adults 'over-scaffold' children with visual losses by initiating many more conversation topics, asking many more questions than usual and requesting more actions. Instead of offering rich descriptions and interpretations to blind children, research shows that adults tend to adopt strategies that limit language interaction and cognitive development (Andersen *et al.*, 1993).

Between children themselves, early social interactions begin by watching one another, and the mutual showing or sharing of objects and toys. Peer interactions and peer scaffolding may also be disturbed by loss of vision. A blind child may be unaware of the efforts of a sighted peer to invite interest

Plate 6.1 Scaffolding. Scaffolding is a metaphor for adult interventions which move children on in their thinking, until they are ready to take over responsibility for their own enquiry

in a toy or participation in a game, if these are based on gestures or visual signals. Difficulties arise when the child with a visual impairment fails to react in the expected way. It becomes easier for everybody when language is used to establish social interaction. However, all young children find it hard to understand the world from another's viewpoint, especially the fact that a play-mate cannot see. Young children's language often lacks semantic specificity and depends on the context for interpretation. Awkward moments can follow when a sighted child points to a coveted object and says to a blind play partner: 'I want that one.' The simple presence of peers may not be enough for the child with a visual impairment to join in social encounters with others. Effective social enterprise may have to be mediated and stimulated by adults, and thus the scaffolding, in some instances, may need to be redesigned.

BRISTOL RESEARCH ON CHILDREN WITH VISUAL IMPAIRMENTS

In this section we describe the research developed at Bristol University that has focused on aspects of social interaction, play and language of children with visual impairments in mainstream schools. This project was intended to provide ideas and guidelines for how to promote opportunities for better social interaction between children. So that teachers could relate this research to their own classroom experience, it was decided to concentrate on a wide range of children with visual impairments, representative of individuals likely to be found in mainstream schools, rather than a highly selective group.

Observing children at play provides a rich source of evidence about ways in which children explore their physical and social environments; develop games, routines and roles; and create social networks that are inclusive or exclusive of play participants. During play, children have the opportunity to experiment with the meanings and rules of real life. They learn how to take alternative perspectives and practise making their intentions clear to others. Playing with others requires a flexible repertoire of social skills. Children are more likely to get what they want from a play situation if they are able to express themselves, if they can negotiate and agree on how the ingredients for a play context should be assembled.

Very few studies have gathered information on play or social encounters of children with visual impairments in their natural settings (see, for example, Ferguson and Buultjens, 1995; Kekelis and Sacks, 1992; Preisler, 1993). Almost without exception, research in this area has focused on children playing alone, in the presence of a caregiver or with parents (Parsons, 1986a). Such research has mainly been conducted in contrived settings that are not typical of real mainstream classrooms. This work has given us some insight into what children do in experimental situations, but these findings can only partly be applied to other contexts. In authentic settings, children with visual losses have to contend with busy, challenging situations where unpredictable events occur, and which may involve fleeting contacts with other children, who may take toys away, and with whom a child has to deal.

Besides observing children – sighted and visually impaired – playing in their natural settings with no formal instructions, we also explored more controlled situations, such as pairs of children working together to perform a task, and children playing at home with their siblings. In each case the objectives were to identify factors that foster social interaction, to examine the characteristics of children that influence their social involvement, and to explore the impact of different contexts on children's social encounters.

The sample of children

Twenty children aged between 3 and 9 years, from six different LEAs, took part in the research. Fourteen boys and six girls were selected on the basis of the presence of a visual impairment from an early age and attendance at a mainstream school. Eight of the children were considered 'blind', and twelve were 'partially sighted'. All the blind children were boys. Five of the children experienced additional difficulties: two children had cerebral palsy, two had learning difficulties, one had a language impairment.

Observation methods

Before the main study started, a pilot project was undertaken with a small selection of children who were observed at regular intervals in their usual school settings, in what teachers called either 'free choice' or 'play time'. Some sessions were filmed in order to iron out any practical difficulties with the observation procedures. As much as possible the observers tried not to disturb the normal activities of the classgroups. Agreement was reached with the class teacher about which sessions would be observed and the procedures were explained.

Target children were themselves asked if they would mind wearing a waist-coat that carried a small radio microphone that would record all that was said by, or in the presence of, the wearer. During the observation period, if children attempted to interact with the observer, only brief responses or explanations were given. In order to deal with children's initial curiosity about the observer's presence, filming was simulated for around three minutes before actually starting, then each target child was filmed for a period of 15 minutes. Each target child was observed for three sessions on different days.

A range of information was gathered about each target child from parents, using a short questionnaire, and drawing on teachers' perceptions. Informal conversations with teachers and general assistants and other observations (occasionally the observer had to wait in the classroom and watched children informally) also occurred, and notes of these sessions were made. For each of the sample of children with visual impairments, we collated data from video and radio-microphone recordings, together with a wealth of information from

Table 6.1 Sample of children in the Bristol study

Child	Diagnosis	Sex	Age	Additional problems	Visual acuity
Elisabeth	Optic atrophy due to haemoptulus meningitis – 5m	F	5y 5m	Premature	3/60
Martin	Norries disease	M	5y 7m	Learning difficulties	nil
John	Norries disease	M	4y 11m	Learning difficulties	nil
Mark	Aniridia	M	5y 6m	–	6/60
Elena	Bilateral microphthalmus with colobomata, nystagmus	F	4y 6m	Language impairment	6/60
George	Bilateral congenital glaucoma	M	5y 4m	–	3/24 RE nil LE
Daniel	Retinoblastoma – 13m	M	5y 2m	–	nil
Anthony	Leber's amaurosis	M	4y	–	nil Light perception on LE
Richard	Cone dystrophy and myopia	M	6y 1m	–	6/36
Kate	Marfan's syndrome	F	6y 7m	–	6/36 RE 6/18 LE
Kevin	Retinopathy of prematurity Totally blind since 3y	M	6y 4m	Premature	nil
Louis	Ocular albinism	M	6y 4m	–	1/60 RE 6/60 LE
Sam	Severely restricted visual fields due to asphyxiation at birth	M	8y 2m	–	2/60 RE 1/60 LE
Charles	Retinopathy of prematurity	M	8y 9m	Premature	nil
Tom	Leber's amaurosis	M	5y 5m	–	nil
Nelly	Retinopathy of prematurity	F	5y 11m	Spastics diplegia Premature	6/60 at 1/3 m on RE nil LE
Christine	Bilateral congenital microphthalmus	F	4y 9m	–	6/36
Alice	Retinopathy of prematurity	F	8y 2m	Cerebral palsy Premature	6/60 RE nil LE
Trevor	Bilateral detached retina due to retinal dysplasia	M	3y 4m	–	nil
Sean	Myopia and restricted visual fields	M	6y 7m	–	6/18 RE 6/24 LE

parents, teachers, assistants and, in some instances, from what the children had to say for themselves.

Data analysis

Once the sessions were filmed, a ten-second time-sampling technique was used that allowed us to determine approximately how much time target children spent on their own, next to, or interacting with others, and how much time they spent in different categories of play. A descriptive analysis of this was then carried out, using a schedule of play categories that analysed the proportion of time spent by different children in various kinds of play, such as role play in the home corner, or building with construction materials. Transcripts of the sessions were also made. These were then used to describe encounters and events, and to code different categories of social function. The descriptions focused on the physical environment; play features such as resources, toys and objects; the group of children present in the vicinity; and the quality of conversational interaction.

Observations were also made of social 'moves' and their function, focused on attentional behaviour (actively initiating attention from adults or peers, or responding to attention-seeking behaviour); resources (getting help, giving information, providing or taking away play objects from others); and activity control (controlling or being managed by others). Observer reliability for the categories of play, quality of interaction and social function was confirmed by using a statistical procedure devised by Fleiss (1971). This measures the amount of agreement amongst many raters applying the coding procedures to the data obtained. Both general agreement and agreement for each particular coding category was found to be over 90 per cent (p < 0.001).

The data from transcripts and descriptions were analysed from different perspectives, focusing on the contexts observed, the content of play activities, and typical characteristics of the social interactions established. We were also able to pin-point particular difficulties or tactics adopted for their solution. One aspect we were interested in concerns the relationship between degree of visual impairment and time spent in different social functions with adults or peers, use of resources, and how activities were managed or controlled.

RESEARCH FOCUS 1: INDIVIDUAL DIFFERENCES AND THE DIVERSITY OF PLAY

Most of the experimental evidence we reviewed in earlier chapters on the play of visually impaired groups suggest some important contrasts with sighted children of the same age. Blind children, particularly, are reported to play less often, and when they do, this tends to be more self-contained and repetitive, less symbolic or imaginative (Parsons, 1986a, 1986b).

The data from our own research, undertaken in everyday play settings, indicate a rich diversity of play behaviours and social interactions. Children engaged in many different kinds of play in a variety of play areas, such as role play in the home corner, constructing objects on a carpet using plastic building bricks and other assembly materials, and manipulative or symbolic play using shapes and dominoes, musical toys, cars, plasticine, water and sand. We did not find a general reduction or narrowing of play in the visually impaired group as a whole, although there were differences between individuals. In this section we examine some of the finer grain details that contribute towards individual differences in creative play, flexibility and social competence, and pose questions such as which contextual factors promote free, complex, interactive play?

In one of the sessions, Trevor, the youngest child in our sample, played in the home corner. He had started nursery very recently and had good language competence, but showed some difficulty in recognising his peers. Trevor got inside a cupboard and opened and closed the doors. His interactions were mainly adult- rather than peer-orientated. In contrast, Anthony, another blind child, but eight months older than Trevor and with more nursery experience, interacted much more freely with his peers while playing in the home corner. He pretended to prepare a picnic, discussing with others what they wanted to take, meeting up with the sighted group later to play-act going out and eating it.

Kevin and Nelly both played with plastic building bricks amongst their peers. While Kevin decided what he was going to make and then finished his model, Nelly changed her mind about what she wanted to build, breaking up the pieces and starting again. Kevin enlisted the help of his peers to find the pieces he needed, discussing how they were going to construct the model. Nelly's play activity was more repetitive and isolated, although she did sustain conversations with peers around issues unrelated to her play, such as planning visits to a friend's house and going to the swimming pool. Irrespective of age or visual loss, all of these children show differing kinds of resourcefulness and sociability.

In terms of the four-quadrant framework presented in Figure 6.1, a few children were simply on the receiving end of other children's or adults' play directives, complying with instructions on how to join in, doing as others required of them, but contributing few ideas themselves. This kind of passive compliance to the initiatives of others we describe as adult- or peer-directed. Some children were largely impassive and preoccupied, showing little interest in materials or individuals around them, and not engaged by adults or peers, which we might interpret in terms of quadrant B. Other children with visual impairments played on their own with toys and materials in self-directed initiatives for a great amount of time, with low involvement of peers and adults, devising personal, non-interactive activities. In contrast to this quadrant C type pursuit, several individuals preferred never to be on their own, demanding openings for joint play and shared activities, which we have described in terms of active learning partnerships.

It is important to analyse how these patterns of play arose and what conditions promoted useful collaborative play partnerships. One important factor is that different schools and professionals varied in their attitudes and expectations with regard to children's play. For example, in one setting a blind child was not expected to play with plastic building bricks because it was assumed he would be unable to locate pieces easily, or to see the models he built. In another context, blindness was never thought to be a limiting factor in using construction materials, and plastic building bricks became one child's favourite activity which he was able to share productively with others. So adults' envisioning of play possibilities has a significant influence on the resources made available, and the range and kinds of play enjoyed. This is an example of how, in socio-constructive terms, specific social contexts tend to develop their own constraints.

Some of the children with more severe visual impairments spent much greater periods of time manipulating objects and resources than in social play with others. This observation was especially true for the two boys who were totally blind and had learning difficulties (Roe, 1996). These children were preoccupied with exploring the features and boundaries of the environment, moving from one area to another, putting things in and out of boxes, and exploring the contents of drawers and cupboards. Some children with severe visual impairments in mainstream settings may require long periods of orientation and familiarisation. Firm friendship links with familiar play partners also take time to build, but appear to be instrumental in shifting from solitary self-contained play to more interactive activities. Continuity and consistency in play groupings are obviously important. Similarly, there may need to be much adult assistance in developing strategies for play and social interaction with sighted children until well into the junior school years.

Martin, for example, was only occasionally approached by another child who would call him and try to show him an object, generally without success. While playing at the water tray, Martin rocked and waved objects and occasionally filled bottles and other containers with water, but was unable to involve others in his play. He appeared to be locked into these repetitive play patterns, whilst adults were generally content with his self-preoccupation and took no steps to intervene or assist. John, another blind child, was trying to fit shapes into the respective holes in a plastic container, when one of his peers tried to help him by pointing to the right holes for each shape. An adult watching from a distance explained what clues John depended on, and suggested that the sighted child guide John's hand to the holes, which was more effective. In this contrasting example, the adult took steps to read both children's intentions, provided information that clarified the task faced by John, together with the help he required, and thereby 'scaffolded' a small instance of co-operative success.

Which adult interventions promoted play and social interaction between the children? Adults have a very important role in providing play suggestions and keeping the child interested in a task, or in the activities of those around them, which we have described as recruitment. In some situations adults can seize openings for more active involvement in shared play. For example, Daniel played on the fringes of a group in the home corner which had become a hospital. Two sighted boys became doctors and were taking care of dolls who needed treatment, while the three girls put on nurses' uniforms. The adult suggested that Daniel became a patient and he was covered in bandages. Later, the children were invited to swap roles and Daniel took the part of a doctor.

Observing children in everyday settings seems to disconfirm the view that there are typically restricted play patterns in visually impaired groups. There are, of course, differences in how inventive and gregarious individuals happen to be. Younger children with more severe visual losses took longer to familiarise themselves with their surroundings and other children, and were more likely to play repetitively on their own. However, this depended to a great extent on the expectations of adults, how they envisaged the play possibilities, and the steps they took to promote collaboration. Importantly, self-contained, unimaginative play patterns are not an inevitable consequence of visual impairment, but often reflect contextual influences.

RESEARCH FOCUS 2: VISUAL IMPAIRMENT, MATURITY AND INTERACTION

This focus examines factors such as children's age and degree of visual impairment in relation to the quality of social interaction. How influential were the characteristics of the children themselves – their maturity and residual vision – in determining the success of social encounters? What kind of behaviour did different children evoke from their interactive partners?

Overall, the younger the children, the more time they spent with an adult on a one-to-one basis (Rho = -0.457, p $<$ 0.05). Also, the more severe the visual impairment, the more time an adult spent in the child's close company, whether or not there were other sighted children around (Rho = -0.490, p $<$ 0.05). In terms of our interaction framework depicted in Figure 6.1, adults responded to the more immature children who had more severe visual losses with an increase in management and control. Adults tended to instruct, demonstrate, direct or restrain an activity, stayed next to individuals or followed them to different locations. For example, when Trevor was sticking bits of fabric and paper together, the adult stayed next to him, instructing him on how to pick up the glue stick, how to spread the glue and so on.

On the other hand, the less severe the visual impairment and the more mature the child, the less children's activity was inhibited, controlled or monitored by adults. With some groups, adults were much more prepared to allow children with visual impairments to mingle with peers without pursuing them, and intervened only occasionally when they thought it was necessary to give assistance, or to offer suggestions that helped to make play more interesting or to move it along. For example, when Sam played a card game with a peer using the CCTV, the children were allowed free reign to solve any problems that arose and adults intervened only on request.

Martin, a blind child of 5 and a half years, with additional learning difficulties, played mainly on his own with shapes and containers. Martin was often watched and approached by adults, mainly for supervisory and management purposes, stopping his more vigorous activity or asking him to tidy up. On one occasion, Martin tried many times to empty a bucket filled with wooden blocks, but the adult always prevented him from doing so because it would make a mess. This could have been approached differently as a teaching opportunity, demonstrating cause and effect: the consequences of tipping a large number of solid blocks onto a hard surface and relocating them amongst piles of other toys!

This episode illustrates a number of issues that we highlighted in Chapter 3 concerning the nature of adult interventions in some school settings. In school, children frequently encounter adults who interact only briefly with individuals and whose main interests are directive or inhibitory. Children with visual impairments seem to be exposed to more questions and commands, rather than interpretative descriptions of events, or interchanges that draw them into new or modified activities with others. Paradoxically, adults seem to restrict, rather than to enlarge, the child's exploration and experience, including the language that accompanies it.

The data reported here add another dimension to the evidence derived from studies of conversational interaction given in Chapter 3 of this book (Kekelis and Andersen, 1984; Andersen et al., 1993). In these studies, adult caregivers responded to children with more severe visual impairments with an increase in verbal requests, questions and directives. This escalation of control in spoken exchanges is mirrored in the adult's occupation of the child's immediate physical space, and in aspects such as restricting certain activities, close monitoring and pursuit. Not only do some adults increase their verbal direction and control in the presence of a child with a visual impairment, they may also escalate their physical proximity and management.

RESEARCH FOCUS 3: CHILD AS RESOURCE

An important aspect of play that we examined was the use of interactive partners as a resource. By this we mean requests children make of one another for specific information, action or objects. The use of play partners as a data source is an important strategy for children with visual impairments, enabling them to capitalise on the broader environmental awareness of sighted peers. By interrogating peers, blind children can confirm identities, locate toys and materials, find out how equipment operates, and gauge others' reactions, intentions or disposition. They utilise what others already know to aid their active exploration and meaning-making. They can create openings for joint play with other children, rather than waiting to be asked.

We can hypothesise that resilience in children with visual losses – the capacity to overcome hurdles and achieve against the odds – in part depends on their persistence in using others to answer questions, to be confident and forthcoming in forging play opportunities and finding things out. In Chapter 3, where we highlighted strategies that children can adopt to facilitate their own learning in integrated settings, key factors were the ability to initiate social contacts, to 'read' the environment, and to be quizzical, curious and assertive. However, there has been no research to date that has addressed these social processes in settings where children with visual impairments are integrated with peers, or that has tried to identify the characteristics of children with visual impairments that equip them for acceptance and success.

An important question, therefore, is how we can assist children with visual impairments to use others as a resource. Conversely, an important measure of how far children with visual impairments are valued as play partners and involved at the hub of events, is their use as a resource by others. Which of our sample of children were approached by sighted peers or adults for purposes such as requests for objects or information, permission to borrow certain toys or equipment, or invitations to join in a venture?

Amongst the visually impaired sample, a strong relationship was found between general maturity and being used as a resource by peers. The older the children, the more they were called on (Rho = 0.560, p < 0.01). There was also a close relationship between the level of visual impairment and being used as a resource. The less severe the visual impairment, the more children were subject to a range of requests (Rho = 0.542, p < 0.01). Almost a third of the approaches made by children with visual impairments to peers, and half the requests made to adults, concerned information: ('What's this?', 'What's it for?'). Approximately 10 per cent of requests to adults and peers called for particular actions to be taken, whilst 22 per cent of requests to peers, and 14 per cent to adults, sought particular objects. A smaller percentage of their requests concerned the identities of partners ('What's your name?'), but not adults, presumably because there were fewer of these around, or it was less vital to know their names. Tables 6.2 and 6.3 give a breakdown of the extent of these interactions for specific purposes with peers and adults.

On occasions, overtures to sighted peers were ignored or unsuccessful, because the addressed child had moved out of earshot, or because a play partner was intent on teasing. For example, when playing on the carpet with a large group of children, Tom had to make a big effort to recognise his peers, which his playmates sometimes confounded:

Tom: Liam? . . . what's your name?
Peer: I'm not Liam.
Tom: What's your name?
Peer: It's . . . ahh . . . Sarah.

Tom: Your name is Charles.
Peer: No, it isn't.
Tom: Yeah.
Peer: Sarah! Sarah!

When we consider how the visually impaired children were used by others as useful funds of data, both peers and adults were generally solicitous with regard to how they were feeling, what they would prefer to happen and whether they were enjoying things ('Do you want a flag?' 'Do you like it?'). Approximately half of both adults' and peers' approaches to the visually impaired sample centred on the individual's response to a current activity. Sighted children occasionally asked blind children if they knew where coveted objects or people could be found, or asked questions such as 'Can you see?'. A very small percentage of the sighted children's requests concerned the current activities of the children with visual losses: what they were doing and why? However, almost all of the adult interjections requested information from the children with visual impairments about their current actions or play, tending not to inspire interest in what others were doing around them.

Trevor, for example, was making a model from boxes and pieces of mate-rial. Every single step was explained to him and there was no interaction with other children. However, Trevor heard a peer saying that he was making a rocket. Subsequently, Trevor also wanted to make a rocket and the adult helped him to find different materials for the fuselage and wings. The adult never thought to bring the two children together to compare their rocket-making efforts.

In all our observations, adults showed difficulties inviting a child with a

Table 6.2 Children with visual impairments using others as a resource

Use of others as a resource	% of overall requests to peers (n = 247)	% of overall requests to adults (n = 59)
Requests concerning identity	5	0
Requests information concerning the localisation of people or objects	14	7
Requests other to take an action	11	10
Requests object	22	14
Requests information concerning the performance of a task	3	2
Requests information concerning other's actions, wishes or feelings	6	3
Requests confirmation (possession of objects, etc)	5	5
Requests other information related to him/herself (asking authorisation)	1	10
Requests other information	33	49

Table 6.3 Children with visual impairments being a resource to others

Use as a resource by others	% of overall requests from peers (n = 92)	% of overall requests from adults (n = 87)
Child was requested to give an object in their possession	7	0
Child was requested to get an object for others	4	0
Child was requested to give information concerning the performance of a task	2	0
Child was requested to give information about localisation of people or objects	7	0
Child was requested to do something for others	4	1
Child was requested to give information concerning the child's own play activity	3	39
Child was requested to give information concerning own actions, wishes or feelings	47	52
Child was requested other information about him or herself ('Are you blind?', 'Can you see?')	9	3
Child was requested other information	17	5

visual impairment to supply or retrieve an object for someone else, in sharing ideas, in providing information or commentary about the play or activities of other children, and in assisting getting something done outside of the immediate focus of the child's own attention and interest. There were no instances observed, for example, of an adult asking a child with a visual loss the whereabouts of other children or particular toys.

The following example also demonstrates how adults may reinforce a child's social isolation, rather than promoting social links with peers. Daniel was shadowed by an adult who stayed behind him at the sand tray and talked to him when requested. Although there were other children playing with sand, Daniel did not interact with them. The adult did not explain what the other children were doing and did not try to extend his play, or to find openings for a joint activity. Daniel's conversation topics moved fleetingly across flowers, trucks, snowploughs, Volkswagen cars, concrete and aeroplanes:

Daniel: Look there is a snow pusher here. A snow pusher.
Adult: A snow pusher? Well, gosh that will be useful when it snows, Daniel.
Daniel: When it melts we'll push the snow.
Adult: That's a good idea.
Daniel: There is a VW . . . there is a VW beetle to be your car.
Adult: Good!
Daniel: (using a spade): I'm making you a new concrete ground.
Adult: Oh! Thank you very much.

212

Daniel kept on turning his back to his peers so that he could talk to the adult, who affirmed each change of interest, without trying to develop his play or involve him in the activities of the group. Consequently, Daniel's play lacked sequence, form or clear objectives, until it seemed as though he simply wanted to hold onto the adult's attention by flitting across topics.

These findings extend some of the observations made by researchers in other experimental contexts (see, for example, Andersen *et al.*, 1993). Mothers observed with their blind children at home tended to make many requests, asked questions and introduced topics related to the child's own current activity. They rarely linked current interests to distant persons or events, or involved the children in activities taking place elsewhere. In other words, the strategies adopted by adults towards children with visual impairments appear to reinforce self-contained, solitary, introverted behaviour, homing in on current actions and feelings, but failing to contextualise these or make links with surrounding children, activities or events.

RESEARCH FOCUS 4: PLAY CONTEXTS, RESOURCES AND ROLES

In none of the schools involved in our research did we expect to find the kind of 'designer' play environments advocated by Schneekloth (1989) where physical space is carefully subdivided, large equipment and real artefacts are in evidence, with routeways, storage places and boundaries clearly marked.

Notwithstanding the realities of many of the play contexts or resources to be found in most mainstream settings, the selection and deployment of appropriate materials is an important factor in promoting play and social interaction. This may seem obvious, but in our study we observed that some children played with toys that were poorly adapted to their needs. For example, a group of children were engaged with a box of dominoes that could be matched in terms of colours and designs. Whilst his peers were puzzling over the designs and pictures, Tom built stables and fields around pretend animals with the dominoes. The fact that Tom did not have access to these materials on the same basis as his peers effectively prevented any further interaction between the children as they were intent on playing different games.

The context in which the children played had an effect on the amount of time children spent playing and interacting with each other. When children played with construction materials, they spent most of their time playing next to, rather than with, other children. On the other hand, when children played in the home corner, they tended to interact more with one another and this was particularly observed when the group of children in the home corner remained the same. The physical layout of objects is also an important factor. Large areas with toys spread out loosely on the floor led children to spend more time looking for things. They ended up playing with whatever they found, rather than choosing what interested them.

Toys such as pegboards, shape puzzles, post boxes, formboards, containers, beads and blocks are designed to establish fine manipulative skills and concepts such as shape, colour, pattern and size. More helpful for promoting imaginative, interactive play are real objects, or equipment of appropriate texture and materials (such as wooden kitchen tools, metal pots and pans, rather than plastic). There are also versatile toys that can be used representationally and in partnership, such as the many kinds of materials available commercially that can be fitted together to build vehicles, race tracks, space stations, pirate ships, forts or marble mazes. Other toys provide a context for joint imaginative play, such as dolls' houses, vehicles, kitchen sets, zoos, farmyards, military depots or science fiction replicas. Imitative play, which perhaps holds the greatest potential for stimulating social interaction, can be promoted by small 'stage sets' and 'props', such as a Post Office counter, workbench and tools, kitchen range, grocery shop or take-away, dressing up clothes and hats, finger and glove puppets, doctor and nurse uniforms and toy medical equipment.

Although children interact more with each other in play sets such as the home corner, these also tend to generate more conflict. Resolving conflicts is an important part of learning how to deal with others, but negotiation must occur and agreements must be achieved if children are to gain from the experience. Adults have an important role in deciding which children will be socially compatible and will make a viable group. Adults may need to step into some situations if there is a misuse of materials, or if a child appears to be disturbing the play activity unduly. In accord with our framework of interaction presented in Figure 6.1, contingent adults who wish to scaffold play positively will be adept at standing back when groups are playing successfully, but perhaps suggesting new resources and play possibilities when the activity appears to be flagging.

Overcontrol of group activities by adults may result in reducing the level of interaction between children. For example, Charles was playing a game with two peers that consisted of finding shapes with either some similarities to, or differences from, another given shape. The adult presented the shapes to Charles so that he knew what the other children were talking about. The adult directed each child's activity and controlled the turn-taking of the children, who were expected to follow directions and answer questions. The adult also controlled Charles' head position, turning him to face in certain directions, and took away any object that Charles might explore during waiting periods. In this highly scaffolded activity the children did not address one another and became anxious about getting the right answers to the problems set by the adult in charge.

With older children, it may be worth identifying the different roles involved in working or playing together and helping a group to take decisions about who will do what. Group activities proper involve listening to others, learning how to make suggestions or enter a discussion, and a willingness to put aside selfish interests in taking turns, waiting and helping one another. It is important for all children, including those with visual impairments, to have the opportunity to choose friends, to negotiate with play partners and to develop a varied repertoire of skills for participating in groups and for resolving conflicts.

RESEARCH FOCUS 5: LANGUAGE AND CONCEPTUAL GROWTH

At several points in this book we have considered the close interweaving of conceptual growth with certain kinds of perceptual experience and the language that both organises and encapsulates it. Play opportunities are often rich in meaning, but children with visual impairments depend on their collaborators to interpret events and to provide verbal descriptions and clarifications that represent play moves in terms that are accessible. If play is to be an effective source of language and conceptual growth, both adults and children have to be mediators of shared experience.

When children play within established groupings it is easier for them to get to know one another's limitations and needs, and to learn ways around obstacles to shared understanding. Many of the play partners of children observed in our study had great difficulty working out how the world might appear to someone who could see little, whilst others were much more competent at providing the extra information required:

Peer: (stands behind the pushchair facing Kevin who is sitting on the floor): We are going out today . . . Would you like to come with us? . . . Do you? . . . Do you want to go in the middle? . . . Do you want to make a visit with us?

Peer: (bends her trunk in Kevin's direction): Do you, Kevin? . . . Do you want to push the pushchair with us?

Kevin: (stands and stretches hand towards peer): Yeah.

Peer: (pats pushchair): Here.

Peer: Mix the sugar.

Daniel: Let me see . . . where is the sugar?

Peer: (holds pot in front of Daniel's face): Here.

Daniel: (reaches for the saucepan): In where?

Peer: (touches Daniel's face with the pot): In here.

A group activity with a common outcome, to which all the children make an active contribution, requires skills in negotiating, bartering, reconciling different opinions, and the reaching of compromise solutions. In the following play scenario, a group is helping Kevin to design a house:

Peer: What about a window?

Kevin: No, it's not a . . . It's a Victorian house.

215

Plate 6.2 Social contact. When children play within established groupings it is easier for them to get to know one another's limitations and needs: note how these children maintain contact

Peer: A Victorian house has windows. . . . A Victorian house has a door and windows doesn't it?

Peer: Yeah. But it's his house.

Peer: I would be sweating.

Peer: Yeah . . . Well, Simon, they didn't have lights, did they? They had candles.

Kevin: Yes, remember? . . . Oh! We need that . . . and a square.

Peer: I've found two flags.

Peer: Oh thank you Simon. . . . We can have two flags on our roof.

Kevin: I don't like flags, it's my house.

Peer: Do you want to put one flag then?

Kevin: No, no flags, they did . . . they didn't have flags on, on, on Victorian houses.

The challenge of this kind of dialogue around a shared enquiry, where children draw on aspects of their experience and are prepared to pursue their own personal perspectives, reveals the close relationship between the shape of children's thinking and the linguistic means they have at their disposal. In Chapter 3 these moments of joint exploration, challenging one another's ideas and assumptions, were described as 'passages of intellectual search' (Tizard and Hughes, 1984). All of the children involved in these kinds of exchanges adjust, hone and remake their own understandings from their efforts to construct things together. Language is not just the means by which individuals formulate their ideas and express them. It is also the basis for individuals to think and learn as a group.

RESEARCH FOCUS 6: RESOLVING CONFLICT

The final research focus is concerned with conflict, defined as the clash of opposing interests. When children recognise a confrontation between viewpoints or actions and take steps to find solutions, there can be important developmental gains, most often defined by researchers in terms of cognitive restructuring (Bearison *et al.*, 1986; Light and Glachan, 1985). These processes usually signal dramatic shifts in the child's thinking and understanding, as the child's repertoire of skills extends to cope with new situations or ideas.

Most studies of conflict in sighted groups have observed children in experimental settings, such as playing 'Mastermind' in pairs. Children who learn most from problem-solving tasks are those who discuss one another's perspectives, who listen and respond to their peers, and who provide clarifications and explanations whenever negotiations falter: they 'scaffold' one another. Very little research evidence has been gathered on how conflicts are resolved when one of the play or task participants has a visual impairment.

In an example taken from our own observations, a group of children could not agree on who should occupy a play space, the roles children should adopt, or the actions to be taken to move the play forward. Elisabeth, a 5 and a half year old with limited visual acuity, bickered with her peers and on many occasions rejected what they proposed. She tried very strongly to control other children physically by pushing them away, by grabbing at objects in their possession, by shouting at them, or ignoring them when they tried to negotiate with her. Elisabeth found it difficult to express what she wanted verbally, often leaving her sentences unfinished and making noises of exasperation, but failing to clarify her point of view:

> Elisabeth:(pulls peers): No, no, no, you don't go in there, you are THE DAD, NO, NO, GET OUT.
> Peer: No, I want to be in here. Elisabeth don't pull, Elisabeth don't.
> Elisabeth:Then you go in the . . . now I was giving you . . .
> Peer: Let's ring the ambulance, quick.
> Elisabeth:NO, I DON'T WANT, I WANT TO . . . (pulls peer) You can be the dad.
> Peer: Alright . . . I'll be the ambulance lady, yeah?
> Elisabeth:I was packing this . . . all this up now.
> Peer: Yeah, and I was the ambulance lady, yeah?
> Elisabeth:NO, I was calling the ambulance.

Adults have an important mediating role within these social contexts, suggesting, explaining, reminding, prompting and clarifying roles and expectations without overdominating. To some extent, careful choice of play partners and familiar routines for play help to smooth play encounters. To participate in play all children must acquire a repertoire of social strategies, such as sharing, negotiation and compromise. All of these dimensions require a decentring from the child: an ability to take other people's needs and perspectives into account. These are the particular aspects of social experience that a visual impairment renders more difficult to acquire and which adults seem unwittingly to be poor at promoting.

IMPROVING SOCIAL ENCOUNTERS

A number of suggestions arise out of these research findings that seem likely to promote more positive social interactions. Learning how to interact socially with others is a demanding task for any child. Many clues that help us during social encounters are very subtle and depend on good vision, such as interpreting and using facial expressions. Initially, children may depend heavily on more experienced social partners, usually adults, to provide information concerning what is happening around them. It is also important for children to have opportunities to investigate and interpret social dynamics by themselves.

A first determinant of play concerns how the physical environment is organised for consistency and security. Children with visual impairments need to know where things are and how they can find them safely and quickly so that they can participate more actively. Unstructured play sessions are particularly difficult when toys and materials cannot be located easily. It is essential that the environment is organised systematically, with specific activities recurring at a certain time, with similar groupings and layouts. Providing opportunities to interact with a small group of children that remains the same for a whole play session helps the child to know who the peers are, how to approach them and how to find out what they are doing.

A second factor concerns how adults' envisioning of play possibilities determines which resources are made available. Our research shows that more creative and interactive play is promoted by certain toys and not others. In some instances, adults discouraged certain kinds of play, such as with construction materials, because they felt that a child would not be able to see the finished product. In addition to this, unless resources are provided (such as adapted games or toys) that children with reduced vision can use on equal terms as their play partners, children may play at cross purposes with their peers. Children with visual impairments may also need more time to learn how to use toys appropriately, together with greater explanation and demonstration of toy functions.

A third influence on social encounters concerns the adult's role as mediator. Earlier we examined some key concepts that socio-constructivism highlights, such as scaffolding and contingency. Adults can encourage engagement in different kinds of play scenarios by being sensitive to moments when to step in or to step back, when to allow play to unfold without interference, and when to propose new directions. The continuous presence of an over-controlling adult who shadows a child for protective purposes may not foster social interaction. Successful adults promote interaction by recruiting children to activities, making suggestions about the help required to understand a task and seizing openings for extending play possibilities, without dominating the proceedings. These aspects of scaffolding encourage children towards more complex and interactive play, whilst gradually handing over responsibility for successful social encounters to children themselves.

Often we observed that when adults tried to assist children with visual impairments, they focused on the child's egocentric activity, wishes or feelings, without helping them to network with other individuals or activities going on around them. Successful adults comment on others' activities, express their own feelings, disagree where appropriate with the child, and stimulate interest in other people's ideas and actions. They help to forge and reward children's own attempts to interact with others. Listening to children during their play encounters helps to monitor breakdowns in communication or conflicts that cannot be resolved. At these points, a sensitive adult assists the play partners by finding alternative ways of proceeding and showing them how to deal with one another. Good scaffolding, in contexts such as these, helps children to understand the intentions, feelings and actions of those who share their world, and the social rules by which they are governed.

SUMMARY AND OVERVIEW

In the field of visual impairment there is a great deal that research has yet to uncover. Although many children with severe visual losses do make sense of the complex social environments in which they live, developing competences in language, personal and academic domains, there is still much uncertainty about optimal teaching and learning conditions, and what should be given priority in a programme of intervention. In this final chapter of our book we have focused on the importance of social interaction for children's development and the experiences that children with visual impairments encounter in mainstream settings, with both peers and adults. How a teaching milieu is designed and organised, and the role of the adult as social facilitator, is perhaps the most important set of factors over which we exercise choice and control.

In the book as a whole we have addressed a wide set of issues that impinge on the learning and development of individuals with a visual loss. Initially, we considered ways in which images of children as learners are influential, and the importance of individual differences in terms of adaptivity, resilience and motivation. We also gave detailed consideration to the terms in which a visual impairment may be defined and identified. The physical and psychological processes involved in any visual condition are highly complex and give rise to perceptual experiences that can be fully understood only in relation to individuals as they cope with the day-to-day contexts of their lives.

There is a strong temptation, which researchers rarely resist, to simplify and homogenise issues, to play down their complexity. In the sections that summarise the existing research literature, we have attempted to give an account of developmental processes and the impact of a visual loss, without categorising children or over-generalising: the 'all blind children . . .' trap. The shift in perspective highlighted is one of rich diversity in the characteristics that different children bring to learning encounters. Our own interest lies mainly with the learning processes through which children do extend their language, concepts and wider understanding, and the special place of vision within these processes. The 'site' in which these processes can be most effectively observed is the social matrix of family, peer group or school, where teaching and learning transactions take place.

It is often the case that knowledge gained from examining the problem-solving and adaptivity of children with specific obstacles to overcome, such as a sensory impairment, can inform the more effective teaching of all children. This particular theme has informed our critique of recent policy and legislation under the Code of Practice for identifying and assessing children's special educational needs. We have examined how current professional practice may contribute towards the raising of individual achievement and the realisation of 'lifelong learning', within the context of visual impairment. The educational needs of individuals with a visual impairment often concern language and cognition, exploration and mobility within the physical world, and the acquiring of appropriate social conventions that permit rewarding relationships and effective participation in the cultures of family, school and the wider community.

The links or 'bridges' that adults and peers make possible between a child's inner world and the world outside, often using the vehicle of language, are an important dimension for those involved with any individual with a visual impairment. The socio-cultural perspective adopted in our studies provides some new and exciting possibilities for understanding how language and learning are essentially social constructions, dependent on both the efforts of the child and the domain in which problems are jointly tackled. Our main aim has been to show how many of these significant concerns can be addressed in a practical way, underpinned by research, without minimising the very real challenges to families, teachers and individuals that a visual loss presents.

APPENDIX: FURTHER INFORMATION SOURCES

American Foundation for the Blind
15 West 16th Street
New York NY10011
USA

Centre for Studies on Integration in Education
415 Edgware Road
London NW2 6NB

ClearVision Project
Linden Lodge School
61 Princes Way
London SW19 6JB

Disabled Living Foundation
380–384 Harrow Road
London W9 2HU

Eye Care Information Bureau
4 Ching Court
Shelton Street
London WC2H 9DG

Guide Dogs for the Blind Association
Alexandra House
9/11 Park Street
Windsor
Berkshire SL4 1JR

LOOK
The National Federation of Families with Visually Impaired Children
Queen Alexandra College
49 Court Oak Road
Birmingham B17 9TG

Moorfields Eye Hospital
City Road
London EC1V 2PD

National Low Vision Advice Centre
3 Colleton Crescent
Exeter
Devon EX2 4DG

Partially Sighted Society
206 Great Portland Street
London W1N 6AA

Research Centre for the Education of the Visually Handicapped
University of Birmingham
School of Education
PO Box 363
Birmingham B15 2TT

Royal National Institute for the Blind
224 Great Portland Street
London W1N 6AA

Scottish Sensory Centre
Moray House Institute of Education
Holyrood Road
Edinburgh EH8 8AQ

SENSE
National Association for Deaf/Blind and Rubella Handicapped
13–15 Clifton Terrace
Finsbury Park
London N4 3SR

SKILL
National Bureau for Handicapped Students
336 Brixton Road
London SW9 7AA

Special Needs Resource Centre
University of Northumbria at Newcastle
Coach Lane Campus
Newcastle-upon-Tyne NE7 7TW

VIEW
Association for the Education and Welfare of the Visually Impaired
York House
Exhall Grange School
Wheelwright Lane
Ash Green
Coventry CV7 9HP

GLOSSARY

Accommodation   Ability of the lens to adjust its shape through the contraction and relaxation of ciliary muscles so that a sharper image falls on the retina. It is the mechanism that allows us to focus on objects at different distances.

Acuity   Ability to distinguish very fine detail. Sharpness of vision.

Albinism   Condition characterised by the absence of pigmentation (skin, hair and/or eyes) which is often associated with low visual acuity, photophobia and nystagmus.

Amblyopia   Lack of some visual functions which results in limited central visual acuity. Usually occurs when the other eye is preferred and it is often associated with a squint.

Aniridia   Absence of the iris resulting in photophobia due to the inability to control the amount of light entering the eye.

Aphakia   Absence of the lens.

Astigmatism   Refractive error caused by irregularities on the surface of the cornea and resulting in distorted or blurred vision.

Binocular vision   Ability to focus both eyes on the same object at the same time and to fuse the two images in one image, enabling judgement of distance and perception of depth.

Blindness   In legal terms, an individual is considered blind if he or she is not able to use vision to perform any work for which eyesight would be essential. This usually corresponds to a visual acuity of 3/60 or less in the better eye and after correction. However, if there is a loss in the visual field, even an individual with a visual acuity superior to 3/60 may be considered blind.

In educational terms, individuals are considered educationally blind when they need to use non-visual means in order to follow educational tasks.

Cataract   Opacity in the lens of the eye resulting in loss of visual acuity.

Choroid   The choroid is part of the middle layer of the eye together with the iris and ciliary body.

Coloboma   Congenital wedge that is missing from the iris usually due to its incomplete growth.

Colour blindness   Limited ability to distinguish between different colours.

Cone   Cells that form a layer of the retina and are responsible for visual acuity and colour discrimination.

Cornea   Transparent and curved surface at the very front of the eyeball. Constitutes the outside layer of the eye together with the sclera.

Cortex   Area of the brain responsible for central processing.

Cortical visual impairment   Inability of the brain to interpret the signals received from the eye.

Emmetropia   Refers to the absence of refractive errors when parallel light rays are brought to a focus on the fovea with the lens at rest.

Enucleation   The eyeball has been completely removed through surgery, following an accident or disease.

Field of vision   The entire area in which an object can be seen without moving the eyes.

Fovea   Small area in the retina to which light rays are brought. It is adapted for the most distinct vision.

Functional vision   Relates to how a person uses residual vision to function in everyday settings.

Glaucoma   Condition characterised by a high pressure in the eye resulting in changes in the optic nerve and field of vision.

Hemianopia   Refers to defective vision in half of the visual field.

Hypermetropia   Refractive error in which parallel light rays are focused behind the fovea. Also called long-sightedness.

Iris   Coloured membrane that changes the size of the pupil and, in so doing, controls the amount of light entering the eye.

Light perception   Ability to distinguish light from dark.

Macula   Area in the retina that, together with the fovea, is adapted for distinct vision.

Microphthalmos   Refers to an eye that is smaller than normal.

Monocular vision   Vision obtained through one eye only.

Myopia   Refractive error in which parallel light rays are brought to focus in front of the retina. Also called short-sightedness.

Night blindness   Condition characterised by dysfunctional rods that results in difficulty in seeing at night and in dim light.

Nystagmus   Involuntary and rapid movements of the eyeball.

Optic atrophy   Condition characterised by a degeneration of the optic nerve that leads to the cortex.

Partial sight   In legal terms, 'partial sight' is defined as a visual acuity of between 3/60 and 6/60. This term is interpreted quite differently in educational terms where it refers to individuals who may use their eyesight to follow educational tasks but will need to have access to some special methods or support. Although in educational terms individuals will need to use their sight in a variety of situations that are very different to those used during an assessment, a Snellen visual acuity of between 6/18 and 6/60 can constitute partial sight.

Peripheral vision   Perception of objects, colour or movement by any part of the retina excluding the macula.

Photophobia   Abnormal high sensitivity to light.

Ptosis   Refers to the drooping of an upper eyelid.

Refractive error   Defect in the eye that results in the inability of light rays to be brought to a focus on the retina.

Residual vision   Amount of vision that a person has left. Widely used term that is not very precise because persons with the same amount of residual vision may function very differently.

Retina   Highly complex membrane that is made up of cones and rods and receives visual stimuli that are transmitted through the optic nerve to the brain.

Retinal aplasia   Mal-development of the retina.

Retinal detachment   Condition characterised by complete or partial separation of the retina from the choroid.

Retinitis pigmentosa   Condition characterised by degeneration and atrophy of the light-sensitive cells in the retina. Affects peripheral vision first and is often a progressive condition.

Retinoblastoma   The most common malignant intraocular tumour of childhood which arises from retinal germ cells. Usually occurs before the age of 5.

Retinopathy of prematurity (ROP)   Condition in which the retina has been damaged due to oxygen inhalation. Most frequent in prematurely born infants of low weight.

Retrolental fibroplasia   See retinopathy of prematurity.

Rods   Cells in the retina that are adapted to perceive motion and vision in dim light.

Scotoma   An area in the visual field that has no vision. A blind spot in the visual field.

Squint or strabismus   Abnormal alignment of the two eyes due to imbalance of the eye muscles.

Tunnel vision   Contraction of the visual field to an extent that only a small area of central vision is left, giving the impression of looking through a tunnel.

Visual acuity   Ability of the eyes to see detail.

REFERENCES

Aitken, S. and Buultjens, M. (1992) *Vision for Doing: Assessing Functional Vision of Learners who are Multiply Disabled.* Edinburgh: Moray House Publications

Andersen, E. S., Dunlea, A. and Kekelis, L. (1993) The impact of input: language acquisition in the visually impaired. *First Language*, Vol. 13, pp. 23–50

Arter, C., McCall, S. and Bowyer, T. (1996) Handwriting and children with visual impairments. *British Journal of Special Education*, Vol. 23, No. 1, pp. 25–29

Baird, G. and Moore, A. T. (1993) Epidemiology of childhood blindness. In A. R. Fiedler, A. B. Best and M. C. Bax (eds) *The Management of Visual Impairment in Childhood.* Clinics in Developmental Medicine No. 128, Cambridge: CUP, pp. 1–8

Barnes, S. B., Gutfreund, M., Satterly, D. J. and Wells, C. G. (1983) Characteristics of adult speech which predict children's language development. *Journal of Child Language*, Vol. 10, pp. 65–84

Barraga, N. C. (1970) *Teacher's Guide for Development of Visual Learning Abilities and Utilization of Low Vision.* Louisville: American Foundation for the Blind

Bearison, D. J., Magzamen, S. and Filardo, E. K. (1986) Socio-cognitive conflict and cognitive growth in young children. *Merril-Palmer Quarterly*, Vol. 32, No. 1, pp. 51–72

Best, A. B. (1992) *Teaching Children with Visual Impairments.* Milton Keynes: Open University Press

Bigelow, A. E. (1986) The development of reaching in blind children. *British Journal of Developmental Psychology*, Vol. 4, pp. 355–366

Bigelow, A. E. (1987) Early words of blind children. *Journal of Child Language*, Vol. 14, pp. 47–56

Bigelow, A. E. (1990) Relationship between the development of language and thought in young blind children. *Journal of Visual Impairment and Blindness*, Vol. 84, pp. 414–419

Bishop, V. E. (1986) Identifying components of success in mainstreaming. *Journal of Visual Impairment and Blindness*, Vol. 80, No. 9, pp. 939–946

British Paediatric Association (1995) *Health Needs of School Age Children.* Report of a Joint Working Party chaired by Leon Polnay. London: British Paediatric Association

Bruce, I., McKennell, A. C. and Walker, E. C. (1991) *Blind and Partially-sighted Adults in Britain: The RNIB Survey, Volume 1.* London: HMSO

Bruner, J. S. (1983) *Child's Talk: Learning to use Language.* Oxford: OUP

Bruner, J. S. (1986) *Actual Minds, Possible Worlds.* Cambridge, MA: Harvard University Press

Burgess, T. (1993) Reading Vygotsky. In H. Daniels (ed.) *Charting the Agenda: Educational Activity after Vygotsky.* London: Routledge

229

Burman, E. (1994) *Deconstructing Developmental Psychology*. London: Routledge

Came, F., Webster, A. and Webster, V. (1996) *Supporting Learning in the Secondary School: Raising Individual Achievement under the new Code of Practice*. Bristol: Avec Designs Ltd

Clark, H. H. and Clark, E. V. (1977) *Psychology and Language: An Introduction to Psycholinguistics*. New York: Harcourt Brace Jovanovich

Clark, R. (1974) Performing without competence. *Journal of Child Language*, Vol. 1, pp. 1–10

Clunies-Ross, L. (1995) *LEA Visual Impairment Questionnaire: Preliminary Analysis*. London: RNIB

Coakes, R. and Sellors, P. H. (1995) *Outline of Ophthalmology* (Second edition). Glasgow: Butterworth-Heinemann

Conti-Ramsden, G. (1994) Language interaction with atypical language learners. In C. Gallaway and B. J. Richards (eds) *Input and Interaction in Language Acquisition*. Cambridge: CUP

Cutsforth, T. D. (1932) The unreality of words to the blind. *Teachers' Forum*, Vol. 4, pp. 86–89

Dawkins, J. (1991) *Models of Mainstreaming for Visually Impaired Pupils*. London: HMSO

Department of Education and Science (DES) (1978) *Special Educational Needs (The Warnock Report)*. London: HMSO

Department of Health (DOH) (1991) *Registered Blind and Partially-sighted People at 31st March 1991, England*. London: Department of Health

Dick, M. (1994) The School Health Service. In J. Solity and G. Bickler (eds) *Support Services: Issues for Education, Health and Social Service Professionals*. London: Cassell, pp. 109–122

Dunkerton, J. (1995) Examination results of visually impaired students. *British Journal of Special Education*, Vol. 22, No. 1, pp. 34–39

Dunlea, A. (1989) *Vision and the Emergence of Meaning: Blind and Sighted Children's Early Language*. Cambridge: CUP

Erin, J. N. (1986) Frequencies and types of questions in the language of visually impaired children. *Journal of Visual Impairment and Blindness*, Vol. 80, No. 4, pp. 670–674

Erin, J. N. (1990) Language samples from visually-impaired four- and five-year olds. *Journal of Childhood Communication Disorders*, Vol. 13, No. 2, pp. 181–191

Ferguson, R. and Buultjens, M. (1995) The play behaviour of young blind children and its relationship to developmental stages. *British Journal of Visual Impairment*, Vol. 13, No. 3, pp. 100–107

Fewell, R. R. and Rich, J. S. (1987) Play assessment as a procedure for examining cognitive, communication and social skills in multihandicapped children. *Journal of Psychoeducational Assessment*, Vol. 2, pp. 107–118

Fleiss, J. L. (1971) Measuring nominal scale agreement among many raters. *Psychological Bulletin*, Vol. 76, pp. 378–382

Fonagy, P., Steele, M., Steele, H., Higgitt, A. and Target, M. (1994) The theory and practice of resilience. *Journal of Child Psychology and Psychiatry*, Vol. 35, No. 2, pp. 231–257

Fraiberg, S. (1977) (ed.) *Insights from the Blind*. New York: Basic Books

Gallaway, C. and Richards, B. J. (1994) *Input and Interaction in Language Acquisition*. Cambridge: CUP

Garton, A. F. (1992) *Social Interaction and the Development of Language and Cognition*. Hove: Lawrence Erlbaum Associates

Good, W. V. (1993) Ophthalmology of visual impairment. In A. R. Fielder, A. B. Best and M. C. Bax (eds) *The Management of Visual Impairment in Childhood.* Cambridge: CUP, pp. 30–47

Greenhalgh, R. (1993) Social aspects of visual impairment. In A. R. Fielder, A. B. Best, M. C. Bax (eds) *The Management of Visual Impairment in Childhood.* Cambridge: CUP, pp. 173–179

Hall, D. B. (1991) *Health for All Children: A Programme for Child Health Surveillance.* Oxford: OUP

Harrell, R. L. and Strauss, F. A. (1986) Approaches to increasing assertive behaviour and communication skills in blind and visually impaired persons. *Journal of Visual Impairment and Blindness,* Vol. 80, pp. 794–798

Harrison, F. and Crow, M. (1993) *Living and Learning with Blind Children: A Guide for Teachers and Parents of Visually Impaired Children.* Toronto: University of Toronto Press

Jan, J. E., Freeman, R. D. and Scott, E. P. (1977) *Visual Impairment in Childhood and Adolescence.* New York: Grune & Stratton

John-Steiner, V., Panofsky, C. P. and Smith, L. W. (1994) *Sociocultural Approaches to Language and Literacy: An Interactionist Perspective.* Cambridge: CUP

Jose, R. T. (ed.) (1983) *Understanding Low Vision.* New York: American Foundation for the Blind

Kanski, J. J. (1994) *Clinical Ophthalmology.* London: Butler & Tanner Ltd

Kekelis, L. S. and Andersen, E. S. (1984) Family communication styles and language development. *Journal of Visual Impairment and Blindness,* Vol. 78, No. 2, pp. 54–65

Kekelis, L. S. and Sacks, S. Z. (1992) The effects of visual impairment on children's social interactions in regular education programs. In S. Z. Sacks, L. Kekelis and R. J. Gaylord-Ross (eds) *The Development of Social Skills by Blind and Visually Impaired Students.* New York: American Foundation for the Blind

Keys, W. and Fernandes, C. (1993) *What Do Students Think about School?* Windsor: National Commission on Education/NFER

Light, P. and Glachan, M. (1985) Facilitation of problem solving through peer interaction. *Educational Psychology,* Vol. 5, Nos 3 and 4, pp. 217–225

Light, P., Sheldon, S. and Woodhead, M. (1991) *Learning to Think.* London: Routledge

Meadows, S. (1996) *Parenting Behaviour and Children's Cognitive Development.* Hove: Psychology Press

Mets, M. B. (1989) The Eye and the Chromosome, in W. Tasman and E. A. Jaeger (eds) *Duane's Clinical Ophthalmology,* Vol. 5. Philadelphia: J. B. Lippincott

Millar, T. (1986) Factors involved in supporting visually impaired children in mainstream schools. *Support for Learning,* Vol. 1, No. 4, pp. 16–21

Miller, G. A. (1963) *Language and Communication.* New York: McGraw Hill

Miller, L. (1992) Diderot reconsidered: Visual impairment and auditory compensation. *Journal of Visual Impairment and Blindness,* Vol. 86, pp. 101–105

Mills, A. E. (1983) (ed.) *Language Acquisition in the Blind Child.* London: Croom Helm

Mills, A. E. (1993) Visual handicap. In D. Bishop and K. Mogford (eds) *Language Development in Exceptional Circumstances.* Hove: Lawrence Erlbaum Associates, pp. 150–164.

Moll, L. (1990) (ed.) *Vygotsky and Education: Instructional Implications and Applications of Socio-historical Psychology.* Cambridge: CUP

Parsons, S. (1986a) Function of play in low vision children (Part 1): A review of the research and literature. *Journal of Visual Impairment and Blindness,* Vol. 80, No. 5, pp. 627–630

Parsons, S. (1986b) Function of play in low vision children (Part 2): Emerging patterns of behaviour. *Journal of Visual Impairment and Blindness*, Vol. 80, No. 6, pp. 777–784

Phillips, C. I., Clark, C. V. and Tsukahara, S. (1994) *Ophthalmology: A Primer for Medical Students and Practitioners*. London: Baillière Tindall

Piaget, J. (1967) *Six Psychlogical Studies*. London: London University Press

Piaget, J. (1971) *Structuralism*. London: Routledge and Kegan Paul

Piaget, J. (1971) *Science of Education and the Psychology of the Child*. London: Longman

Piaget, J. and Inhelder, B. (1969) *The Psychology of the Child*. London: Routledge and Kegan Paul

Preisler, G. M. (1991) Blind infant–sighted mother interaction during the first year. *International Journal of Rehabilitation Research*, Vol. 14, No. 3, pp. 231–234

Preisler, G. M. (1993) A descriptive study of blind children in nurseries with sighted children. *Child: Care, Health and Development*, Vol. 19, No. 5, pp. 295–315

Roe, J. (1996) Social Interactions of Children with Visual Impairment in Integrated Settings: paper presented at Mary Kitzinger Trust Vision Research Workshop (unpublished)

Roe, J. (1997) Peer Relationships, Play and Language of Visually Impaired Children, Unpublished PhD thesis, University of Bristol

Rogoff, B. (1990) *Apprenticeship in Thinking: Cognitive Development in Social Context*. Oxford: OUP

Rosenblith, J. (1992) *In the Beginning: Development from Conception to Age Two*. London: Sage Publications

Royal National Institute for the Blind (RNIB) (1994) *Looking into PE: Curriculum Guide for Teaching PE to Children with a Visual Impairment*. London: RNIB

RNIB (1995a) *Improving Environments for People with Visual and Learning Difficulties*. London: RNIB

RNIB (1995b) *Play it My Way: Learning Through Play with Your Visually-impaired Child*. London: HMSO

RNIB (1995c) *Making Your Voice Heard: Helping Parents to Secure Educational Support for their Visually-impaired Child*. London: RNIB

Schaffer, H. R. (1977) (ed.) *Studies in Mother–infant Interaction*. London: Academic Press

Sheridan, M. (1976) *Manual for the Stycar Vision Tests*. Windsor: NFER

Schneekloth, L. H. (1989) Play environments for visually impaired children. *Journal of Visual Impairment and Blindness*, Vol. 83, pp. 196–201

Short, F. X. and Winnick, J. P. (1986) The influence of visual impairment on physical fitness test performance. *Journal of Visual Impairment and Blindness*, Vol. 80, pp. 729–731

Snow, C. E. (1995) Issues in the study of input: finetuning, universality, individual and developmental differences, and necessary causes. In P. Fletcher and B. MacWhinney (eds) *The Handbook of Child Language*, Oxford: Blackwell, pp. 180–193

Spencer, C., Blades, M. and Morsley, K. (1989) *The Child in the Physical Environment: The Development of Spatial Knowledge and Cognition*. Chichester: Wiley

Stephens, B. and Grube, C. (1982) Development of Piagetian reasoning in congenitally blind children. *Journal of Visual Impairment and Blindness*, Vol. 76, No. 4, pp. 133–143

Stone, J. (1995) *Mobility for Special Needs*. London: Cassell

Tizard, B. and Hughes, M. (1984) *Young Children Learning: Talking and Thinking at Home and at School*. London: Fontana

Tobin, M. J. (1993) The language of blind children: communication, words, and meanings. In M. C. Beveridge and G. Reddiford (eds) *Language, Culture and*

Education: Proceedings of the Colston Research Society, Bristol. Clevedon: Multilingual Matters

Tobin. M. J. (1994) *Assessing Visually Handicapped People: An Introduction to Test Procedures.* London: David Fulton Publishers

Tobin, M. J., Tooze, F. H., Chapman, E. K. and Moss, S. (1979) *Look and Think: A Handbook on Visual Perception Training for Severely Visually Handicapped Children.* London: Schools Council/RNIB

Trevarthen, C. (1979) Communication and co-operation in early infancy: a description of primary intersubjectivity. In M. Bulowa (ed.) *Before Speech: The Beginnings of Human Communication.* Cambridge: CUP

Vernon Report (1972) *Education of the Visually Handicapped.* London: DES

Vygotsky, L. (1978) *Mind in Society: The Development of Higher Psychological Processes.* Cambridge, MA: Harvard University Press

Walker, E. C., Tobin, M. J. and McKennell, A. C. (1992) *Blind and Partially-sighted Children in Britain: The RNIB Survey, Volume 2.* London: HMSO

Walker-Andrews, A. S. (1988) Infants' perception of the affordances of expressive behaviours. In C. K. Rovee-Collier and L. P. Lipsitt (eds) *Advances in Infancy Research*, Vol. 5. Norwood, NJ: Ablex

Warren, D. H. (1994) *Blindness and Children: An Individual Differences Approach.* Cambridge: CUP

Webster, A. (1992) Images of deaf children as learners: the influence of adults' perceptions on assessment and intervention. In T. Cline (ed.) *The Assessment of Special Educational Needs: International Perspectives.* London: Routledge

Webster, A. (1994) Hearing impairment. In J. Solity and G. Bickler (eds) *Support Services: Issues for Education, Health and Social Services Professionals.* London: Cassell, pp. 151–169

Webster, A. and McConnell, C. (1987) *Children with Speech and Language Difficulties.* London: Cassell

Webster, A. and Wood, D. J. (1989) *Children with Hearing Difficulties.* London: Cassell

Webster, A., Beveridge, M. C. and Reed, M. (1996a) *Managing the Literacy Curriculum: How Schools can Become Communities of Readers and Writers.* London: Routledge

Webster, A., Came, F., Webster, V. and Price, G. (1996b) *Supporting Learning in the Secondary School: Raising Achievement under the new Code of Practice, Volume 2: Issues for Practitioners.* Bristol: Avec Designs Ltd

Wells, G. (1981) *Learning through Interaction.* Cambridge: CUP

Wells, G. (1985) *Language, Learning and Education.* Windsor: NFER-Nelson

Wells, G. (1987) *The Meaning Makers: Children Learning Language and Using Language to Learn.* London: Hodder & Stoughton

Whitmore, K. and Bax, M. (1990) Checking the health of school entrants. *Archives of Diseases in Childhood*, Vol. 65, pp. 320–326

Wood, D. J. (1988) *How Children Think and Learn.* Oxford: Blackwell

Wood, D. J. (1992) Language, learning and education. In P. Gray (ed.) New concepts, new solutions. *Educational and Child Psychology*, Vol. 9, No. 2, pp. 17–25

Wood, D., Bruner, J. S. and Ross, G. (1976) The role of tutoring in problem solving. *Journal of Child Psychology and Psychiatry*, Vol. 17, No. 2, pp. 89–100

Woodhead, M., Carr, R. and Light, P. (1991) *Becoming a Person.* London: Routledge

World Health Organisation (1980) *International Classification of Impairments, Disabilities and Handicaps: A Manual of Classification.* Geneva: WHO

INDEX